The Future of Christian Marriage

The Future of Christian Marriage

MARK REGNERUS

OXFORD
UNIVERSITY PRESS

OXFORD
UNIVERSITY PRESS

Oxford University Press is a department of the University of Oxford. It furthers
the University's objective of excellence in research, scholarship, and education
by publishing worldwide. Oxford is a registered trade mark of Oxford University
Press in the UK and certain other countries.

Published in the United States of America by Oxford University Press
198 Madison Avenue, New York, NY 10016, United States of America.

Library of Congress Cataloging-in-Publication Data

Names: Regnerus, Mark, author.
Title: The future of Christian marriage / Mark Regnerus.
Description: New York : Oxford University Press, [2020] |
Includes bibliographical references and index.
Identifiers: LCCN 2019059950 (print) | LCCN 2019059951 (ebook) |
ISBN 9780190064938 (hardback) | ISBN 9780190064952 (epub) |
ISBN 9780190064969 (online)
Subjects: LCSH: Marriage—Religious aspects—Christianity. |
Marriage—Social aspects.
Classification: LCC BV835 .R445 2020 (print) |
LCC BV835 (ebook) | DDC 248.4—dc23
LC record available at https://lccn.loc.gov/2019059950
LC ebook record available at https://lccn.loc.gov/2019059951

1 3 5 7 9 8 6 4 2

Printed by Sheridan Books, Inc., United States of America

Contents

Acknowledgments

A word of particular appreciation is in order for my data collection site coordinators: Daniela Delgado Gutiérrez in Guadalajara, Fernando Pliego Carrasco in Mexico City, Tomasz Adamczyk and Wioletta Szymczak in Lublin, Chady Rahme in Beirut, Franca Attoh in Lagos, Raquel Martin Lanas in Pamplona, and Yana Mikhaylova in Moscow. Laura Wittmann conducted interviews in Austin, Texas, and Howell, Michigan.

I owe a particular debt of gratitude to the Social Trends Institute, and Carlos Cavallé and Tracey O'Donnell in particular, for underwriting half of the data collection costs for this project. Eric and Keri Stumberg, Sean Fieler, Greg and Kelly Anderson, Vicente Segu, and Kevin and DeAnn Stuart all contributed with additional material assistance and/or moral support, for which I am grateful. My editor at Oxford, Cynthia Read, continues to be fair and more than kind.

Dorothy Morgan's assistance with survey research analyses was top rate. Catherine Pakaluk, Brad Wilcox, Mary Bathon, and Chad Pecknold offered excellent late-stage advice. Betsy Stokes, Amy Hamilton, and Jennifer Lind provided critical editorial assistance. I am grateful to Meg McDonnell, Nick McCann, Joe Price, J. P. De Gance, Bryan Richardson, Luis Tellez, Timoteusz Zych, Katarína Baginová, Miriam Kuzárová, Patrik Daniska, Juraj Sust, Jakub Lipták, Željka Markić, Ivan Munjin, Joanna Banasiuk, Anna Janczyk, Bishop (of Oyo) Emmanuel Adetoyese Badejo, Tugdual Derville, Caroline Roux, Axel Rokvam, Ivan Pavluytkin, Ivan Zabaev, Daria Oreshina, Masha Goleva, Samar Azzi Rahme, and Enrique and Katharina Gomez Serrano for engaging conversations and/or country-specific assistance. (And my apologies to those I've accidentally omitted.) A shout-out to my family for enduring my occasional absences and interminable dinner-time conversations about this project.

My employer requires me to say this: "A researcher who is involved in this study, Dr. Mark Regnerus, receives monetary payment for providing writing, editing, evaluation, and networking services to the Witherspoon Institute. The business interests of Witherspoon Institute relate to the topic of this study." Despite that, the Witherspoon Institute did not actually underwrite any aspect of this book project, nor did they weigh in on—or even know about—any analyses or conclusions of mine.

Finally, this book is submitted in praise of Deeann Regnerus, whose grace, faith, and commitment have taught me much about Christian marriage. (You are so much better at this than I am.) And it's dedicated to St. John the Baptist, whose life was demanded from him because of a marriage. (It must be important.)

1

Introduction

Evgeni lives alone now in his Moscow apartment. He's a 30-year-old engineer employed in the city, with a degree in robotics and complex automation. Compared with many other Muscovites, Evgeni has a stable position that comfortably pays the bills. Nevertheless, he's nervous about the economic health of the country. About the moral condition of the nation, he's flat depressed. "[T]hey have distanced themselves from God, unfortunately," he laments. "I am an example myself." Evgeni then admitted to having "wrecked my marriage." He left his wife of 10 years to pursue another woman. It didn't work out. The reasons why only made sense to him in hindsight: "Naturally, you cannot build anything on passion. I had all sorts of dreams, fantasies, that you could build your life in a different way." He thought there would be happiness, but it proved elusive. Evgeni is able to see his 4-year-old daughter once a week. He found solace and reconciliation with God in the Orthodox congregation he attends in Moscow. It's where he discerned what he had lost. He deeply regrets the affair and longs for a second chance. "I would like to obtain mercy from my wife," he levels. So far, no luck.

The social support necessary for sustaining marriage has eroded in Evgeni's country, such that the end of the Soviet era could boast more stable families than today's Russia. Exiting your marriage had been long frowned upon in a political system in which courting unwanted attention from the government was foolish if not outright dangerous. And as recently as the 1980s, divorce required formal committee approval. In other words, marriage was not a private concern. It was a public one. Not so much anymore: if both parties agree, a divorce can be secured for a minimal fee in one month. Since Evgeni had first-hand experience here, he could offer unique insight:

> In the Soviet times . . . people were not involved with the church, but there was more stability, and more understanding of responsibility toward one another. As the propaganda of such values as freedom and a comfortable life is increasing, family is dying at full pelt. Now there is this trend that

young people generally do not understand why family is necessary and they consider it something which just gets in the way of their life.

Living by himself in a city of many options, Evgeni could readily meet someone new. But he wants someone old.

I'll lay my cards on the table. I am a fan of marriage. It has been good to me, despite its tall demands and my half-hearted efforts to excel at it. I think marriage has served many others well, too, and is a profound source of developmental benefit for children. Intact married families bring significant value to society. My interest in this subject, however, is not about a return to some theoretical previous golden era of matrimony. And I have no interest in making an idol of marriage as society's panacea.[1] But when marriage patterns change among Christians, the matter deserves attention.

This is a book about how modern Christians around the world look for a mate within a religious faith that esteems marriage but a world that increasingly yawns at it. It is not a book about *how* to get married, or about being married, staying married, or being happy in marriage (although one hopes this is the case). While I touch upon the biblical and theological history of marriage, I only do so in order to situate the reader in preparation for the book's aim—to understand the challenges that Christians face in today's "marriage market."

Some of the challenges are mathematical—for example, there are far more women than men in congregations—while others are ideological, such as the popularity of short-term relationships and the penchant for keeping one's options open. Other concerns are economic: Is marriage prudent when good, reliable jobs seem to be shrinking? Is marriage less attractive after a financial downturn?[2] I have studied American relationship patterns for over a decade now, which has made me wonder if my questions are truly global or just domestic. I wanted to know how Christians in different countries are navigating both old and new challenges to marriage. So I decided to ask them—evangelicals, Catholics, Orthodox, and Pentecostals. My research took me to seven countries, where my team spoke with just under two hundred young adult Christians.

While most of the world still values the institution, marriage must now compete more than ever with other life priorities. Demographers increasingly speak of the second demographic transition (SDT).[3] In developed societies—especially, but not only, those that exhibit lengthy economic prosperity—it is believed that men and women alike are beginning to lose the motivation to marry and have children, and so they increasingly delay or avoid one or both. Indeed, the act of getting married, something humans appear to have done for millennia out of economic practicality if not always out of love, is growing less common—quickly.[4] Standards in marriageability have risen, too, in step with women's increasing labor force participation. When women no longer feel the need to marry—but still wish to marry— they are going to be choosier and will tend to wed later than they otherwise might have. As I document here, Christians around the world are increasingly accommodating these wider shifts in marriage trends. But there's also resistance, and it's rooted in vibrant, productive religious groups and organizations.

While secularization is at work, and the age at marriage is rising along with it, pastors, priests, and lay leaders are trying to keep marriage on the radar. "There are courses on communication in relationships, talking about emotions, dealing with emotions in a relationship," observed Wiktoria, a 24-year-old speech therapist from Krakow, Poland, who is getting married in three months. In Krakow, there are many masses said for those seeking "a good wife or husband," and there are "home churches" for married couples— the Polish equivalent of the American small-group Bible study.

Wiktoria is still well below the median age of marriage in Poland, yet she and her fiancé did not rush things: "We regarded the marriage commitment as so serious that we wanted to be sure that it was all fine between us, that we were certain of everything," she explained. "So yes, it was a rather slow process," one that began for her at age 19. When your parents and grandparents are still together—and when you live in the least secular part of Poland—it's just not that hard to envision married life. In fact, I stumbled upon a wedding less than two hours into my first ever visit to the country. How appropriate— I thought at the time—a wedding in a country whose piety quite possibly outpaces every other Catholic-majority nation in the world, a country that produced one of the most articulate recent apologists for the good of marriage and family life—Pope John Paul II. It dawned on me that I had not attended a Catholic wedding in the United States for at least five years, despite my obvious interest in the subject matter.

Doubtless, the trials of the twentieth century have fostered a more resilient Church in Poland. Cultural resistance—in this case by honoring traditions that predated its occupiers—paid off. Beauty, dignity, and family recaptured what had been first despoiled by cold rationality and then later bled by state-sponsored secular ideology. Today, the country is a far cry from the

Soviet-era version of itself and now features a surging economy—and with it, greater choice. The aggressive atheism of Poland's communist era elite—successfully resisted by the Church—has given way to a tacit "apatheism" fed by consumerism, which may be more difficult to contest.[5] Practices once considered almost obligatory are now becoming options, including faith and family. While weekly church attendance in Poland hovers just above 40 percent of the population—a figure double that of the United States—young adults predictably pull down that average.[6] Only 26 percent of under-30s attend regularly, compared with 55 percent of Poles over age 40. The difference is striking.

Marriage, too, has become more optional there. For every 100 marriages in Poland, there are now 36 divorces (not too far off from the 42 per 100 in the United States).[7] That 36 figure was just 6 in 1960—only 6 divorces for every 100 weddings during the heart of the communist era. Even as recently as 2010, it was only 27 per 100. Perhaps the free market has been hard on marriage in Poland, fostering an acquisitive and consumptive mentality whose principles are no respecter of matrimony. Wiktoria can see it: "In the past, getting married . . . becoming a wife and mother was more important than now. . . . Women [today] do not want to live as their mothers did." And while most interviewees still equate marriage with having children, many historically Christian nations—including Poland and Spain—display meager fertility rates. The average number of births per woman in either country was 1.32 in 2015, a rate that forecasts obvious population decline in the absence of immigration.[8]

Other changes are afoot as well, including the recognition of same-sex marriage in a growing number of Western nations.[9] However, although it remains a hot topic in the United States, most of the world's Christians live in countries where talk of same-sex marriage is only on the lips of tourists, local activists, or Western diplomats. In such countries, divorce rates are also much lower than we are used to seeing in the West.

The M Word

"Marriage is not a popular topic," asserted the late University of Chicago ethicist Don Browning, a scholar noted for both his acumen and his genuine concern for the institution of marriage. He elaborates: "It is often referred to as the 'M' word, almost in the same category as other dirty words. Of course, it is not a dirty word, but it is a word that makes people uncomfortable as a topic of serious conversation."[10] Add Christianity to marriage, and you get the holy grail of unfashionable pairings in the scholarly world.

Browning felt this way back in 2003, and the situation has only gotten more awkward. To talk seriously about marriage today in the scholarly sphere is to speak a foreign language: you tempt annoyance, confusion, or both. As a result, there is a tug of war going on over what is known with confidence about marriage, what can be said about it, and who is authorized to say it. To its many and vocal modern critics, marriage is legalized slavery, antifeminist,[11] and a receding institution whose dying grip on society cannot come soon enough. In the past, psychologist Bella DePaulo claims, "marriage dominated not because it really was the best way to live for everyone, but because it was uncontested." "That marriage is dead," she celebrates.[12] More standard critics are simply agnostic about it. For them, marriage is out of fashion or uninteresting (unless somehow you are contesting its institutional status by marrying someone of the same sex). Interlocutors want clarity up front, to ensure that you are inclusive in your definition of marriage but modest in your regard for its genuine significance. To *esteem* marriage? That's simply too much.

All this is more than a little disconcerting, considering how good marriage has been for both individuals and their communities, Christian or otherwise. The data on marriage remains solid, even if few want to go on record admitting it. Marriage is by far the optimal context for childrearing. Married men and women accumulate more education and wealth and are more likely to own a home than are unmarried adults, even similarly situated cohabiting or single adults.[13] They are also more likely to have jobs at all, even when controlling for other factors, such as race and education.[14] Marriage also consolidates expenses—like food, child care, electricity, and gas—and over the life course drastically reduces the odds of becoming indigent or dependent on the state. And those are just the *economic* benefits of marriage. Recent high-quality research suggests that marriage is associated with higher life satisfaction, greater happiness, better mental and physical health, and greater longevity, even after controlling for baseline health. Marriage is connected to higher levels of meaning and purpose in life, more positive relationships, less loneliness, and greater social support, even controlling for baseline financial status and education.[15] Cohabitation reflects uncertainty and diminished commitment while splitting up lends itself to emotional and financial struggles.[16] I could go on.

Sadly, most of marriage's fans have largely gone quiet, hoping that it will somehow survive its current unpopular phase. (It will.) Few social scientists or theorists concern themselves with the decline in marriage rates. They most certainly do not collect data with an interest in identifying best practices for fostering the institution.

Research Questions

If one were to speak of these trends in economic terms, it would make sense to say that Christian marriage in the West appears to be experiencing a recession. Given the historically tight connection between institution-alized religion and family, this poses an intellectual—and a theological—problem: Does the increasing flight from marriage affect the practice of Christianity? Just how central *is* marriage to Christianity? There are other more practical questions, too, including the following:

1. How do lay (nonclergy) Christians talk about the marriage recession? Does it concern them?
2. How much clarity is there about the meanings and purposes of marriage?
3. What do Christians expect from marriage? Are expectations largely the same the world over?
4. Are there good ideas or "best practices" for making marriages happen in particular congregations or families? And are there particularly toxic norms, too?

Marriage and family correspond to "a yearning that is part and parcel of human existence," Pope Francis holds. It is among our most basic desires. He remains confident that despite "all the many signs of crisis in the institution of marriage, 'the desire to marry and form a family remains vibrant, especially among young people.'"[17] Is he right? Does the marital impulse remain vibrant? It's an empirical question.

The answer depends in part on your definition of *vibrant*, as well as upon the context you're investigating and the one you're using for comparison. The marital impulse in Helsinki is not what it is in Warsaw. But perhaps contrasting secular Scandinavia with Catholic Poland is like comparing apples with oranges. Montreal and Warsaw, on the other hand, are both historically Catholic cities. Still, the former is nothing like the latter in terms of present-day religiosity and marital impulse. Even in the United States, marriage rates (per capita) in Rhode Island, Connecticut, New York, Massachusetts, New Jersey, and Florida are *less than half* of those in less-populated Utah, Alaska, and Wyoming.[18] But what about among Christians, regardless of where they live? Is the marital impulse really still vibrant among them? That's what I wanted to know.

Research Methods

In this book, I combine major-survey analyses of the state of marriage around the globe with my in-depth interview project.[19] Between September 2016 and October 2017, my research team and I talked with 190 church-going, young adult lay Christians (average age 27) in seven countries: the United States, Mexico, Spain, Poland, Russia, Lebanon, and Nigeria. Why these places? Because they represent much of the diversity of Christians across the globe, and because each either fits a particular niche or represents an emergent trend:

1. The United States is the major source of globally concerned evangelical Christianity and exports copious amounts of culture (Christian and otherwise) through technology and media.
2. Mexico is a traditionalist country with an emergent economy, amid a history of migration to its northern neighbor. Its Catholic culture contributes to a general esteeming of marriage.
3. Spain features a Catholic monopoly alongside low-grade conflict with a large secular population. It also suffers from elevated unemployment, which tends to suppress marriage rates.
4. Poland is one of the most Catholic countries in the world. As a nation of survivors with a strong sense of history, it has outlasted brutal oppression from multiple neighbors.
5. Russia is my sole source of Orthodox interviews. While exhibiting elevated marriage *and* divorce rates, Russian Orthodoxy is framing itself as a cultural protector of Western civilization and values.
6. Lebanon features the Middle East's last sizable Christian minority. The faith there is ancient; many believers trace their roots to the original converts.

7. Nigeria has it all—Muslims, Catholics, Pentecostals, and evangelicals—together with an antagonism toward what it perceives as Western imperialism on matters of sexuality.

What does the situation of an unmarried 28-year-old Russian Orthodox Muscovite have to do with that of a 31-year-old Maronite Catholic from Beirut or a 27-year-old evangelical from Austin, Texas? Plenty, actually. It's not that Orthodox, Catholic, and evangelical worship experiences look similar. (They do not.) It's that each increasingly shares common experiences and overlapping interests in today's rapidly globalizing world. They're more similar to each other than many of them would ever guess. And in this particular study, another priority unites them together with millions of Christians elsewhere: the desire to participate in Christian marriage.

One of the reasons I became interested in the "marital impulse" abroad is because of the rapid retreat from—or delay of—marriage in America.[20] As recently as 1970, 80 percent of Americans between the ages of 25 and 34 were married. My parents were among them. But by 2015, that 80 percent had shrunk to only 40 percent, with no sign of recovery or even leveling off. Never-married young Americans now notably outnumber their married counterparts.

Churchgoing Christians make up a sizable share of the American young adult population—somewhere between 15 and 30 percent (depending on how the survey defines them)—and what happens around them is apt to affect them. However, it seems logical that one should not *expect* to see a wholesale flight from marriage among active Christians. There have long been reliable Christian arguments for marriage and developed theological thought about the vocation of and call to holy matrimony, which ought to weather social trends. And there remains significant social support for marriage among Christians of all stripes. Yet, as my research on Christians and their thoughts on marriage expanded into a wider assessment of marriage itself (and its future), it became evident that Christian marriage patterns are not *that* distinctive from wider trends. And so this project—a book about marriage among Christians—has inadvertently led me to also explore here the nature of marriage itself, regardless of creed or country.

The Interviews

My research team aimed to conduct twenty-five in-person interviews in each country. Men and women are largely evenly represented in the sample. The text of the interview questionnaire (available in Appendix A) was translated into the language of the interviewers and interviewees. Some countries feature interviews from more than one area; others were all conducted in the same city.[21]

The names of all interviewees quoted or described in this book have been changed to protect their confidentiality. Ages, marital status, religious affiliation, and employment sector are presented accurately.

The interviews do not reflect a random sample. The particular cities were often selected because they were home to a similarly interested scholar—commonly a social science professor from a nearby university. These scholars were compensated for overseeing the conduct of high-quality in-person interviews there. I visited most of the sites (some more than once) myself, conducting follow-up conversations with several interviewees, asking for clarification about some responses, and learning about subsequent events since their first interview. While survey data would be easier to display in a bar chart, it simply cannot get to the core of my research questions. (For that reason, you will see very few tables in this book.)

This is also not an unbiased sample. First, I intentionally pursued church-going lay Christians as respondents. And it is likely, despite efforts to the contrary, that the sample is more middle class than it ought to be. I did make numerous efforts toward including poorer and working-class persons in the sample, and the Lagos site contains more such interviews. That said, norms about marriage tend to flow from the top down, so what the middle class and elites think and do about marriage matters, often for everyone.

Added to the 190 interviews with churchgoing lay Christians are additional extemporaneous interviews I conducted with religious leaders in various countries. Typically shorter and less personal, these interviews focused on their experiences in their organizational roles: What do they see happening with marriage in their congregations, dioceses, and denominations? What are their organizations doing about the marriage recession, if anything?[22]

Three Definitions: Christian, Marriage, and Christian Marriage

Talking about Christian marriage—the point of this book—implies a working definition of what it means to be a Christian, and also what marriage is. I am using the term *Christian* here generally—to include those persons who profess and practice some form of Christianity. In other words, I'm referring to Catholic, Orthodox, or various types of Protestant. I encourage readers not to get hung up on finer distinctions and to be open to learning from other Christian traditions and perspectives.

I tried to avoid interviewing people who were Christian in name only and not in practice. In all of the interview settings except one, I asked my site coordinators to privilege weekly (self-reported) church or Mass attendance as an interview criterion.[23] (In Moscow, monthly attendance sufficed.) Not surprisingly, during follow-up conversations, some of the interviewees turned out to have not been as faithful in their attendance patterns as they had originally stated.[24] This unwittingly turned out to be a very helpful variable, since their marital attitudes and relationship actions tended to differ from the more fervent attenders, and this alone tells us something.

Now to another complicated question: What do I mean by *marriage*? Am I talking here about marriage among Christians, or about Christian marriage? And is there something essentially different between the two things? I believe there *is* a difference, but it is more pronounced in some locations and traditions than others. In the United States, for example, many Christians can marry on a beach, have their vows solemnized by a "minister" ordained online for the occasion, and call it good. Their marriage will be accepted as legitimate in very many congregations. If a Catholic couple did that and wanted to participate in Catholic life, they would need a convalidation, a ceremony by which a civil marriage is made valid by the Church.

In some other places, the distinctions matter even more. In Russia, you *know* if you're marrying in the Orthodox Church. It's quite distinct from a civil marriage, which many interviewees there referred to as getting "a stamp in the passport."[25] In Lebanon, civil marriage simply does not exist; Christians there who wish to marry must do so in a church. In France, by contrast, marriage is primarily a civil matter, one that must precede any religious ceremony. It's the law—a legacy of the French Revolution's triumph over Church dominance.

Given this diffusion of authority, it becomes increasingly difficult to speak intelligibly of something called Christian marriage. What I am talking about is *marriage among Christians*. This is not to be confused with studying *married Christians*. In fact, the majority of this study's respondents are unmarried. Some are divorced. Those who are married were recently so—within the past few years. Some had married in a church (or intended to one day); others didn't or didn't expect to. If they were married, their spouse did not have to also be a practicing Christian. I also considered remarriages as valid marriages (not requiring explanation from the interviewees). There were no polygamous marriages studied, nor same-sex relationships.[26]

The Western Recession in Marriage

What can we learn from the big numbers—the population-level data on marriage and marital timing? Keeping in mind that survey information like this varies in quality across countries, let's start with the West. The countries in Table 1.1 have been historically shaped in various ways by forms of Christianity (with Japan, a nation with very few Christians, thrown in for comparison). The table displays the percent of ever-married women ages 25 through 29, along with the average age at first marriage for women. Why measure women, and at these ages? Thirty is the age at which women's fertility tends to begin a slow decline[27] and is generally a popular benchmark in the minds of many women.[28] Estimates of men's marriage patterns are not shown but are publicly available.[29] Across the world, men consistently marry at older ages than their female counterparts.

As you can see, marriage before age 30 has receded dramatically in much of the West. We can map the free fall over a few decades—the blink of an eye in the history of marriage. In Italy, the share of women under 30 who have ever been married dropped from 77 percent to 24 percent between 1981 and 2016. Marriage during the high-fertility years has quickly shifted from expected to unusual. In this table, only Poland and Romania were exceptions to this trend; around 60 percent of women in each had ever been married by age 30. But a swift and linear decline is still obvious—28 percent in Poland and 33 percent in Romania—in just a few decades. Czechs are the least religious among Eastern and Central Europeans, and their plummet is the most profound—a 71 percent drop since 1980.[30] Scandinavian countries are the only nations where the 1990–1991 figures were already below 50 percent,

Table 1.1. Percent of Women Ages 25–29 Ever Married, and Mean Age at Marriage

Country	Percent Ever Married				Mean Age at Marriage		
	1980–1981	1990–1991	2000–2002	Latest	1994–1996	Latest	Change
Australia	80.9	67.4	46.4	35.1	27.7	29.9	2.2
Czech Repub.	91.1	89.1	61.1	26.3	23.9	32.0	8.1
Denmark	68.4	42.5	32.6	21.4	25.1	31.8	6.7
Finland	66.7	48.2	36.9	28.0	29.6	30.4	0.8
Germany	—	63.4	38.8	26.5	27.5	31.5	4.0
Greece	79.3	72.5	55.2	38.6	24.5	29.2	4.7
Italy	76.6	60.9	43.6	24.4	26.1	29.2	3.1
Japan	76.0	59.6	46.0	38.7	27.7	29.4	1.7
Netherlands	80.6	58.9	35.4	24.8	28.6	32.3	3.7
Norway	76.5	53.8	31.7	23.4	29.9	31.9	2.0
Poland	84.9	83.1	70.2	61.5	24.4	26.6	2.2
Romania	—	88.7	69.2	59.4	22.1	26.6	4.5
Spain	77.8	61.3	37.4	—	26.0	27.7	1.7
Sweden	51.2	37.2	23.6	23.1	31.5	31.0	–0.5
Switzerland	67.4	55.9	39.9	30.1	27.7	30.6	2.9

Notes: Latest figures are as early as 2010 or as late as 2016. Wherever possible, consistency of figures (from country census or estimates) was maintained across rows. In a few instances, however, particular rows display both census numbers and estimates. A few countries' mean age at marriage estimates were only calculated in 1991 and 2011.

Source: World Marriage Data 2017 (New York: United Nations, Department of Economic and Social Affairs, Population Division, 2017).

and Sweden seems to have bottomed out at 23–24 percent, an estimate that remained stable from 2000 to 2016. Norway, Italy, the Netherlands, Sweden, and Denmark all report their most recent estimates as between 20 and 25 percent. Perhaps that is the floor. Time will certainly tell.[31]

The mean age at marriage is also rising in nearly all of these countries; the two measures typically move in tandem. By 2014–2016, women in numerous countries displayed a mean age at first marriage of over 30. In most countries featured in Table 1.1, the average age at marriage climbed at least three or four years in just two decades. The Netherlands displays one of the highest average ages at marriage for females in the world, at about 32.3 years.

This particular statistic will not likely climb much higher, even if marriage rates continue to tumble, so long as marriage remains closely associated with childbearing. Still, cohabitation has outpaced formal marriage in Scandinavia. In the Danish 2011 census data, 36 percent of women ages 25 through 29 reported being in a consensual union, well above the 24 percent who said they were married.

Table 1.1 only tells us about the retreat from marriage in terms of its pace—marrying later, if at all. There are other signals of change, too, including exiting from marriage by divorce. Recall from the start of this chapter that for every 100 marriages in Poland in 2015, there were 36 divorces. In the United States, that figure is 42 per 100. (This is the statistic that leads many Americans to claim that "nearly half of all marriages end in divorce.") As recently as 1960, few if any countries exhibited a divorce-to-marriage ratio exceeding 0.1. In other words, about sixty years ago, there were at least 10 marriages for every divorce. That is no longer the case, often by a long shot. Beginning around 1970, the ratio began to climb. Spain, for example, now records nearly 7 divorces for every 10 marriages—a surge brought on, in part, by a new law easing and speeding up the divorce process, approved by Spain's socialist government in 2005.[32] Yet even after pent-up demand for divorce was satisfied, the Spanish divorce rate still remains twice as high as before the law was instituted. (A similar pattern was visible in the United States after a series of no-fault divorce laws commenced in 1969.) And it's not just happening in Spain. The number of divorces recorded in Lebanon shot up 61 percent between 2000 and 2011.[33]

While Italians may be delaying marriage, as Table 1.1 certainly suggests, divorce there remains comparatively low. And Mexico is the only country featured in this book where there are still fewer than 2 divorces for every 10 marriages. The ratios of a variety of countries—France, Russia, Germany, the United States, the United Kingdom, Canada, and Sweden—now cluster near 0.5 (5 divorces for every 10 marriages).

Obviously, where marriages are receding, only the more committed are actually getting married, so it stands to reason that we should expect divorce rates to eventually tumble alongside marriage rates, as in the United States. But a return to 1960s divorce-to-marriage ratios in the West is unlikely.

Church records reveal similar stories. For ease of interpretation, let's just look at the largest of them. Catholic marriages plunged 59 percent in the United States between 1965 and 2017.[34] Worldwide, the decline in these marriages is still steep but not as severe—a 32 percent drop since 1970. In raw numbers, it means there were 1,060,000 fewer Catholic weddings on the planet in 2015 than there had been in 1970. Back in the States, Catholic funerals had already outpaced Catholic marriages in 1965, though they were still pretty even at 9 weddings for every 10 funerals. By 2017, the ratio had dipped to 3.7 weddings for every 10 funerals.[35]

Christianity and the Marital Impulse in Seven Countries

The World Values Survey (WVS) enables us to assess agreement on a variety of questions about religion, marriage, and family around the world between 2010 and 2014.[36] Table 1.2 displays predicted probabilities—two columns each for men and for women—mapping the likelihood of Christians being married at age 25, 30, 35, and 39 in each of the seven countries where we conducted interviews.[37] There are a lot of numbers there, so I'll stick to what jumps out at me when I study them. Those who attend church services regularly ("more observant") have a better shot at being married—almost at every age—in most countries. But the predictions vary widely among countries: 76 percent of religiously observant Polish women are expected to be married by age 30, and 88 percent by age 35—about 10 percentage points in front of devout women in the United States and Spain. Marriages in Mexico, however, are expected to top out below 70 percent, including among the most devout. The gap between churchgoers and everyone else is especially striking in the United States and in Spain, averaging around 20 percentage points at each age (for example, half of American men who don't regularly attend church are expected to be married at age 35, well below the 72 percent prediction among their churchgoing counterparts).

In two countries—Nigeria and Russia—religiousness is less important for predicting marital status. In Nigeria, marriage is so common that church attendance doesn't add much to the cultural imperative to marry. In Russia, the difference is similarly negligible, but for quite different reasons. Elevated religiousness is uncommon, and observant Orthodox seem to be at least as cautious as—if not more than—the rest of the population in their choice to marry or not.[38] Compared with the other nationals featured here, Russians are the *most* likely to be married by age 25 and the *least* likely to be married at age 39. Due to high divorce and adult male mortality rates, the probability of being married in Russia is actually predicted to diminish as respondents near age 40, unlike in most other countries featured here. According to data from the

Table 1.2. Likelihood of Being Married, by Country, Age, and Level of Religious Observance

Age	Men		Women	
	Less Observant	More Observant	Less Observant	More Observant
Lebanon				
25	9%	15%	18%	29%
30	30%	44%	49%	64%
35	47%	62%	67%	78%
39	49%	63%	68%	80%
Mexico				
25	31%	42%	33%	44%
30	47%	59%	50%	61%
35	53%	64%	55%	66%
39	48%	59%	50%	61%
Nigeria				
25	13%	12%	32%	29%
30	37%	34%	64%	61%
35	66%	63%	86%	84%
39	82%	80%	93%	92%
Poland				
25	16%	25%	21%	32%
30	55%	69%	64%	76%
35	73%	83%	79%	88%
39	69%	80%	76%	85%
Russia				
25	44%	48%	50%	54%
30	63%	67%	69%	72%
35	62%	66%	68%	72%
39	47%	52%	54%	58%
Spain				
25	6%	16%	13%	31%
30	24%	48%	42%	67%
35	39%	65%	59%	80%
39	38%	63%	58%	80%
United States				
25	16%	33%	21%	40%
30	37%	60%	45%	68%
35	50%	72%	58%	78%
39	49%	71%	57%	77%

Source: World Values Survey, Series 6 (2010–2014), http://www.worldvaluessurvey.org/wvs.jsp. The estimates are predicted probabilities (displayed as percentages, for readability).

Organisation for Economic Co-operation and Development (OECD), 5 percent of Russian marriages fail during their first year, and just over 40 percent of them are over within five years.[39] Other former Soviet republics, including Azerbaijan, Georgia, and Moldova, all display similarly high risks of early divorce, well above those in other nations. This pattern is decidedly out of step with marriage rates in former Soviet satellite states (like Slovakia), where age at marriage has soared, which lowers risk of prompt divorce.

So why do so many Russian young adults like Evgeni jump into marriage only to promptly exit? "We don't reflect on this," one sociologist there told me. "We forget sacrificial love," leveled another. "People think of it as formalized cohabitation. They are not thinking of it as family." Evgeni agreed: "I did not appreciate [my marriage], did not work [at it], did not try. I was not tolerant. I was self-seeking." In subsequent conversations, sociologists further attributed high levels of divorce in Russia to elevated rates of substance abuse (long a problem in the country), weak models of fatherhood, and few models of prosperous marriage. Each of these weaknesses is exacerbated for those who lived through the traumatic collapse of the Soviet Union. It certainly remains a paradox, however—comparatively early marriage in a nation populated by far more agnostics and atheists than practicing Orthodox Christians.

Other statistics jump out from Table 1.2, including the high percentage of marriages (at least eventually—by age 40) in the United States, Spain, Poland, Lebanon, and Nigeria. Mexico displays a pattern similar to Russia, but the gap between the churchgoers and everyone else is more pronounced—consistently around 10 or 11 percentage points. The gender gap in marriage in Mexico at identical levels of religiosity is narrow, whereas the gap is wider elsewhere: in Spain, just under half of 30-year-old male churchgoers would expect to be married, while just over two-thirds of churchgoing women should be married by then. Lebanon and Nigeria are similar.

The big picture is this: being active in church matters for marriage in most countries, for both men and for women, but the faithful have a better shot at being married in some countries than others. Over time, of course, the gap in marriage between the more religious and the less religious adds up.

A Guide to the Rest of the Book

The book covers significant territory. Chapter 2 briefly tours the history of Christian marriage before highlighting the importance—often overlooked—of distinguishing between religious and civil marriage. I raise a variety of questions and answer them with the patterns—and in the words—of young adult Christians across seven countries. What do the interviewees think marriage is? What is its purpose? Is there a degree of unity about marriage in the minds of regular Christians from around the globe, or is there more diversity than anything else? The chapter concludes with an explanation of the global shift in the meaning and timing of marriage, from understanding the union as laying a foundation for life success to viewing it as a "capstone," an accomplishment in itself. This has affected Christians as much as anyone.

The subject matter of Chapter 3 is the male-female relationship. Women's criteria for a mate have risen everywhere, in step with their greater labor force participation, but the link between economic egalitarianism and marital pessimism (or delay) is far from straightforward. I explore what economic and sociological data say about men's marriageability and the declining marriage rate, before discussing how Christian men and women in each country talk about each other and about sex role expectations in their relationships.

Confusion about key aspects of marriage and their association with church and state have invited strong assertions about the social construction of the union—that is, since we *made* marriage, we can unmake it, or refashion it as we wish. Not everyone agrees, including a good deal of the globe's population and not a few classic social theorists. Toward the end of Chapter 3, I introduce an "observed" model of marriage—not so much a definition as a discerning of the core, and key expectations, of marriage *as it is practiced*. These, so far as I can tell, are not nearly as subject to social construction as are other aspects or traits commonly attached to marriage.

In Chapter 4, I turn my attention to the price of sex and the price of marriage. The former seems to be declining everywhere, while the latter seems to be rising. Sex is easy to get, according to the interviewees. Marriage? Not so much. I explore the mathematical challenge facing young adult Christians in congregations, in which women tend to outnumber men, and investigate whether the technology-generated hazards I outlined in my 2017 book, *Cheap Sex*, are—in the same ways, and for the same reasons—affecting relationships outside the United States. Many interviewees recounted the early sexualization of relationships and stalled relationship progression.

Chapter 5 documents how high expectations for marriage have mixed with limited means to achieve them, yielding chronic uncertainty. Our interviews revealed much about Christians' logic for marrying and the temptation to solve uncertainty and anxiety by committing to something short of marriage—cohabitation.

I also reflect on how marriage has fared under both communism and capitalism, with an eye on the emerging "gig" economy (that is, temporary jobs or additional part-time work). Globalized capitalism has elevated expectations of what marriage should be like, and we are privy to far more information and options than ever. Americans invented online dating to improve their odds when seeking a partner—albeit often not a spouse. Do Christians elsewhere use these tools? Some do, but not many, at least not yet.

I also describe at length one of the key barriers to marriage in some countries—social expectations about costly weddings. Many Christians with whom we talked felt caught up in a web of tradition, but without the benefits (social support, connectivity) that once accompanied meeting the expectations of family, friends, and neighbors. Speaking of family, most interviewees the world over have an opinion about how their parents have shaped their relationship development—both how they help and how they hurt.

One of the goals of this book is to smile at the good, not just frown at the bad. In Chapter 6, the most practical one, I focus on what facilitates the marital intentions of the world's Christians. We asked every interviewee about particularly helpful programs and initiatives—governmental, community, university, and congregational. I discuss at length eight ideas worth consideration.

The title of Chapter 7 is identical to that of the book *The Future of Christian Marriage*. There is plenty that can be changed about how Christians approach marriage. But there is much that cannot, or will not, change—and must, instead, be navigated. For example, the capstone model of marriage that I describe in Chapter 2 is now nearly universal. All but a small minority of the world's Christians see marriage as something to build toward rather than build upon. That's a massive change occurring over a mere two generations. This comes with both possibility and peril, including the unavoidable reality that fewer Christians will marry at all.

I assess two competing theories borrowed from the sociology of religion: Rodney Stark's "moral communities" paradigm and Christian Smith's "embattled and thriving" thesis. The first of these holds that the marital behavior of the surrounding population ought to powerfully shape the marital behavior of Christians therein. The second thesis, drawn from Smith's earlier work on American evangelicalism, suggests that a (Christian) minority can be embattled—in this case, by collapsing national marriage rates—but still thrive, that is, witness a vibrant marriage culture despite its context.[40] The evidence points more toward the former than the latter.

How central *is* marriage to the future of Christian faith and practice? Very, I argue. Can it recede in popularity without damaging the reproduction of the faith? Not much. Christianity thrives, in part, because it organizes and channels human sexual relationships. I also reflect in greater detail on the collapse of familism, and how social science unwittingly assisted its collapse by running silent about the optimal outcomes of stable families when they had the data to argue otherwise. Finally, I conclude with five predictions for what we should expect next.

2

From Foundation to Capstone

Farah is the 25-year-old unmarried daughter of a Maronite Catholic priest living in Beirut. (Unlike in the Latin rite of the Catholic Church, it is not unusual for priests in the Maronite rite to be married.)[1] Around 35 percent of Beirut's two million people are Christians, and the vast majority of them are Catholics of the Maronite rite. I met Farah, who works part-time for the United Nations, at the diocesan headquarters in northern Beirut after an already eventful day. (It had included a stalled vehicle in the hills above Byblos, my first hitchhiking experience in decades, and a kind lift from a Shiite Muslim with a small statue of the Virgin Mary stuck to his dashboard. Hospitality knows no religious boundaries in Lebanon—for now.)

Farah's father cares a great deal about marriage and has counseled many struggling couples at their apartment. (It's a small place, so Farah overhears the conversations.) She is more than prepared to be married, but there are no suitors on the horizon. She doesn't seem concerned, however. Lots of devout Lebanese women wait. It's a better option, she maintains:

> Honestly, if I see a couple getting married and I feel that they are happy together, this is something that gives me a lot of happiness. So if they are happy with marriage, great. But if they're getting married just because they [feel they] have to, I think it's better not to. . . . It's very annoying that three-quarters of the people are getting married just because they don't want to stay alone. So they run and ask to have a match with anyone, to avoid being alone, and share the cost of expenses, and other economic reasons that lead to marriage.

Despite her comparatively new logic, Farah considers herself "old fashioned" about marriage. She believes marriage to be ordained by God, but she doesn't automatically appeal to religious/biblical arguments to support her opinions about it. Rather, she emphasizes her own emotional responses: She feels "a lot of happiness" when she agrees with a couple's marriage decision but finds it "very annoying" otherwise. She seems to appreciate the Apostle Paul's opinion of marriage as inessential, insisting that sometimes "it's better not to [marry]." I pressed her on the topic, and she continued: "My friends [either] think marriage is a fairy tale, or else [that] they'll lose their freedom. For me, it's sharing life with somebody else. . . .You can be free, *with* somebody." Her perspective on marriage as another *kind* of freedom is not yet rare in Beirut, but it is certainly becoming less common among Lebanese Christians, who are experiencing secularization pressures similar to those felt by their European and American counterparts.

Once widely considered the Paris of the Mediterranean, Beirut is largely foreign territory for Americans now, a place associated with bad memories: the Lebanese Civil War of the 1980s, high-profile assassinations, and particularly the bombing of the Marine Corps barracks in 1983, which claimed the lives of 241 Americans and 58 French peacekeepers. More recently, many associate Beirut with the emergent power of Hezbollah, the Iranian-backed Shiite movement labeled a terrorist organization by a variety of Western powers. Most Americans—including the vast majority of Christians—need hear no more to conclude that Lebanon is suspect territory. And yet it is the Middle Eastern nation with the highest share of Christians. This is due in part to the comparative decimation of Christian communities in Egypt, Iraq, and Syria—an unintended consequence of the prodemocracy Arab Spring movement of the past decade. Muslim dictators, in hindsight, kept the peace between Christian minorities and Muslim majorities far better than have democratic elections since then.

In reality, the Beirut of today is a rare beacon of hope for Christians in the Middle East, and it is a rather different place than most Americans imagine it. A power-sharing agreement between Christians and both Shia and Sunni Muslims continues to hold. Ongoing grievances with government corruption and economic entropy appear nonpartisan. A strong Hezbollah militia deployment to eastern Lebanon squelched a nascent Islamic State (ISIS; Islamic State of Iraq and Syria) insurgency as recently as 2017, protecting the Christian community of East Beirut. Common enemies make for uncommon coalitions.

Much of Beirut is remarkably Western. One could easily mistake its combination of skyscrapers, hills, palms, and miles of suburbia along winding ocean-view roads for Southern California. It's an apt comparison in more than just topography, for the Christians in Beirut find themselves increasingly Western in their worldviews and actions. (The average age at first marriage for women in Lebanon was 28 at last count, nearly identical to

American women, and the oldest in the Arab world.)[2] About childbearing, Beirut's young adult Christians share far more in common with Americans than with their more traditional Muslim neighbors, whose stricter sex roles and elevated birthrates foretell the future of Lebanon.

Biblical Marriage

There is certainly an arc to the history of Christian marriage, one that leads away from understanding women as the property of their husbands, and toward the development of what Christian ethicist Don Browning called an ethic of "equal regard."[3] But there is no question that the Hebrew Scriptures made sense of sex and marriage largely through the lenses of property and purity—and within an honor/shame complex that many of the globe's Christians now find foreign.[4] Lifelong celibacy in the ancient Jewish world was quite rare; most married. A man's wife was considered a form of property, and there were grades of sexual ownership, ranging from wife to concubine to slave woman. Kinship was a person's primary identity (and source of social division), and households were stratified into obvious and extensive hierarchies. For a good example of this, look at Genesis 14:14: "When Abram heard that his nephew had been taken captive, he led forth his trained men, born in his house, three hundred eighteen of them, and went in pursuit as far as Dan." This rather large number of men characterizes what Harvard sociologist Carle Zimmerman identified as "trustee familism," a system in which the family is considered perpetual, its solidarity paramount, and its authority entrusted to the patriarch as head.[5] Hence, the oversight and protection of family members was a profound priority. (The cavalier manner in which many in the West today allow their young adult children to attend college hundreds of miles from home would have been unimaginable in this system.)

Abram's wife, Sarai, was not his only sexual partner. He had concubines as well—including but not limited to Hagar—with whom he fathered children.[6] Because of such household complexity, sex and marriage and relationship hierarchies were domains laden with moral gradations and tension, as the antagonistic relationship between Sarai and Hagar makes evident. Still today, jealousy remains a hallmark of polygynous societies.[7]

The Torah appears to have given the right of divorce to husbands but not wives.[8] Moreover, a man's marital status was not at issue in adultery; only her marital status counted. Adultery with a married woman was considered a property violation. Indeed, the ninth of Ten Commandments warns against coveting, among other things, "your neighbor's wife." Many read into the original text an assumption that the same goes for a wife's coveting of her neighbor's husband, but that would be an eisegetical—or at least more modern—reading of the text. If a man violated (e.g., raped) an unbetrothed virgin, he was to pay the bride price to the woman's father and marry her, and he could henceforth never divorce her.[9]

But this type of familist (and polygamous) system is shown the door by the beginning of the era of the Christian Church. Jesus himself chided his listeners—and their ancestors—for disregarding how marriage was meant to be from the beginning: permanent, but not eternal.[10] He also pressed marriage toward greater equality between the sexes—by asserting that a man, too, commits adultery when he divorces his wife and marries another woman.[11] *His* marital status—not just hers—now matters. And in the post-resurrection kingdom of God, Jesus declares that marriage—together with its accompanying status concerns—will simply not exist.[12] I'm sure his audience was taken aback at imagining such a scenario. Some scholars interpret this as a divine disregard for marriage and family, and a golden opportunity to trumpet new relational and family forms.[13] I see no compelling reason to perceive it that way, and plenty of reasons to suggest this is a gross misinterpretation. After all, Jesus endorses marriage with his appearance—and first recorded miracle—at a wedding. That matters.

It is, therefore, ironic—and a remarkable accomplishment of contemporary interpreters—that Jesus is now considered by many a morally flexible figure here, content with the loosening of marriage bonds and casual toward Christians' intimacy choices. Forgiving? Of course, as the account of the woman caught in adultery signifies.[14] But lacking standards and open to whatever relationships his followers wish to accommodate? That makes no sense. The rulings of the Jerusalem Council, soon after Christ's ascension, make evident that sexual and marital behavior remained a key component of moral law at the time.[15]

Meanwhile, the missionary convert Paul is popularly considered to have been more scrupulous than Jesus was on marital and sexual matters. This, too, is unfortunate—an anachronistic misinterpretation of the sexually toxic Greco-Roman world in which Paul proselytized as a religious minority. Some scholars hold, in fact, that the more sober and attentive approach to marriage fostered by Paul among Christian communities held a particular appeal to neighboring pagans and was a winsome factor in conversion and growth.[16] N. T. Wright, long one of the most popular expositors of Christian texts, highlights Paul's radical distinction from the surrounding society: "He insists that the husband should take as his role model, not the typical bossy and bullying male . . . but Jesus himself."[17] And so, today's disparaged, supposedly "sex-negative" Christian traditionalists were the first century's countercultural radicals offering women greater honor, equality, and social status.[18]

Paul is also well known for his endorsement of celibate singlehood, male headship of the wife, spousal self-sacrifice, and sexual satisfaction for both husbands and wives. He denounced sexual permissiveness and "irregular" unions, characterizing marriage as akin to Christ's sacrificial love for his bride, the Church. Paul did permit a certain no-fault divorce in cases in which only one spouse had converted to Christianity and the non-Christian, therefore, desired to leave the union. (It was not unilateral, however; if the non-Christian was willing to stay, however, no divorce was permitted.) In the case of two married Christians, Paul does not budge an inch, stating that God desires marriages to last and that Christian spouses who split are to either remain unmarried or reconcile.[19]

The end of the biblical era began nearly 2,000 years of church history—and with it no shortage of wrestling over the boundaries and details of Christian marriage. Competing voices vie for authority as new and distinctive realities, contexts, cultures, technologies, and disasters affect this most primal of arrangements. The age of first marriage has risen notably of late, but about this topic, the Scriptures are silent. As for what distinguishes a marriageable man or woman, there is little more guidance than several proverbs and the previously discussed Pauline counsel. Modern economies that feature new opportunities usher in both possibilities and challenges, with little direct biblical guidance for marriage-minded career women.

Farah could plainly see this magnified in the lives of Christians she knows in Beirut. Husbands and wives both work, on average. It's just assumed. (Filipino and Ethiopian nannies are common.) It's also very demanding. Weekends are overloaded with domestic responsibilities, Farah laments:

> When both spouses are working, they come home tired . . . even before
> kids come into the picture. So even before they have kids, the couple don't
> have the time to sit together, so they delay their discussion time. They delay

things to Saturday usually, so Saturdays, or weekends, become overloaded, which becomes very tiring.

Such arrangements have their costs and benefits, she figures. It's the new way of doing marriage in her community:

> Couples used to sit together more, over dinner and other situations where they could be together, free at the same time, rather than having one of them finish work at 5 p.m. while the other finishes at 7 p.m. This change might also have some positives, which is that they both share expenses. This challenging condition is creating a new image of marriage.

Today's Lebanese television shows portray marriage as they tend to in the United States—embattled, temporary, and obsessed with relational and sexual freedom. It is as if skepticism about marriage is a viral infection spreading eastward and southward from the West. I could detect it from Mexico City to Moscow to Beirut to Lagos. It is plainly obvious that something is afoot with marriage, if not the marital impulse, among the globe's young adult Christians. Nothing about the process of marrying can be taken for granted anymore. For now at least, Farah's commonsensical approach is resisting the media's "depressive" portrayals of matrimony as a prison. "In reality," she reasons, "life has the good and the bad, the sweet and the bitter."

Civil? Religious? Valid? Legal? Who "Owns" Marriage?

Most Christians, like Farah, hold that marriage was ordained by God. While empirically that claim is impossible to confirm or disconfirm, it pays to remember that marriages can be solemnized in church as well as in your backyard or down at City Hall. In other words, the irreligious of the world have long valued marriage, too. Marriage does seem to serve some very old civic and protective purposes, including the care of children (and eventually of parents by their children), the ownership and inheritance of property, and the legal right to act on behalf of an incapacitated spouse. As a result, Christians tend to affirm marriage for both the religious and the irreligious, perceiving the union as an obvious social good.[20] Geoff, a 24-year-old Baptist from Austin, Texas, is a part-time electrician and full-time university student. He typifies a common position when he states, "I think and believe that marriage is better, even for someone who's a nonbeliever. I'm just trying to think why." Geoff supposed that civil marriage commitment levels are probably lower and the definition of marriage murkier, but "there's still an understanding that you are entering into a covenant with this person for life, where you're committed to loving this person for your life and caring for this person for your life." In other words, Geoff holds that civilly married persons typically act in good faith when they marry. They intend to stay married, and he thinks that's a good thing.

Geoff is onto something. In the 2018 American Political and Social Behavior survey, two out of every three Americans—but far more among the most religious—disagreed with the opinion that marriage is "an outdated institution."[21] There remains wide goodwill toward marriage. This raises a pair of questions that few ever consider: Are the irreligious doing something different from Christians when they get married? Who retains oversight of marriage in general—and what does that even mean?

Don Browning wrote that the Protestant Reformation "made marriage a public institution but one that could be blessed by religious institutions."[22] Most agree with Browning that this was a game changer for religious oversight of marriage, though it didn't often alter how marriages functioned.[23] The magisterial Reformers (like Luther and Calvin) tended to argue that marriage was not a sacrament but *was* ordained by God. To them, marriage was not a "natural institution" made sacramental by the Church's elevation of it, but a human institution—and, hence, subject to the jurisdiction of civil authority that was itself somehow answerable to divine law and principle. With this, marriage comes to be understood widely as a contract, because contracts are what civil authorities adjudicate. In other words, the Reformation politicizes marriage.

Church and state would thereafter compete as authorities over marriage law. In hindsight, it is a remarkable concession—to give a secular institution authority over what includes moral questions involving sexual expression, childrearing, and the care of family members. In Calvin's Geneva, it may not have seemed like such a large leap from the church to the city council. It does today.

Conservative Presbyterian sociologist David Ayers acknowledges the consequences of Protestantism on marriage law: "We cannot deny that Protestantism helped to pave the way for the explosion of divorce, and secularization of divorce law, that we have seen since the early twentieth century. However, the Reformers did not anticipate this, nor would they have supported it."[24] Agreed. Nonetheless, division creates confusion, and what the magisterial Reformers did not share was a uniform policy on how to regulate marriage. That is, who is to say when a marriage exists or does not exist? Could a marriage be legal but not valid, or valid but not legal? In the United States, there remains considerable confusion about the distinction.[25] In brief, legality *is* validity in civil marriage, but not *necessarily* in religious marriage. (It depends on your Christian tradition.) Historically, Christian marriage in the United States—and perhaps other locales—has been widely thought of as a spiritual dimension added to an earthly reality that is typically (but not always or entirely) adjudicated on secular terms.[26] The result is a blend of authority—more secular than religious—with individual pastors or committees becoming arbiters of acceptable marital practices in their organizations and congregations. Their attempts to adjudicate and enforce their own rules about divorce and remarriage, however, are hamstrung by the ease with which disgruntled or "disciplined" members can simply change churches.

My own father, a minister in the Reformed Church in America—a small, mainline Dutch Calvinist denomination—told me he would rather bury people than marry people, a sentiment the Southern Baptist Convention's Russell Moore commiserates with in his book *The Storm-Tossed Family*.[27] It sounds unkind, but what my father meant was that he found the oversight and interpersonal dynamics of funerals far easier to navigate with a sense of the sacred intact than the perceived rights and petty squabbles that often characterize weddings (and their preparation). He required known cohabiters to live apart for a time before he would agree to officiate, and neither bride nor groom (nor their parents) tended to appreciate his intervention. Martin Luther himself didn't much enjoy the subject:

> How I dread preaching on the estate of marriage! . . . The lax authority of both the spiritual and the temporal swords has given rise to so many dreadful abuses and false situations, that I would much prefer neither to look into the matter, nor to hear of it. But timidity is no help in an emergency; I must proceed. I must try to instruct poor bewildered consciences and take up the matter boldly.[28]

This would prove to be a tall order, especially since Luther believed that everyone who was able to do so should marry, including clergy. (Calvin was particularly adamant about the latter principle.)

Today—as an indicator of the effectiveness of the Protestant Reformation—most Christians treat civil marriages as equivalent and interchangeable with religious marriages. But who is to say a marriage can or cannot be dissolved, and a new one formed? And who would do the dissolving—church or state? What if the state becomes a poor guardian of marriage—as many Christian leaders are now asserting with the emergence of civil same-sex marriage?

Farah's home country, Lebanon, poses an interesting test of some of these questions, because it is an unusual nation that does not offer civil marriages to its citizens. All marriage matters in Lebanon are religious by definition. (A civil marriage can be entered into outside the country, but this remains a contested political matter.) The same goes for the end of a marriage; if a religious organization permitted you to marry, then they must adjudicate your divorce. This is hard for many outside the Middle East to comprehend today, but church historian John Witte, Jr. notes that in early Protestant circles, this was standard operating procedure: "Couples who wanted to divorce had to announce their intentions in the church and community and to petition a civil judge to dissolve the bond."[29] That is almost unimaginable today. A divorced Presbyterian woman in Austin once lamented to me that her divorce, which her husband had pursued against her wishes, went officially unnoticed in her church. People knew about it and felt sorry for her. But she wanted more—some formal acknowledgment of the injustice of the matter. But no avenue existed for such a thing.

To split in Lebanon, Maronite Catholics appear before a Maronite court, and Muslims before an Islamic court. These courts make decisions about child custody as well as financial support for children and spouses. And there is no such thing as equal treatment under the law in Lebanon regarding family matters. There are as many as fifteen different marriage and divorce codes in the country—including Shia, Sunni, Druze, Maronite, Orthodox, and Baptist. Further, men and women don't always experience comparable treatment, regardless of code. In some cases, pursuing a divorce can mean completely waving rights to one's children.

For Maronites, there is no divorce. Being Catholics, their recourse is annulment, a judgment that the marital bond never actually existed. Grounds for annulment must be plainly proven. The process takes time.[30] Appeals can seem interminable, shelving the decision into limbo until all considerations are resolved.

All around the world, remarriage after divorce remains fuzzy ground, religiously—especially since divorce is nearly always a civil matter (countries like Lebanon notwithstanding). In the States, Christians often count on their congregations to recognize the religious and civil validity of their new marriage. (Seventeen years as a Presbyterian provided me ample opportunity to witness this phenomenon.) Many remarrying Christians don't give "validity" a second thought.

This all means that there is far more to marriage oversight—let alone its encouragement—than many Christians tend to recognize or appreciate. Marriage is important—of that they have no doubt. But beyond this common ground, differences quickly emerge. Since most Christians still wish to marry despite the civil and religious confusion, then what they think marriage actually is, and what it entails, matters a great deal.

What Do Christians Think Marriage Is?

The Bible begins and ends with a marriage.[31] Jessica—a vivacious 31-year-old Catholic, who was unmarried at the time of the interview but has subsequently married—made sure that we knew that. This nonprofit organization manager from Austin had plenty to say about marriage:

> So like God tells us of his, like, eternal plan for us in marriage, you know. It's like a marriage isn't meant for us in and of ourselves . . . It's meant to prepare us to be united with God forever. From that marriage, the couple, and the children who come out of that marriage, become a symbol and a sign of God's eternal plan of love for them, for everyone else that they meet.

At least in Jessica's case, the Catholic Church has succeeded in communicating its party line. And she is sold on it all: marriage as a symbol and a sign; matrimony as one aspect of a divine plan; the union at least partly about preparation for heaven; the close association of marriage with children.

There was more—plenty more—in Jessica's expansive vision for what marriage is and can accomplish:

> When we are married, we're not just this sort of abstract sign and symbol of, like, Christ's love for the church, which is beautiful. It's beautiful to think about. But it's like a very concrete [thing]. Every beautiful good act of love that I do in my marriage transforms the entire world, you know. And that's

the power of grace in a marriage, you know. . . . The goal is to transform the entire world, basically.

That's a substantial goal. And marriage won't be easy, she acknowledges. On the contrary, "It's painful. It's sacrifice. It's struggle, you know?" That is why, Jessica thinks, many are waiting to marry or forgoing marriage altogether. But they're missing out on spiritual resources, she ventures:

> I think when we learn to rely on God and we learn that even though our spouse is intended to give us emotional support and help us to be finan- cially stable and help us to raise children, I think in a Christian marriage, when you invite God in . . . it creates a healthy kind of detachment.

Faith helps people see the bigger picture. And marriage can help Christians have a healthier view of this transient world. That's not all; Jessica is con- vinced there is also real, spiritually powerful help funneled through mar- riage: "God offers us so much grace, and it's, you know because it [marriage] is a sign of his faithful love for us." One reason that people have given up on marriage is that they have given up on this "grace" from God: "People have stopped trusting God, and they stopped believing that he has a faithful love for us. They stopped believing that he can heal their wounds." If Christians expect their marriages to thrive without spiritual nurture, they shouldn't be surprised when it doesn't happen.

Varied Definitions of Christian Marriage

Of course, church splits and missionary ventures have multiplied the influ- ential voices about Christian marriage since the time of the apostles. A great many traits and tolerated practices appear throughout history: dowries, bride prices, betrothals, engagements, the acceptance of common-law and other nonconformist unions, the permissibility of divorce and remar- riage, and degrees of consanguinity (kin relation) of potential spouses. In fact, while we in the West take this requirement for granted today, it actu- ally wasn't until the twelfth century that Christianity witnessed the emer- gence of the free mutual consent of the marital party as an imperative in marriage—as distinct from the will of parents or the community. These is- sues, however, are growing rather than shrinking in number as Christianity becomes more popular in the Global South than in the postindustrial West. [32]

As discussed above, the Reformation multiplied disputes about legitimate authority over the regulation of marriage among Christians. It also raised anew the question of what marriage actually is and what it is for. The Catholic Church holds that matrimony is one of seven sacraments—a visible way in which God gives grace—and is lifelong. Marriage's whole-life union is provided for the good of the spouses, the taming of concupiscence (the human penchant for lust), and the procreation and education of children.[33] It is also about sacrifice—the same kind of sacrifice that Jesus made for humanity. It's equated with the sacrifice made by a priest receiving holy orders, who devotes himself to live a celibate life, married to the church.

Most Protestant leaders would agree with much, but not all, of the Catholic view. Rather than a sacrament, most conservative Protestants usually emphasize marriage as a *covenant*. According to evangelical (Presbyterian) pastor and apologist Tim Keller, "the essence of marriage is that it is a covenant, a commitment, a promise of future love."[34] The Southern Baptists elaborate:

> Marriage is the uniting of one man and one woman in covenant commitment for a lifetime. It is God's unique gift to reveal the union between Christ and His church and to provide for the man and the woman in marriage the framework for intimate companionship, the channel of sexual expression according to biblical standards, and the means for procreation of the human race.[35]

Russell Moore summarizes the twin aspects his denomination's definition outlines: "A cross-shaped marriage, like a cross-shaped gospel, is defined by both covenant and connection."[36]

These are not formally at odds with Catholic notions, given that their catechism describes marriage as a covenant twice in its definition.[37] Some versions of Protestant thought further emphasize marriage as a pathway to mutual support of husband and wife in their interests and callings. While there are different visions for marriage, most Christian organizations' descriptions of matrimony are not all that distinctive.

Even if a certain Christian tradition *has* established its own thoughtful explanation of marriage, it is a sure bet that this definition is inconsistently expressed in the words and lives of their own faithful. Nonetheless, it's precisely these words and lives that interest us here, so we posed applicable questions to our interviewees. Their answers yielded some consistency amid considerable diversity, but with significant overlap in major themes.

So what exactly do Christians think marriage is and does? We already heard from Jessica, who invested it with a great deal of meaning and importance. Here is a collection of short answers from our young adult Christian interviewees. While not exhaustive, it is a pretty thorough sample of what marriage *is*, to Christians across seven countries spanning four continents:

- A sacred covenant and a reflection of the unity of the Trinity and the love story and covenant God has for his people (30-year-old woman, Beirut).
- The starting of a family, and the continuity of humanity (26-year-old man, Beirut).
- It's about entering the project that God established for the human being, which is to grow and develop with a partner whom he loves, as God loves, and to let this love become real, not just remain an idea, but to get incarnated and become fruitful through the openness to life (30-year-old man, Beirut).
- A creative love relationship that was created to challenge everything difficult in life through God's presence in it (27-year-old man, Beirut).
- The union of two people who are open to life, and the purpose is to love each other as Christ loved the Church (24-year-old woman, Pamplona).
- To experience love. Finding love for your partner, but always alongside the love of Jesus Christ (26-year-old woman, Pamplona).
- The unity of a man and a woman and fidelity until death do they part (29-year-old woman, Pamplona).
- The union of two persons in the face of the society and God, who . . . passing though their life together . . . become a single whole and reach the divine perfection, becoming a single entity together, in unison (24-year-old woman, Moscow).
- A domestic church (32-year-old woman, Moscow; repeated verbatim by two others in Moscow).
- A unity of people based on mutual desire and blessed by God and committed with the blessing of parents and close people (30-year-old woman, Moscow).
- Marriage is the coming together of a male and female that is approved by God himself. The purpose of marriage [is] companionship and reproduction (26-year-old man, Lagos).

- The main purpose of marriage is companionship, because in the beginning, God created Adam, and Adam was tending to the garden, and later God was like, man should not be alone, so he needs a helpmate. So God created Eve to be a helpmate and a companion to Adam (36-year-old man, Lagos).
- That companionship: procreate, have your own children, build up your own family, leave your parent's house and build up something for yourselves (24-year-old woman, Lagos).
- A legal union for a man and woman to procreate and care for one another (26-year-old man, Lagos).
- The bond between two people for the rest of their life (26-year-old woman, Guadalajara).
- A stage of getting to a maturity level of a relationship. It's already very different than being just a couple. You want to spend life with the other, getting to know families. You accept the other person, you love each other, you support each other (25-year-old woman, Guadalajara).
- Something that is a covenant before God, that is a sacred relationship, that really is the bedrock of culture and family (33-year-old woman, Austin).
- To reflect God, His image, His relationship in our lives, between each other. And for me to lead my wife as Christ leads the church. And it is a sacred bond in the sense that just as God has His covenant with all the prophets, with Israel, and with the church, marriage also is a covenant between me and my wife, that I will understand God through my marriage (24-year-old man, Austin).
- Two people coming together and doing life in order to glorify God (21-year-old woman, Austin).
- A covenant. It's like a binding kind of promise between you, your spouse, and God, and then everything that you say in your vows, that's a promise they are making. That's really what marriage is. It's not always about being happy—it's not. It's really a choice more than a feeling, and a decision you are making together that you want to spend the rest of your life together, support each other no matter what, and work through whatever challenges come your way (24-year-old man, Austin).
- For people who will be together till the end of their life, to aim at salvation and sanctity by dealing with daily problems together, accepting each other, and practicing their love (21-year-old woman, Lublin).

- Learning love toward the other person, regardless of what she is like. First and foremost, it's real, unconditional love (32-year-old man, Lublin).
- Our closest home, our biggest sense of security. It's also a partnership, assistance, a moment when everything else can cease to matter. It's also a gift, because only we can declare in front of God that we want to be together forever. It's also a gift for us (24-year-old woman, Lublin).
- Children, love, fidelity, chastity, being with each other irrespective of any problems the other person might have. Irrespective of mental sickness, physical, or if she grows fat with time—these are not reasons to separate (27-year-old man, Lublin).

Besides the inevitable diversity, what do we learn from this long list? First, there is idealism in some accounts, and pragmatism in others. Curiously, there is "legal" language in only a small number of them.[38] There are a handful of consistent themes: (1) enduring bond, (2) love, (3) procreation and generations, (4) stable commitment, and (5) spiritual support for each other, occasionally dubbed a "domestic church." That term has its origin in the writings of John Chrysostom, an early Church Father who wrote at length and enthusiastically about marriage.[39] A handful of definitions make explicit reference to the notion of a covenant, though other answers imply it. A few hint at sacrament. Several popular notions about marriage are missing here, including explicit references to "best friend" or "soul mate." (This is a short list of descriptions, of course.)

It's remarkable what *has* remained stable within talk about Christian marriage. Marital affection and self-sacrifice are still valued ideals. Marriage remains widely equated with having children. And despite the obvious secularization at work in the social circles of many of our interviewees, there is no evidence whatsoever suggesting radical ideas to intentionally undo marriage in favor of some other norm for organizing intimate relationships. It's just not there. At worst, a small minority of Christian young adults are simply uninterested in marrying. Finally, there is a sense that marrying means you are embarking on something bigger than yourself or your spouse. It's a participation in an intergenerational social phenomenon, an institution whose rules aren't subject to your whims.

Whether the institutional Christian Church, spread throughout the world, knows it or not, its young people are not uneducated about what marriage is. This list is no litany of Hollywood-inspired myths. Most understand that marriage requires sacrifice. They recognize that they would be building something together, including a household with children whom they must educate. Most understand marriage as having divine purpose. They may eventually have real troubles living up to the standards and descriptions they cite, but I don't think they are way off base about what marriage *is*—whether the young person is an Orthodox bank teller in Moscow, a Maronite attorney in Beirut, a Baptist schoolteacher in Austin, or a Pentecostal shoe salesman in Lagos. It is impressive, really.[40] And I was surprised and encouraged to see it.

There are still tall boundaries to closing the deal—that is, actually getting married. But let's not lose sight of this: churchgoing Christians around the world are expressing understandings of marriage that are consistent with historically Christian perspectives. Most of them are not remaking it up as they go along, as some fear.

The early Church Father Augustine (354–430) would be pleased. Perhaps the central pre-Reformation figure on Christian marriage, Augustine affirmed marriage as the first natural bond of human society in his book *On the Good of Marriage*. In it, he distinguished between those goods that issue from marriage in general—sexual faithfulness and children—while understanding marriage itself as uniquely involving divine grace, and as a sign of the union of Christ and the Church (following Paul's declaration in Ephesians 5:32). Indeed, Augustine's "three goods" of marriage—fidelity, children, and the unbreakable bond—can be glimpsed in many responses. He also wished to foster the nonsexual aspects of marriage, and from the brief descriptions offered above, I'd say Augustine's message is getting through.

The responses from my Russian interviewees were, in some ways, the most heartening. When the early Soviets sought to weaken marriage and family ties in Russia, they sponsored meetings in nearly six thousand villages, factories, schools, and other local organizations, all with the intention of debating the very meaning and purpose of marriage. Disagreement and confusion reigned within this country that had formally, legally eliminated a religious perspective on marriage.[41] In light of that concerted-but-failed effort to rebrand the marital relationship, the wide Christian consensus in Russia on key components of marriage is all the more remarkable.

Has Marriage Changed?

The most illuminating question we posed in the interviews, however, turned out to be this one: *Has anything about marriage changed today, or do you think marriage is comparable to what it has long been before?* I will return throughout the book to the answers this question yielded, but it's worth noting briefly that virtually everyone said that marriage is different today than it was in the past. In fact, only about 3 percent of interviewees with whom we spoke answered "no" when they were asked the question. Geoff was one of these. When pressed, however, the 24-year-old Baptist from Austin could clearly see shifts in how people thought about marriage:

> Yes, as far as what society thinks of marriage, it has absolutely changed . . . It almost seems like society is trying to get rid of [marriage], or is moving in the direction of the lines between what marriage is and what it isn't, and there's just no more lines. I mean it can be anything now. . . . . I even saw a video news story about a woman who wanted to marry herself, and she actually had a ceremony where she married herself. There's another one where she wanted to marry a playground, and so it's just like, "What in the world?!"

But the essence of marriage? That is stable, he maintained:

> I think marriage hasn't changed and never will change. And the fact that marriage is something that was given from God to display his glory and to show what the relationship between Jesus Christ and his people—the church—is like. . . . Yeah, that's never going to change: what marriage is. And marriage is a covenant between the man and woman where they are fully, absolutely committed to each other before God.

Carlos, an unmarried 30-year-old from Mexico City, agrees: "Marriage has not changed. What changed is society."

We didn't ask interviewees whether they believed that the definition of marriage they had offered us was, in fact, stable, or whether it, too, had changed. Given the historic continuity displayed in many of their answers, many of them may agree with Geoff—that the essential core of what marriage is has not changed. But that may be the only part that hasn't.

New Expectations about Marriage for (Nearly) Everyone

It is easy for most Christians to cite ways in which marriage has changed during their own lifetimes. Most are aware that divorce had surged, and that many couples live together before marrying. Sex roles have certainly shifted, as I will detail in Chapter 3. Recent moves to approve same-sex marriage in a number of countries—including several in which we conducted interviews— have revealed that the internal structure of the union can be legally altered, at least in the eyes of the state.

Some family scholars have claimed that the deinstitutionalization of marriage is underway, meaning that marriage as we have long understood it is receding, and an alternative system of relationships—including, but not limited to, marriage—is slowly taking its place.[42] It's worth evaluating the evidence. They may be onto something. How most Christians schedule and anticipate marriage has changed considerably, and it doesn't much matter whether you're Polish, Lebanese, Nigerian, American, Catholic or evangelical, a liberal or a conservative. As sociologist Andrew Cherlin has detailed in his work, and as I have portrayed in Figure 2.1, marriage is now widely perceived as a capstone rather than a foundation.[43] This means that marriage is now something individuals aspire to, rather than something a couple enters in order to help them fulfill their aspirations.

Cherlin's nomenclature is illustrative: A capstone is the finishing touch of a structure. It's a moment in time. A foundation, however, is what a building rests upon. A foundation is essential; a capstone, not so much. A foundation is necessarily hardwearing. A capstone is an accessory that can be replaced if necessary. Similarly, when people are "building" their lives, marriage is

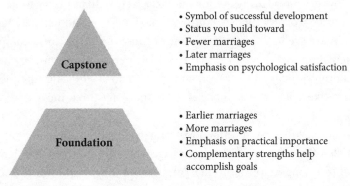

Capstone
- Symbol of successful development
- Status you build toward
- Fewer marriages
- Later marriages
- Emphasis on psychological satisfaction

Foundation
- Earlier marriages
- More marriages
- Emphasis on practical importance
- Complementary strengths help accomplish goals

Figure 2.1. Capstone and foundational visions of marriage.

widely understood today as an achievement attained by each, not the beginning of constructing an adult life together.

Most no longer think of marriage as a formative institution but, rather, as
the institution they enter once they think they are fully formed. Increasing
numbers of Christians think likewise. When marriage was considered foundational to the adult life course, more people entered into matrimony and
did so earlier than they do today (typically by several years). There was an
emphasis on building something—a family, a household, perhaps career and
financial success. Foundational marriages were commonly characterized by
love but were intended to be practical—two people taking shelter together
and celebrating what achievements they could muster as a team, even if their
roles were distinctive (and they often were).

The shift has gone largely unnoticed over the past half-century. Parents
advise their children to finish their education, to launch their careers, and
to become financially independent, since dependence is weakness. "Don't
rush into a relationship," they caution. "Hold out for a spouse who displays
real godliness." "First loves aren't apt to be the best fit." "You have plenty of
time!" "Don't be dependent on a mate." As a result, many Christian young
adults sense that putting oneself in the trust of another person may be foolish
and risky. Many choose to wait out the risk—sometimes for years—to see
how a relationship will fare before committing. Consequently, the focus of
20-somethings has become less about building mature relationships and fulfilling responsibilities and more about enjoying oneself, traveling, and trying
on identities and relationships. Chloe, a 27-year-old from Howell, Michigan,
working in neuropsychological testing, drew a blunt dividing line based on
age: "You have your twenties to focus on you and then [after your twenties]
you try to help others."

We now get ourselves ready for marriage, rather than marry to get ourselves poised to accomplish common objectives—a home, job, family.
Instead, marriage itself has become one of those objectives, an accomplishment signaling that they have "made it." This perspective is now by far the
most common today in the West, and it has made significant inroads into
countries like Nigeria, Lebanon, and Poland—my three most traditional
locales.

Agnieska, a 26-year-old woman working in a Lublin insurance company's
call center, voiced the new logic of marriage when she observed that "it might
be good [for couples to wait to marry], because they would like to become
self-reliant first, buy a flat, order their life, and then think about getting

married, be it in church or the registry office." Julia, a 24-year-old working in the legal department of a Lublin manufacturing company, was even more emphatic: "People don't want to get married until they have a well-paid job. . . . You have to gain credentials, a well-paid job to make your family happy. Happiness is fully based on the economic factor." In Julia's experience, it's not only your finances but also your character that is reflected in your job position: "It is said that a mature person has to be self-reliant. Self-reliance is synonymous only with a good post [job]. A minor post in civil service, in the office, is not so much appreciated anymore." She also recognized the added difficulties of the changing economy, the risks of entrepreneurial enterprises and the sacrifices and time they require: "So, he thinks about establishing his own company, which absorbs so much energy that he only focuses on founding this company."

At the same time, Agnieska doesn't believe this new way of thinking has made people better at marriage. If anything, it's the other way around: "In the past, in my opinion, relationships were more mature than today." Julia, too: "My father has always told me that he started with my mother from the beginning. They've achieved something." It's rubbed off on her: "You mustn't wait with that [marriage] till you're 30 and get your dream job. I think it's worth going through next stages with that chosen person." Their remarks, like those offered by numerous others, signal changing expectations of men and women, greater uncertainty about their relationships, and higher expectations for marriage—key ideas upon which I dwell later in the book.

Thinking of marriage as a capstone to a successful young adulthood is considered a safety mechanism, reinforcing the independence of the spouses rather than encouraging their interdependence. These are two adults who don't need each other. But they want each other. We have certainly become what a team of sociologists call marriage "planners" rather than marriage "naturalists," who more characteristically married in their early to mid-20s.[44]

I cannot overemphasize how monumental, consequential, and subtle this shift is. Marriage is morphing away from being a populist institution— a social phenomenon in which most of the world's adults participated and benefitted—to becoming an elite, voluntary, consumption-oriented, and oft-temporary arrangement. As demographer Daniel Schneider observes, "owning a home, a car, or having some savings becomes a way to cross a symbolic boundary and qualify for marriage."[45] If you can't afford these things, the thinking goes, then you aren't ready for marriage. Schneider and Pat Hastings, using U.S. Census Bureau data, verify that "poor women have high, nearly unattainable, economic standards for marriage."[46] (This, despite the fact that marriage per se costs very little.) As another study's authors put it, "Marriage, but not cohabitation, requires economic and residential independence, which boils down to having enough money."[47] Most people still want to marry, but only some can "afford" the new capstone vision of marriage. One interview-based study simply concluded, "one does not marry if one is struggling financially."[48]

It is no surprise, then, that we observe growing inequality in the West, prompted, in part, by the marital divide between rich and poor. The advantaged consolidate their wealth and income by a marriage between two successful people, while the disadvantaged are left without even the help of each other. The capstone vision has unwittingly turned marriage into an unaffordable luxury good. It may sound outlandish, but it's not: marriage is the social justice issue of our time.

The capstone vision of marriage has become a Western export, too, as I have learned from interviewees. Of course, it plays better in some locales than others. As the authors of *Understanding Family Change and Variation* point out, and as our Nigerian interviewees confirm, this kind of "individual-first" approach to marriage and family is not always welcome and may "fit poorly" in many African nations.[49] (And not just Africa.) The capstone vision doesn't travel alone, though. It arrives—in the words of University of Michigan demographer Arland Thornton—as part of a cultural and political "package of ideas" that imply that prosperity and power will follow upon the adoption of Western family- and marital-expression norms, timing, and forms.[50] Such developmental idealism, Thornton notes, can collide with powerful indigenous social and cultural systems with competing visions for family and social life.

Pope Francis, thought by many to be rather liberal in matters of marriage and divorce, nevertheless reserves harsh words for what he calls "ideological colonization." "There is a global war trying to destroy marriage," he claimed in 2016, one fought not "with weapons, but with ideas."[51] It's a soft form of oppression and colonialism being pushed upon "developing societies by affluent ones, especially the West, through imposing an alien worldview or set of values on poorer societies, often by making adoption of those values a condition of humanitarian or development aid."[52]

Demographers, on the other hand, tend to hold that culture change of this sort is simply inevitable. They maintain that much of the West has already entered a second demographic transition (SDT). The first one occurred well over 100 years ago when the death rate began to drop in the West, mirroring an earlier decline in the birth rate.[53] The characteristics of this second transition, however, read like a primer not only in the capstone vision for marriage but also in secular progressivism:

- fertility postponement and rising nonmarital fertility and childlessness
- efficient contraception, prompting revolution in sexuality and women's roles
- declining marriage and remarriage rates and increasing divorce rates
- emergence of "needs" such as individual autonomy and expression
- secularization
- flexible life course organization
- tolerance (of identities, relationship choices, and sexual decisions) as a prime value

This package of norms is easy to spot in Spain, Lebanon, and Mexico, where secularization among the Christian population is quite visible, as are a recession in social solidarity, the postponement of fertility, and the rising age at marriage. The shift affects the heart of what it means to be human: the purpose of life, the role of relationships (the place of the other vis-à-vis the self), and the point of sexuality. Marriage and family are still valued, but the narrative around what they should look like, when you should enter them, and why, has changed. In theory, that means more people could marry and have families. In reality, fewer are marrying, and even fewer will.

Is There an Ideal Age to Marry?

The province of Navarre in northern Spain is one of the most Catholic parts of what is historically thought of as a rather Catholic country. The truth, of course, is more nuanced. Spain sports both significant Catholic and secular populations and has for a long time. The Spanish Civil War in the late 1930s demonstrated (and exacerbated) violent polarization between the two. While Navarre is not known for political strife, Basque separatists have staged attacks in Pamplona as recently as 2009.

Pamplona, in the north near the French border, avoided much of the worst of the fighting. At a population of nearly 200,000, it is much smaller than Madrid or Barcelona, and it lies tucked at the edge of the Basque country, amid the scenic foothills of the Pyrenees. Pamplona tends to be a recipient—rather than a sender—of the frustrated employment ambitions of young adults from other Spanish provinces. Spain's experience in the global recession that commenced in 2007 was darker, deeper, and longer than that felt in the United States and in a variety of ways marks it still. "When the crisis came," one native told me, "nobody had money." What they had instead was substantial mortgages and car loans, with no means to pay them. Many returned to live with parents (who had little money, too). The recovery was slow, uneven, and incomplete. In Spain, the experience of the global Great Recession lingers. "It changed the mind," one interviewee described:

> Before we didn't think about tomorrow, because the economy was abundant. Now we say just the opposite. We're very, very cautious, because you don't know what's going to happen. Before we didn't think about problems; now we think about them too much.

Religiously, Pamplona is disproportionately represented by the Catholic organizations Opus Dei and the Neocatechumenal Way, both of which are known for their devotion. The influence of each was discernible in the lives of some interviewees, and indirectly so in the lives of others. Diego, a 27-year-old engineer working for a marketing company, characterized it this way: "People in the north are more conservative" but "in the Mediterranean area and the south, people do what they want." Others would agree. At the same time, old-town Pamplona is known internationally for its raucous San Fermin festival, a ten-day party featuring lots of alcohol and the early-morning "running of the bulls," a ritual in which (mostly) young men dress in white with red bandannas to run through the narrow streets of the city, chased by six bulls who eventually meet their end—the bulls, that is, save for an occasional gored runner—in the arena that awaits them. In sum, Pamplona is a pretty Catholic place: lots of opportunities for confession, and plenty of scheduled Masses. Other parts of Spain? Not as much.

Like most European countries, Spain is witnessing pronounced secularization, a process several theorists believe accelerated after the end of Franco's dictatorship in 1975.[54] The current prime minister, who took the oath of office in 2018, is an avowed atheist. Recent analyses of Spanish time-use surveys reveal a dip in average Sunday Mass attendance between 2003 and 2010, from 16 percent to 14 percent, but pronounced gaps between age groups, with only 4 percent of those 18 to 29 reporting weekly attendance, compared with 31 percent among those ages 65 or older.[55]

But it's the skyrocketing age at first marriage that drew my attention to Spain. It has increased by 5.4 years, on average, over just two decades. And the share of under-30 women who are married has plunged 69 percent since 1980. Both patterns are less pronounced in Pamplona, though still present.

So is there an ideal age at which to get married? I am asked this question a lot, and mass-media outlets regularly revisit this topic.[56] The intelligent follow-up question is, "Ideal for what?" For minimizing risk of divorce? For attracting an optimal spouse? For long-term marital happiness?[57] For healthy pregnancies and the best chance at avoiding birth defects? For the best chance at active grandparenting? These are quite different outcomes, but they're all related to the question of age at marriage. (I like to joke that waiting until you're age 75 to marry is probably the best way to guarantee your marriage will last for the rest of your life.)

But this quest to discover the ideal age at which to marry also betrays a common misconception about social science—that we can give you the answers for what you ought to do in your own life and relationships. No— we can only offer our best observations of how one pattern of behavior—in this case, age at marriage—is associated with some desired outcome (like avoiding divorce), and only across a particular population. There are always qualifiers to our results, including (1) the association may be real but rather weak, (2) it may operate differently among different populations (for example, among women only), and (3) the association may be an indirect one, that is, a circuitous pathway rather than a straight line. For example, young American men—ages 18 to 20—often display a high probability of marital failure. In the National Study of Family Growth, almost half of men who married at 18 were divorced within five years. Why? It's not because there's anything assuredly problematic about being 18 but, rather, because men of that age are notably less likely to have matured emotionally, to have selected a reliably committed mate, and to understand well how to sacrifice, communicate, and solve problems cooperatively. They are also less likely to be earning enough of an income to sustain a family. And yet there are some 18-year-olds who can do all of these things, especially if they are surrounded by family and friends who want to help their marriage succeed. It's just an uncommon scenario, and an even rarer mentality. (Some men can't do these things even by age 40.) Still, a few more years of maturation tend to help young men figure out how to be better husbands, communicators, and problem-solvers.

But again, we're talking about probabilities, never certainties. And the splitting up of those who marry young can have much to do with external forces, like legal shifts in family law, poor marital examples from their parents, or the emotional toll of job loss or a child's death. I could go on. Nevertheless, people continue to think that social science research can wisely counsel individuals about what to do in their own relationships (or what to blame for their failures). But it can only give general observations, not specific advice. What social science can do well is wake people up to the ocean of trends and forces they are swimming in, and to the realization that their decision-making isn't nearly as "independent" as they might like to believe. Before they can truly swim against the current, they need to know to where the tide is trying to pull them.

The current trend of rising age of marriage didn't have to be revealed to our interviewees. Almost to a person, they were already aware—even in locales where the average age had only inched up, such as in Nigeria. Peter, a 26-year-old shirt designer from Lagos, sees it:

> I will say marriages have changed today because people don't get married early. Generally, it has been a trend that people marry early, especially in this part of the country . . . but these days we find people of about 30, 35, yet to get married. And there has been a change in the trend for the past few decades.

Sonny, a 28-year-old auditor from Lagos, agrees:

> People planning to get married late now are following the trend of the change in society. I believe that since there is no stipulated age for you to get married and people are now [more] conscious of their environment [more aware of opportunities], I think so many people don't want to settle for less.

Nigerians who are struggling to make ends meet were more likely to consider marriage a capstone today rather than a foundation. To wait is smart, Sonny told us, especially in light of the current economic shift to less reliable sources of income:

> The reason why a guy might want to get married [later] is, one: he needs to accumulate a lot of money so as to start a home. Second: a man is not supposed to . . . be depending on only the financial status of his company

of employment; he has to be creative and have a different source whereby he gets money. In terms of this Nigerian economic [situation] that we are facing now, it is not very safe for you to just enter into marriage at a certain age. You need a lot of things, which you should have done and prepared before you enter into marriage.

Forty-eight percent of our interviewees told us that there was no ideal age to get married. The Spanish and Polish interviewees, in particular, felt this way. Keep in mind, however, that saying there is no ideal age at which to get married is not saying that any age is as good as another. It's commonly a way of saying that it ought to be up to the individual. Among those who did offer a specific age, the number averaged 26 for Nigerians, Mexicans, and the handful of Polish interviewees who specified. Russians preferred the later age of 29. For American respondents who gave us a number, the average was 28.[58] Very few interviewees who responded with a number offered an answer that was below age 25.

Three themes emerged repeatedly in the interviews when we discussed ideal marital timing: (1) the need for time to launch a career, or at least to acquire some assets or fiscal security, (2) time to mature, but not so much time as to become resistant to accommodating a spouse, and (3) the reality of a woman's "biological clock," or age-related fertility concerns. These are not poor motivations to hurry or to wait. But none of them were linked by the respondents to their Christian faith. Interviewees wanted to marry fellow Christians if they could, but there was no discernible religious influence on *when* they would marry.

That said, had this interview project not specifically targeted young adult Christians, I suspect the biological clock argument would have been less common. But we seldom heard our interviewees dismiss infertility risks. A response like the one from Evgeni, the 30-year-old divorced Muscovite we heard from in Chapter 1, struck a common tone. First, he thought waiting was best—an unsurprising response from someone whose first marriage had failed. (I cannot recall a divorcé from any of the seven sites counseling anything but caution.) But he considered waiting too long a unique risk for women: "She needs to give birth to her first child preferably before she's 27, or at least before 30, naturally. But I won't say that there's some specific age." Since most interviewees only want two or three children, however, voicing of the fertility-timing motivation was uncommon among people under 30.

In fact, a solid majority of the young adult Christians with whom we spoke did not believe the rising average age at marriage posed any problem; they themselves typically wanted to wait. It is irresponsible to do otherwise, as Sonny explained when he described marrying younger as "not very safe."

Ariana, a 24-year-old college graduate who works in finance for a multinational company in Guadalajara, typifies this understanding. She holds that the rising age at marriage is ideal. She hopes to marry by 30, and she finds the question itself rather invasive: "Each one decides what works or not. If they don't want to get married, then enjoy. What each one decides is okay." Alejandra, a 26-year-old student in the same town, feels similarly motivated to wait, in part because her own career has failed to launch: "The truth is that I would like to develop professionally before committing to marriage." And with age, she believes, will come maturity, which means better chances for her marriage long-term. Farah, the 25-year-old Lebanese woman interviewed earlier, is hopeful about marriage, but reticent to rush it. About how a relationship should ideally develop, she had this to say: "In a year, you see a bit of the person, then in two years you see a bit more, but it's important to discover more about the person. . . . To me, if you just met them, four years' minimum is required to decide."

Not everyone is going along with the trend toward later marriage, of course. Severiano, a 31-year-old Peruvian physician-in-training currently living in Spain, thinks that it's best to marry by age 23 or 24. This is surprising. If anyone could imagine the wisdom of delaying marriage, you would think it would be a medical student, harried by long hours and little time to spare. But Sevé himself hopes to marry within about a year's time, nearly eight years after his ideal. Why does he regret waiting? So far as I can tell, it's about the clash of cultures between his native and adopted countries, and his admiration for making family a priority:

> I have seen that people are getting married when they are quite a lot older, especially in Spain. My brother, who did a master's degree here, got married young, when he was 24 and his wife was 22. When she gave birth here in the clinic, she didn't feel that people's first reaction toward her was entirely positive. Maybe they thought that my brother had gotten her pregnant— that it was an accident. It didn't occur to them that they had [intentionally] married young.

The confusion was not limited to the baby's mother and father, either:

My parents came over when the baby was born, and often when they were out walking the baby, people thought they were the parents, not the grandparents. So—you get the idea. And I have to tell you that this was one of the reasons, not the main reason, but this cultural difference was one of the reasons why my brother didn't look for work here but chose to go back to Peru—because his wife didn't feel comfortable here. People would say things like, "You could have gotten further professionally."

One of the most interesting exchanges on this subject came by way of a conversation between a pair of newlyweds in Russia. They were bereft, by their own admission, of good marital exemplars. Alexander, who works in the Kremlin, lamented "no living examples to look up to." In fact, "there's nothing to look at besides Christ and the gospel, and the [stories]." His wife, Anya, concurred: "It is very difficult to create your own family now, because there are no behavior models." She hoped for some mentors, saying, "It would be great to find a family that could give us some idea" of how to make marriage work well. This was not to be found in her parents: "My dad had four marriages, and my mom had been married twice."

Russia's latter Soviet and post-Soviet eras bred a secular materialism that could not conceive of sustained self-sacrifice for another person. Getting married? Yes. Staying married? No. Alexander, who at 35 has been active in his Orthodox faith for the past decade, observed that both their sets of parents could not understand the "one flesh" union of which Jesus speaks in Mark 10: "Our parents had no idea about this, so they reduced everything to work: earn more money, achieve something in life, become something, be worth something. Those are the terms they used." A happy marriage and healthy family life didn't count as one of these achievements. Hence, Anya's wish to stay at home with their newborn makes no sense to her mother-in-law. "My mother is pretty sure I have suppressed poor Anya," Alexander joked. Anya agreed: "She cannot believe that it can also be my choice to give birth to children."

The couple could serve as poster children for the foundational vision of marriage, and this was made even clearer when we posed the question, "What do you think—what is the optimal age to get married?" Alexander answered, "When I was 21, I thought it was 35. Now that I'm 35, I think, of course, it's 21." Anya explained that "when a person is already 35 or so, he or she does not want to attune to anyone," and Alexander agreed: "The person becomes rigid."

This is a challenge, or perhaps a conundrum, many young adults articulate. It is as if there is a sweet spot in the mid- to late 20s, when the immaturity of dependence upon parents is over but you've not enjoyed so much sustained independence as to find a genuine *inter*dependence difficult to welcome. It's a point before, as Anya put it, "such a person lives in his or her mind . . . and in selfishness." Clearly, to sustain a marriage, spouses must be able to get outside of themselves and enter into the perspective of the other. But is there truly a point where you can't teach an old dog new tricks?

Valentina, a 30-year-old also in Moscow, no longer thinks in terms of age ideals, though she once did. Neither does she subscribe to what we'd call the capstone model of marriage: "To me it seems weird—to get married later only because I need to earn money, buy an apartment, or achieve something in my life. Put it off not to burden yourself with a family? That's something I cannot understand." She, too, is talking about interdependence—whereby husbands need their wives, wives need their husbands, and children need them both. The actively Orthodox, she observed, concur: "It's seldom among the Orthodox people that they go out for too long [before marrying]." Tatiana, a 27-year-old Muscovite, has grown pessimistic about marriage but nevertheless agrees that overpreparation isn't the solution: "What gets in the way is probably the fact that we are all waiting for some ideal conditions to come about. And those conditions are not coming."

Will Waiting to Marry Mean Fewer Marriages?

Demographers, while infrequently given to studying marriage, are nevertheless keenly interested in whether fertility rates are truly in decline, or just delayed until later. It's a fair question. The key concern is the difference between what is called a "quantum" change and a "tempo" change: Is real change happening (quantum), or is the change we think we're seeing simply a delay (tempo)?[59]

The same question can be posed for the study of marriage. Is real decline occurring in the number of marriages, or are the marriages just being delayed? Some demographers and sociologists claim we are simply witnessing a tempo effect—nothing to fret about. They contend that since the trend to delay marriage is fairly recent, we're seeing the most major effects now. And when marrying later in life becomes common practice, we will find that the number of marriages are still about the same. But the second demographic transition perspective would suggest that quantum change is happening to marriage. Which position is correct?

Well, I'll tell you. It's quantum. There *are* fewer people marrying today (and I have every reason to believe this is happening among Christians as well). Table A2.1, in the appendix, displays a series of regression models[60] predicting the effect that the general postponement of marriage will have on the number of actual marriages around the world.[61] I looked first at everyone ages 25 through 44. Then I focused in on those people who are marrying later (at age 35 through 39, and then at age 40 through 44). What did I learn? In short, marital delay matters. Postponement drags down marriage rates in all regions of the world. For every one-year increase in the average age at first marriage in Europe, the rate for Europeans between the ages of 25 and 44 having ever been married decreases by 3.44 percent. Recall from Table 1.1 that the increase in average age at first marriage in a variety of European countries has been considerable, ranging from 2.6 years in Switzerland to 6.3 years in the Czech Republic. In the latter, that alone would spell a 22 percent decline in the rate of people who ever get married.

It's not just happening in Europe. Every single region of the globe reveals marriage postponement as having a significant influence on overall marriage rates, and this remains the case whether we assess the entire pool of people or just focus on the adults in their early 40s. The most pronounced effects appear in South America, where a one-year increase in the mean age at first marriage is associated with a decrease of 5.24 percent in the ever-married rate for South Americans ages 25 to 44.

I cannot assume from what appears in this table that the age delay in marriage is *causing* fewer marriages to happen, just that the average age at first marriage and the ever-married rate are definitely moving together—one upward, one down.

Bouncing again off the fertility theories of demographers,[62] some are concerned about the possibility of a low-fertility *trap*. This is a scenario in which a full generation of a country's citizens experience high levels of childlessness and fertility postponement in such a way that the dramatically low fertility levels there become harder to break out of. Here again, one might wonder the same about marriage, given the significant—and now sustained—marital delay patterns highlighted in Table 1.1.[63] Might there be a low-marriage trap that need concern us? I doubt it. Marital decisions are not subject to the same age concerns that fertility is. While there is such a thing as a "biological clock," there is no "matrimonial clock." A person can always get married. But it's increasingly clear that fewer will marry in the future.

Conclusion

Marriage has come a long way since biblical times. Across much of the Christian world, women are no longer thought of as property, and practices like polygamy or arranged unions are widely rejected among Christians in a way they were not in the Old Testament era. There is still plenty of confusion to go around, as the Reformation pushed marriage away from the authority of the Church and toward that of civil government. Even today Christians struggle over the question of marital authority and how marriage can be two different things—civil and religious. Despite this quandary, whose ramifications are underestimated, Christians from around the globe tend to hold perspectives on marriage that have much in common, albeit with particular differences. Marriage, we heard, is about sacrifice, covenant, sacrament, a setting for children, a domestic church, a pathway for holiness, and an expression of committed love. But what has changed recently, almost without notice, is the vision for an ideal marital timetable and compelling reasons for marrying. Marriage, even in the minds of most Christians, has become much less about a foundation to build upon and more of a capstone that marks a successful young adult life. Marriage is now something individuals aspire to, rather than something a couple enters in order to help them fulfill their aspirations. What it certainly means, however, is that fewer people—Christians included—will ever marry at all.

3

Men and Women

Rachel is a 33-year-old mother of twin girls who married a little over two years ago. Two years before that, she had moved to Austin after receiving her Ph.D. in psychology at a university in the upper Midwest. She is now a self-employed psychologist who does contract work, including with the state of Texas. Like many, she sees a connection between her educational aspirations and her marrying after age 30: "Adult life tends to start later" than in previous generations. For her, the educational phase of one's life isn't really part of being an adult. It is associated with freedom and independence, not the interdependence of marriage.

Austin itself is considered a politically liberal and culturally permissive oasis in a relatively conservative (though diverse) state. "Keep Austin Weird" is the city's mantra. Its population has surged in recent years, just like other metro areas in the Sun Belt states. The city itself is now surprisingly the eleventh largest in America, home to just under one million people—not counting suburbs. With help from venture capital, Austin has become a technology hub and is considered one of the best places to live in America today. The impulse to pursue twin incomes has certainly surged in the central city, once a reflection of—and now contributing to—soaring home prices.

Austin's religious scene is a mixture of the evangelical Protestantism for which Texas is well known, Sun Belt Catholicism—growth of which comes largely via higher Mexican American fertility—and the occasional off-beat spirituality movement. There is certainly a significant dose of secular culture. Rachel had been largely unreligious for the first thirty years of her life, but she now belongs to one of Austin's many evangelical congregations—Southern Baptist, in her case.

Before completing her Ph.D. at age 29, Rachel had met many men in academia, but none were ready for a serious relationship (even though most of them were well into their 30s). She doesn't entirely blame them: "Men have gotten rightfully confused about what the heck women want. And aren't really sure how to date women." She met her husband on the dating site OkCupid, "because I'm cheap," she laughed, "and it was free." She admitted, after cautioning her interviewer to remember that she wasn't active in her nascent faith at the time, that she and her husband had slept with each other on their third date and cohabited during their engagement—an arrangement she would do differently today (though their tough economic position at the time helped make sense of living together). It's a near-miracle that the relationship persevered, given the low rate of success that accompanies early-relationship sex.

What she had long lacked was an orienting perspective—one with deep roots. Finding God helped a lot, Rachel told us. In particular, it was evangelical Christianity and its emphasis on the Bible:

> What I've come to realize is that without that framework in your life, without that [biblical] guidance, you're left to your own devices, and you're left to decide what you think is best at any moment, based on whatever your emotions are, whatever your current circumstances in life are, whatever you're hearing from your friends, from your family, whatever. And that is so unstable . . . [T]here's a message in the Bible about what works in every aspect of our life and my experience has been that if you play by that rule book, so to speak, things work out a whole lot better. Life tends to go a lot better—relationships, your own emotional health and well-being.

Her marriage preceded her conversion, and yet the two events seem to her, in the end, a package deal. Before becoming a Christian, Rachel wanted the commitment of marriage, but she still viewed it as something that could be severed at will if need be, since it was reducible to a piece of paper issued by the state. Today she believes marriage is a covenant before God, a sacred relationship, even if her own pathway to it was unconventional for a Baptist.

But even more than marriage, it was the arrival of their children that matured the love between Rachel and her husband. Rachel wants her children to benefit from a strong Christian family life, something neither she nor her husband experienced while growing up. Starting a family had felt natural to her. And it's functional for men, she holds:

> I think men are meant to be the providers. You know that's kind of what they're designed for. And if they have no one to carry out that role for, I think it's easy to feel kind of lost, without a purpose. And that's why I think sometimes you see men who maybe are very immature making a lot of bad decisions.

Rachel's right. Between 1996 and 2016 in the United States, men ages 25 to 34 exhibited the largest leap in labor force nonparticipation, from 6.7 percent to 11.3 percent.[1] Such men, Rachel holds, are living in their own small, selfish world: "It's not a healthy place to live, for so many reasons." Nevertheless, she observed, good can sometimes result: "Some of them get a woman pregnant, and that is often the thing that causes them to go, 'Wait, I gotta get my act together. I gotta make sure I have a job.'"

Rachel gave voice to tensions that are evident everywhere—including about the new, more level playing field, wherein men and women compete (and hopefully cooperate) in terms of education, economics, and career expectations. In fact, interviewees commonly noted shifting sex roles and expectations as the most obvious way that marriage has changed.[2] Many brought up the full-time labor force participation of women, and we heard extensive commentary about the ramifications of this both before and within marriage. But interviewees seldom described anything like a high-conflict "battle of the sexes." Rachel sure didn't. Instead, it was about the challenges of integrating increasingly similar types—a male and female worker—within a union that had long witnessed sex roles, the expectations that men and women have of each other (*as* men and women) in their lives together. Since many roles are flexible in nature, some call them gender roles.[3] Other roles—like childbearing and breastfeeding—are not flexible, but bodily and sexed.

The New Normal

Nadine, a 30-year-old unmarried accountant living in Zouk, a northern suburb of Beirut, had thought a good deal about roles and how they have changed. She repeatedly returned to the matter, endorsing the new normal:

> The man cannot now deny the existence or the importance of the woman, or undermine her. He has to be like her. Both do housework, raise kids, etc. The man cannot come and sit once he arrives home. He has to be active at home, since both him and the woman are working outside, so they share responsibilities inside.

Nadine's family had moved to Zouk from Chouf, a district south of Beirut that had been devastated during the civil war. Christians had been purged from Chouf but allowed to return after the reconciliation—though with little local political power. Nadine's father spends most of his time in Chouf, while Nadine spends most of hers in Zouk, with her mother, who is not employed. Her parents are not divorced, but according to Nadine, they don't seem to mind spending nearly all of their time apart. Nadine expects more one day from marriage, and from a husband, than what she witnessed growing up. To begin with, she sees it as an absolute must for both a husband and wife to work: "Couples nowadays are depending on each other financially," she leveled. Like for many in Beirut, times are lean for Nadine, especially because she helps her parents financially as well:

> Things are getting more and more expensive, and my salary is not increasing. I get paid around $1,000 USD [per month], so I feel I am going backward. I tried to ask for a raise, but no answer from my employers. I have to settle bank installments for the car loan and spend some pocket money, and this is barely enough. If I had no family and were independent, it might have been sufficient. But in the condition where I help my family, it's very little money.

Over seven thousand miles away, in Guadalajara, Juliana is a 25-year-old graphic designer. She would agree with Nadine about the two-earner household: "The majority of women already work, in part because the economic situation is not enough for a man to be the support of family. Now you need both salaries." Ariana, 24 and a recent college graduate, also lives in Guadalajara and feels the same. Ariana had no personal experience with marriage while she was growing up—her father was already married to another woman when her mother gave birth to her and to a sibling—but she, too, could still discern a shift in roles:

> Before, you didn't see a woman working. Now, it's practically impossible that a marriage survives without both working. Before, you saw families with fourteen children, and now, I think nobody can say they are going to have fourteen children and make it. I think that with two [children], it's difficult. But [even] apart from that, it's not the same. Since both are working, they see each other less, or maybe they like to take trips and wait to have children. I think it's completely different—the institution as such, or sacrament, if you will.

What we heard from these young adults was not a his-versus-hers perspective. Men and women largely agreed on the role-sharing realities of modern marriage. Enrique, 28, an industrial engineer in Guadalajara, has nothing but compliments for the women he's seen flourishing in the labor force, recognizing their struggle to balance work and family:

> I think women are much better at work than men. I'm completely convinced of it. But by their very nature, if they want to have a family, they may see their careers cut short. What do I think? Well . . . I don't think there is a right or wrong answer. I think that for the family, there has to be the right balance. I know there are very hard-working girls, but they are very generous in doing whatever possible to combine their family and their work.[4]

I could add dozens more comparable endorsements, or at least expectations, of the dual-income family. As far as expressed standards go, this one is now typical among the average churchgoing Christian in all seven countries. This new normal—two jobs, two incomes—may not be considered ideal among all the interviewees, but it was certainly thought to be necessary by most. And most considered it an improvement over more traditional norms.

Many, like Nadine and Ariana, contrasted the current state of affairs with the very different one in which they grew up. Unlike Ariana's, Nadine's mother remains committed to the older, more traditional model of courtship, which doesn't include being too picky when choosing a mate. This adds tension whenever the two discuss Nadine's relationship frustrations:

> She feels I don't want marriage, . . . because I usually meet guys with the idea of "no" prevailing in my mind. That's why Mom tries to tell me not to think like that. I am trying to change this in me. Mom tells me not to keep this idea in my mind, because my life alone will not be a happy one. Though I myself find that both ways, there is something negative—whether you get married or stay single.

At age 28, Esteban owns a failing advertising agency in Guadalajara. He explained to us his theory about intergenerational tensions: "The thesis is our grandparents, the antithesis is our parents, and the synthesis is us." I asked for clarification. He said that it means his grandparents' era was marked by strict gender roles and a machismo mentality among men. His parents' generation ushered in an uneven dismantling of those norms—which often yielded divorce among those who could afford it. His own generation has more of the right idea, he believes. They honor women's workforce contributions and are more egalitarian in marriage. However, they face the challenges of a highly competitive economy and few examples of how to live this new model of marriage. This results in considerable uncertainty—more than in the past, even though the economic outlook then was commonly far more modest than today.

Interestingly, in no site did I hear a sustained description of marriage as a means to combat or mitigate economic uncertainty. Marriage was always the victim of uncertainty—less attainable now because of it—rather than a reliable tool to combat uncertainty.[5] This, more than anything, reveals the deep infiltration into the minds and hearts of Christian young adults of the capstone model of marriage (as described in Chapter 2). A foundational model would consider marriage as a way to reach the goal of financial stability; a capstone says that marriage is a prize for having achieved that stability on your own.

Reason observes that two incomes are better than one. Sharing expenses reduces each person's recurrent liabilities. Moreover, marriage is said to be good for psychological and physical health, as the evidence continues to suggest. So why aren't we seeing more marrying instead of less? Because, at some primal level, men—the ones who are still doing the asking—don't want to. Understanding why this has occurred is hardly straightforward, but part of the reason is that they feel unable to meet women's rising expectations.

Higher Expectations for Lifestyle and Marriage

Material expectations have surged in a rapidly globalizing world in which media readily displays how the other half lives. Consequently (as just discussed), one income will not accommodate what many young adults, Christians included, want for their early married life. Have we truly entered the era of what some psychologists are calling the "suffocation model" of marriage, wherein too much is expected of fallible humans?[6] I suspect so. Marriage seems increasingly a "vehicle of self-actualization" rather than a setting for self-sacrifice, Russell Moore fears.[7] "Simply put," Presbyterian minister Tim Keller suspects, "people are asking far too much in a marriage partner."[8] They're onto something. Regardless of the research site, I heard few Christian young adults professing expectations for marriage that were modest. That's not a value judgment. It's just a fact. High material and psychological expectations accompany the capstone vision (and timing) of marriage.

Nadine, the unmarried woman from Beirut whose parents live apart, is not just concerned about making ends meet in a country facing seemingly endless economic challenges. She wants a nice financial cushion: "Before, people used to be content with anything," she explained. "Now people require more things. . . . As for me, I think that if I want to get married, I need to be financially comfortable." Her reasons include the possibilities of children: "If I get pregnant and stop working, we will be in financial trouble." She is also trying to avoid divorce by ensuring financial stability before marriage. "If I were living the life of my mother," she told us frankly, "I would have divorced a long time ago." Still, she understands her parents' priorities, even though she doesn't share them: "They lived the times of war. Many of them did not get a lot of education. Their only concern was to be part of a family."

When asked what she thought of the rising age at marriage in Lebanon, Nadine was ambivalent. Her broadened horizons (compared with previous generations) have in a sense improved her life but also complicated it in regard to marriage:

> I can't really evaluate if it's a good thing or not, but I can say that since girls became educated, their requirements became higher. The girl wants at least to keep her economic standards when she gets married. She wants to preserve the standards she got used to in her [single years]. She might have barely enough money, but she can't sacrifice more, starting a family with the same income. The girl thus has more requirements relative to before, and the [standard of] living is getting very difficult, so marriage is becoming harder.

Elias, a 32-year-old Maronite Catholic living in Beirut, has been married three years and relies on gigs to augment his and his wife's income. He had waited five years to be able to afford to marry: First, it took him about three years "to get the down payment for my apartment so that I get the housing loan. Then I had to wait for about a year to get it furnished, and a year to get money for the wedding." Elias's viewpoint parallels Cherlin's capstone model of marriage (see Chapter 2). There isn't a sense in Elias's discourse that he and his wife might have done well to marry younger and then tackle the challenges of housing and furnishings as a team, with a combined income.

As for children, they are happy to have their one child, but since times are so tight, Elias says he doesn't want a second: "I come back home at 11:00 p.m. If we have another child, how long will I have to work?" Surprisingly, the ornamental and cultural expectations of his faith are among the reasons he finds fatherhood such a financial burden:

> If you want to baptize your child, you will have to spend a lot on white clothes [for the child] and a reception. You might tell me that I can get my child baptized without all this, but at the end of the day, everyone is doing this, so why should I be different? The ones who invited you earlier to their baptismal ceremonies, you need to invite them. . . . All the families are having to go through this burden. If we stay like this, there will be no Christian families in the country in about ten years.

To feel that you can't afford to be a Christian anymore—the faith that began in an animal's feed trough in a dirty stable not so far from Beirut—seems tragically ironic. Amid this paradox, it was unsurprising to hear Elias subsequently claim that people are not as contented in marriage today as in past generations. His sentiments were repeated by others in his country.

Agata, a 23-year-old from Lublin working in a veterinarian's office, is married civilly (not in the Church). She didn't mince words about her own elevated expectations. And like Elias, she definitely doesn't want more than one child, "due to financial reasons." Even educating one child can mean going into considerable debt:

> I don't complain about my earnings. But I would like to see the world, not just spend my life taking care of children. If I were to send my child to university, pay back the loan, and have another child who would also go to university, I wouldn't travel. I would struggle to make ends meet every month.

When Kingsley, a 29-year-old evangelical and personal assistant to the head of a private school in Lagos, was asked whether or not marriage today is different, he didn't have to think hard either. His comparison of modern relationships to those of his parents' generation wasn't only about different amounts of money but also about an entirely different attitude toward money—one that seems to erode what he calls "true love":

I remember growing up, Daddy didn't have much. Likewise, Mum. But they tend to help each other; you won't see them argue over money. I have never seen my mum argue over money with my dad. It has never happened. No matter how [much] misunderstanding they have, Dad has never resulted to violence. We were just comfortable with the one room we were living in, good food, good clothing, and that is it. But these days a lot of things have changed. The world has changed a lot of things . . . You don't see what you can call true love. Even boyfriend and girlfriend argue over money, and they are not even married.

What has caused this dramatic shift in just one generation, in Kingsley's opinion? He refers to "the world" as the culprit. We could call it globalization, the media, or simply expanded opportunities—and with them, expectations—all over the planet. But here again, we hear no reference to Christian faith as a source of resistance against these changes. "The world" seems to be winning.

Christian or not, young adults are determined that marriage not curb their premarital material lifestyle. Renowned economist Richard Easterlin hypothesized as early as 1973 that young married couples tend to compare their standard of living to that of their parents when the former (the young married couple) were teenagers. That's much different than comparing their situation to that of their parents when the latter were newly married. According to Easterlin, this unequal comparison prompts declining fertility because young marrieds care more about comfort and status than they do about how many children they'll have.[9] Today—with the now firmly entrenched capstone standard—this tendency of young couples does more than hamper fertility; it slows the generation of marriage in the first place.

This is not simply a phenomenon exclusive to the prosperous West, either. Ndidi, a 28-year-old unmarried Pentecostal from Lagos, was clear about the conditions under which she would marry: "When I have everything I want. When I am able to achieve everything I want to achieve for myself. Then I will get married." Another 24-year-old unmarried woman from Lagos concurred: "Oh, please! [Laughs] I can't marry and suffer." Jonathan, a 24-year-old Pentecostal entrepreneur and university student in Lagos, did not disagree:

Yes, that is how all girls are. I am generalizing [about] all of them. If you have money, they will stay. And if you don't have [money], they will go . . . Women these days are not ready to suffer. They can't stay in an environment where there is a mosquito, a centipede, a house they can't take a selfie of and post on Facebook, you know.

What do these heightened expectations about standard of living have to do with changing sex roles in marriage? The two phenomena are siblings: Part of the reason much of the world expects both men and women—husbands and wives—to work has nothing to do with feminism or the long-overdue emphasis on education of girls and women. It has plenty to do with notably higher material standards than our grandparents had, and two incomes are a faster path than one to achieving those standards. This is not the *primary* reason women's labor force participation rate has surged; genuine equality of opportunity is valued by many, Christians included. But I would be remiss as a sociologist if I were to ignore the influence of our growing material expectations—whether found in Lubbock, London, or Lagos.

In some places, unreasonably high lifestyle standards are framed as the result of Western exports—new, nonnative norms increasingly corrosive to marital life. One Lebanese man noted, "People are trying to apply the European lifestyle," which he claimed concerns the pursuit of money and pleasure. He impugns his fellow Lebanese Christians who "think this lifestyle is the correct one." "We want to imitate the West," he observed, "thinking the Western people are right and we are wrong." Magdalena, a 21-year-old recently married woman from Lublin, echoed his thoughts, maintaining that "Western ideologies that are imposed on our system of beliefs are trying to destroy our concept of family."[10] Likewise, Paweł—a 24-year-old graduate student in Krakow—had little love for relationship advice coming from the West (i.e., "the U.S., U.K., and France"): "A lot of Catholics here in Poland don't realize this, or even if they do, they think those patterns that come from the outside are good. They don't really think critically about them. The arguments from the Church don't attract them."

John Thomas, a 20-year-old Catholic college student in Lagos, blames globalization for the marital recession he perceives in Nigeria: "People are getting accustomed to the culture of other people so well that they are adapting so easily to them" and in so doing, "forgetting" their own cultural heritage. He went on to highlight America as an example of an exporter of relational norms that were never native to Nigeria. And the local Christians are picking up what the United States is doling out: "We also see that, in the church where we are today."

The Specter of Poverty

Men and women have historically responded to temporarily tough economic times by delaying marriage and childbearing. What today's couples seem universally uninterested in doing, however, is lowering their material expectations. This, too, is a sign of the capstone standard's primacy. In the contrasting foundational vision, being newly married and poor was difficult, expected, and (typically) temporary. In the capstone standard, being poor is a sign that there's something wrong with you; you're not yet marriage material.

Not everyone perceived poverty as a marriage-killer. Paweł (quoted above) and Marta are a recently married couple living in Krakow. He is 24, and she is 29—a five-year gap in an unusual direction. Marta is a full-time mother to their 1-year-old daughter, while Paweł is in the middle of graduate studies in philosophy at a nearby university. They bucked the norm by marrying and having a child while Paweł is still in school (and relatively young). When I asked them whether or not they thought marriage had changed, Marta was blunt about the material aspect of the shift:

> Yes. It's now about comfort in marriage, looking for comfort, [more] than it was twenty to thirty years ago. When I think about my family and parents, they didn't have [much] money or [own] a home. When my mother tells me some stories from the past, I'm very surprised that they had children. I think now, and with our friends, if you want to get married, it's good to have a house, a car, work—you definitely need to have a job. [*Your parents had none of that?*] Work, yes.

Paweł then jumped in: "I can share a very similar story about my parents. They were not on their own [when they married], renting a flat, and didn't have a stable job." But today, he says, especially among workers in the big corporations, "people there are very focused on the material." He described a typical age-measured expectation among his peers and how he went the countercultural route instead, marrying before he had reached these milestones: "When you are 32, you need to have a car and two flats, with one rented out. When I got married, I was still studying, and renting a flat." Like Nadine, Paweł could understand the perspective of earlier generations, and he ascribed political reasons to his own generation's drive to obtain:

Our fathers lived under communism. They didn't have a car or flat of their own. We, or our parents, were brought up with the idea that you need to secure yourself, to have your own things. That's why people elsewhere— Netherlands, France, Germany—can rent, but here we have to own.

The current Zeitgeist in Poland is, as Paweł relayed, a consequence of having lived under a government that had owned both your labor and your residence. Private ownership is thought to build a hedge against a future government expropriation. But since owning things takes time, marriage waits.

Men, Money, and the Waning Motivation to Marry

Many sociologists hold that the key to understanding lagging marriage rates lies in wages and employment stability—and similar factors like employment status, job security, and education.[11] They think if these elements were more secure, men would pursue marriage—simply because they always have. Unfortunately, most scholars don't often report the kind of statistics that would tell us just *how* influential economic factors actually are. Does a good job raise the average man's likelihood of marrying in the next couple of years by, say, 50 percent or 5 percent? One trio of researchers attempted a learned estimate and concluded that lessened employment and earnings explain a little over 20 percent of the decline in educated American men's marriage rates since 1969. And they account for about one-third of the decline in marriage among less-educated men.[12] In other words, a large share of the decline (and delay) in marriage has apparently nothing to do with income and employment.[13] Like so many social scientists studying marriage, the authors of this study merely acknowledged the possibility that "the changing normative climate played some role in the decline."[14] I think it's far more than a possibility.[15]

I have no trouble whatsoever affirming that a stable and adequate income helps encourage men of marriageable age to tie the knot. I don't doubt that ideal work schedules and health insurance are good for marriage. But holding onto the presupposition that there is still a strong, primeval impulse among men to marry—with all that marriage entails—if only they could afford it? Globally, that assumption makes little sense today. The situation has grown far more complicated. Harvard sociologist Orlando Patterson, in personal reflections published in an obscure volume in 2002, foreshadowed my own skepticism:

> One common explanation for the low rate of marriage is joblessness, but I have a problem with that. I think employment rates are one factor, but a minor factor . . . If joblessness is what accounts for low rates of marriage, high divorce rates, and paternal abandonment, then one would expect to see massive familial problems in other populations like India and Asia, where there are high rates of unemployment and poverty. You don't get that . . . It just doesn't add up.[16]

His Harvard colleague William Julius Wilson comments similarly. In his landmark 1990 book, *The Truly Disadvantaged*, he had concluded that declining marriage rates among African Americans could be attributed to poor economic opportunities for men.[17] Since then, he's moderated his assessment:

> There may not be a significant increase in marriage, because we're running up against strong currents in the broader society, where marriage is no longer an institution that is considered to be strong and viable and stable.[18]

A third Harvard sociologist, Kathryn Edin, sees it, too: "[M]en's education, employment, job stability, and income do make a difference in transitions to marriage, but not as much as one might expect."[19]

Even if marriageability were only about money, it would be about more money than it once was, given the rising expectations described above. A 2019 study of American marriage markets revealed what economic levels would move women from being unmarried to married. The authors estimated that unmarried men's income would need to rise by 55 percent, and their employment level by 26 percent.[20] This means that more men are now considered unmarriageable. Both highly educated careerist women and undereducated working-class ones are at elevated risk of not marrying in spite of their desire to do so.

It's not as if such men have asked women to marry them and been turned down. My interviews widely suggest that even marriageable men are stalling. Why? It's partly a numbers game. If men are outnumbered by women in the "marriageable" portion of the wider mating market—and they are—then men have more power, and more time, to navigate their way toward marriage in ways and on timetables they prefer. Veronica, a 28-year-old preschool teacher, sees this at work in Guadalajara:

> I have a lot of friends just waiting for [men] to ask them to marry. . . . They [the men] always say they want to be more stable in their jobs before they make a commitment like that. [*Why is that?*] Because in Mexico, in the end, even if we've evolved a little, we still see the man as the person who has to have a better income and support the family economically.

Natural experiments—when nature or markets create some type of upheaval—enable scholars to watch what naturally happens in response. Several such experiments are particularly relevant here. One is the fracking boom in the shale oil fields of North Dakota.[21] Men are far more apt than women to work in this gritty, dangerous, and physically demanding field of drilling for, extracting, and transporting oil and gas. So a lot of men enjoyed financial success as labor needs soared. However, a study found that increased income in those places did nothing to boost local marriage rates.[22] (It only raised fertility rates—both marital and nonmarital births.) The authors contrast this with the Appalachian coal boom of the 1970s and 1980s, when an increase in earnings prompted an equivalent surge in marriage. Why the difference between then and now? Here, too, the authors offer no more explanation than a reference to "social norms."[23] What they refer to, I fear, is that men are losing the motivation to marry.[24]

Artur, a 22-year-old Catholic from Lublin who is engaged to be married within the year, maintains that "People who are planning to establish a family and get married should think that money is the only obstacle." But it's not. Numerous forces are curbing men's interest in marrying, he believed: "In general, people are losing some values which I think are very important," including a respect for family and faith. In their place, Artur perceived competing values—work, career, and experimenting with relationships—all of which seemed to him to enjoy more peer support than marrying at age 23.

Another compelling natural-experiment study in 2018 found that manufacturing decline in male-dominated industries deterred the formation of marriages in America, while decline in more female-intensive employment domains had the opposite effect.[25] When the job outlook became tougher for men, fewer married. But when the same happened for women, more marriages happened. This sheds some light on why women's earning power, while valued, has not been consistently applied by researchers as a marker of women's own marriageability.[26] In fact, women's earning power can backfire. In a landmark 2015 study appearing in the *Quarterly Journal of Economics*, a trio of economists concluded that marriage rates decline when the likelihood of women outearning men rises.[27] You might rightly think this shouldn't be the case, but it is, and it is not unique to Christians. So just how common is this scenario? In the United States, the wife earns more than the husband in 26 percent of couples under age 65, a rate that has held steady since 2010. It surged during the first decade of the twenty-first century but has since slid 2 percentage points to rest where it currently stands.[28]

While progressives might see this as stalled movement toward strict equality in the workplace, the authors of the study detected more personal priorities at work, suggesting that couples actively try to avoid the situation in which the wife earns more than the husband.[29] Why? To prevent conflict. Couples in which the wife earns more than the husband tend to be less happy, report greater marital strife, and are more likely to get a divorce.[30] The mere fact that she earns more than he does was found to increase the likelihood of divorce by 50 percent.[31] To be accurate, the effect is only found when husband and wife are more educated. But ouch—gender equality in households may come at a steep price.

Marriages in which women outearn their husbands typically display another source of disparity: unequal household labor. In the seminal study on the matter, high-earning women actively spent more time on chores and child care than did their husband. This (domestic) work required *after* work has been long dubbed "the second shift" and generally falls more heavily on female shoulders.[32] Aleksandra, a 40-year-old engaged physician in Warsaw, feels the tension on this subject, but she has a plan to deal with it:

> You have to strive to let a man be a man. You have to learn that. You can see that in minor things. You have to let him take care of you . . . I know that I [would] do many things better, yet I restrain myself. . . . Because of my job, I won't be a housewife who will do everything while the man will perform his strictly masculine role. We have to complement each other, and we talk about it.

Magdalena is taking college courses while looking for summer work between semesters. She endorses the nobility of women's labor force participation, but she takes for granted that there will be no overhaul of domestic roles:

Now, there are many women who can simultaneously work and take care of the house. So I think a lot has changed in this respect, which I think is positive. If a woman wants to work, nobody should forbid her that. If she wants to stay at home, then it's also good.

Becker's "Exchange" Theory of Marriage

The *Quarterly Journal of Economics* study I mentioned previously—about women earning more than men—mentions "Beckerian forces," which the authors believe are still at work in the contemporary household (to the chagrin of most sociologists of gender).[33] The reference is to the late economist and Nobel laureate Gary Becker's landmark 1973 article, "A Theory of Marriage," which shed light not only on the existence of a marriage market but also on the distinctive "gains from trade" that men and women typically exhibited when exiting the market upon marrying.[34] Becker's theory held that men and women bring their differences—strengths and weaknesses, skills and needs—into marriage. After the Industrial Revolution, many couples capitalized on the division of labor according to sex, with the husband working in the paid labor force and the wife staying home to manage the household and raise children. In so doing, they were being efficient and, hence, raising the "value" of the marriage itself.[35]

But Becker was not writing about Christian marriage. His concern was less about state or religious recognition of marriages than about the actual behavior that composed male-female unions inhabiting a single household. Cohabitation was common-law marriage, in Becker's mind.[36] Peter, the shirt designer in Lagos, seemed almost to agree with Becker when asked to distinguish between marriage and cohabitation:

> Marriage is a legal form of cohabitation, because there is nothing really unique in marriage; you have been dating the same girl over and over. This time around, you are settling with the lady you have been dating for maybe two to three years, and the whole essence of the marriage is just to make it legal before the general public that this person is actually going to be my wife.

Keep in mind, however, that Becker was writing before the masses began perceiving marriage as a capstone or achievement rather than a foundation from which couples accomplish things by uniting their distinctive efforts. If the latter were still the case, the long-term stability of cohabiting unions might be comparable to those of marriage. They are not, in nearly all societies.[37]

Insofar as marriage concerns the transfer of earned money in return for other valued resources (a well-managed household, children, care, sex, security, etc.), marriage rates should remain stable. But if marriage begins to have less to do with the movement of desirable and distinctive resources *between* spouses and more to do with simple joint consumption of resources, the social practice of marriage should recede. Where spouses are functionally interchangeable and basically independent, they simply do not need the marriage. (The two may yet wed and remain together, perhaps even happily so. But this scenario is serendipitous—a product of privilege, not scarcity. It is not the substance of marriage.) Most marriages reveal differences and interdependence, even if only over time.

When University of San Francisco economist (and evangelical Christian) Bruce Wydick reflected on why he observed a 15 percent increase in the cohabitation rate following a 10 percent growth in women's labor force participation, he responded that "women and men don't 'need each other' as they did when marriage fulfilled a more functional, economic role. Yet the desire for partnership and emotional intimacy remain—hence the rise of cohabitation."[38] Researchers find this reality internationally as well; high levels of women's employment are associated with lower marriage rates, higher levels of cohabitation, and mixed effects on divorce rates.[39] Even the respected naturalist writer Wendell Berry seems to concur when he notes that marriage "is now on the one hand an intimate 'relationship' involving (ideally) two successful careerists in the same bed, and on the other hand a sort of private political system in which rights and interests must be constantly asserted and defended." In other words, he quips, marriage "has now taken the form of divorce: a prolonged and impassioned negotiation as to how things shall be divided."[40]

I mean no disrespect when I say that my contemporaries who vociferously claim that the notion of complementary exchange has nothing to do with marriage are out of step with a good deal of the globe's population. It's the couples who eschew the exchange philosophy who are ambivalent about marriage. When exchange relationships are no longer compelling on a wide scale, marriage should recede significantly and alternative relationship patterns rise in popularity. In the West, it is happening now.[41]

But why is it happening more to the people who need marriage most—the working class and poor? The more that marriage is repackaged and sold in the West as a capstone rather than a foundation, the higher up the social ladder it climbs. Today marriage increasingly appears as an upper-middle-class symbol. Uniting two lives together isn't how you afford things anymore. It's another thing you aim to afford, because marriage itself has become a cultural marker of prestige in the minds of most—Christian or otherwise.[42] However, marriage still has the power to increase wealth, encouraging couples to spend responsibly and save for the future, allowing them to invest together in housing and other appreciable assets.[43] Even married people with *little* education enjoy these monetary advantages.[44] In fact, women from disadvantaged backgrounds are much less likely to fall into poverty if they get and stay married.[45] So it would stand to reason that those who are the least prepared for a rainy day would be the most likely to run for the cover of marriage. But that's just not how it works anymore.

It's not that poor and working-class women don't like the idea of marriage or of the notion of exchange. In fact, they are more apt to endorse both than are the middle and upper-middle classes. But they simply do not see how the men in their life will live up to it. So they hedge their bets, waiting, cohabiting, having children—with few great expectations for a lifelong mate.[46] (This is even more tragic for these communities than it first appears. When a child's parents aren't married—even if they are living together—that child is automatically at increased risk for a heap of negative outcomes, like drug use, delinquent behavior, domestic violence, and parental breakup.[47] Add those risks to the inherent frailty of life in poverty, and it's no surprise when the cycle continues.)

A Case of Cultural Lag?

Perhaps what is occurring among men is simply cultural lag, that is, people failing—but only for a time—to synchronize their attitudes and social behaviors with new realities.[48] In this case, the new reality is women's dramatic success in education and their surge in labor force participation. Marriage need no longer be a foundation. In fact, marriage isn't necessary, but it is still desired. A cultural lag explanation would claim that (1) these changes are inevitable, (2) they're just slow and uneven in their uptake, and (3) marriage will survive just fine and stabilize once the new norms come to dominate. The idea is that since both work outside the home, so both will take a comparable role inside the household, resulting in egalitarian marriage—if they marry at all.

Is this the case? The new reality of equal or near-equal employment of men and women is certainly beginning to sink in. Marriage is being delayed widely in the West, as Table 1.1 demonstrated. Will the transformation of marital norms and expectations follow everywhere? And will we all eventually wonder how we could ever have thought and acted differently? Maybe. Maybe not.

Husbands *have* become more domestic and attentive to children's needs, on average. In the United States, today's fathers have nearly tripled the number of hours spent on housework and childcare since 1965, while mothers' housework efforts on these have declined 25 percent—with no decline in child care.[49] But data from the Monitoring the Future study in the United States reveals that Americans may have reached the border of their enthusiasm for dual-income households. In the years after 2010, slightly more high-school seniors favored the husband as the achiever and decision-maker in the family, when compared with the same question posed in the late 1990s.[50] And that's in the United States.

Lagos, Nigeria, is one of the world's largest and fastest-growing cities, a representative of sorts for the Global South. The city is an extraordinarily interactive experience. There are, after all, lots of possibilities to interface in this metro area with a population estimated at twenty-one million and counting. No one's really counting, however. One of the many sources of tension in Nigerian politics is just how many people live in Lagos and who exactly they are. Rough estimates are all anyone has.

Lagos is Western in its ambitions but African in culture, a setting ripe for conflict over competing values. Despite popular impressions to the contrary, Lagos is a place of profound contrasts—just like many Western cities. Muslims and Christians—mostly Pentecostals and Catholics—coexist largely peaceably in Lagos, unlike in northern Nigeria, where tensions thrive and violence is common. (Boko Haram's insurgencies are well known there and abroad.) Lagos, however, feels far removed from interreligious violence.

Peter, 26 and unmarried, is a self-employed shirt designer. Like many of the interviewees in Lagos, he is sympathetic to the push for women's increased representation in the labor force:

> In this part of our country, there has been too much of an emphasis saying that the woman's role is in the house to take care of the children and the

kitchen, while the man goes out to . . . make provision for food, clothing, shelter for the entire family. . . . With the way the society is now, male and female being educated, both of them have to go out to work. She wouldn't want to sit at home, because she is equally educated.

Interviewees were generally poorer in Lagos than those in other sites, including Lebanon and Mexico. But they were not universally so. A number of them are self-employed, reflecting the ability to operate one's own business but also signaling a scarcity of access to established workplaces and, hence, more stable income. Mirroring American mentalities, Nigerian interviewees who are struggling economically and those who are "making it" communicated comparable perspectives on marriage—elevated expectations of companionship and status achievement—even though the poor are in a far less optimal position to "afford" this mentality than are Lagos's middle class and elite.[51]

Solomon is 26 years old, unmarried, Catholic, and working in advertising in Lagos. While he notices the rising age at marriage and the financial difficulties of becoming a marriageable man (men have to pay a "bride price" as well as reveal adequate earning power in a wildly fluctuating economy), Solomon, too, is convinced that the shift in gender roles within marriage is beneficial. He recounted to us a certain saying from the past: "If [women] acquire every education in this world, it will [still] end in the kitchen." But it doesn't seem to have turned out that way: "Women are now out there working like men, too. You even see them in politics. You see them everywhere, unlike before."

And yet Solomon doesn't believe that this shift has fundamentally altered how Nigerians think about marriage today. Men are still seeking some measure of headship in marriage, and that is getting harder to find:

These days, I will say that men find it difficult to marry a lady who has established herself, somebody who has a comfortable job, has her own house—even if it is a rented apartment—and she lives well. She might not be a submissive type. . . . You will see some men finding it difficult to marry such type of person, because that respect might not be there.

"Some men," Solomon said. Perhaps fewer every year, if a cultural lag explanation here proves correct. But even Peter anticipates potential unrest: "In a situation where there is no understanding [about this], there might be conflict over gender roles." Isaac, a 27-year-old unmarried evangelical who is self-employed in Lagos as a shoe salesman, was more blunt: "If the woman is career-oriented and she is not ready to play her role at home, there will be a problem. So, I think gender roles really have an effect on who young people think to marry."

No amount of cultural lag will ever convince Geoff, the 24-year-old evangelical from Austin, that there's no such thing as sex-specific roles in marriage. More readily than most interviewees, Geoff turned to the Bible for evidence:

> In Genesis, you see God bringing the woman to man as his helper. And you know they are both created equally, but they have different roles. And so I think God designed it that way, and he designed it that way for a purpose. And I think you see when there's a deviation from that, there's problems.

Geoff anticipates benefitting himself one day from the sex-specific roles he perceives in Scripture. He feels fatigue from carrying out some of the household tasks that distract him from his work commitments:

> It's tough being a single guy, because . . . you've got to do everything! I mean you've gotta pay all the bills, you've got to be responsible for getting all your meals put together. You are responsible for, you know, taking care of the house and everything. . . . You can't focus as much on your arena of expertise.

He returned to the subject later in his interview, crediting misinterpretation for the societal pushback that his perspective receives:

> People in society see the gender roles of men to lead, protect, and provide— and see that leadership or headship role where the man is in authority over the wife as something that is repulsive, because it makes the wife or female inferior. . . . They don't make the distinction between roles and worth, whereas the biblical understanding would be that we are both equal in worth because we are both made in the image of God . . . Scripture puts those two realities as existing side-by-side to where you can have different roles yet be equal in worth.

Geoff went on to compare interactions in marriage to the very Godhead, granting matrimony a tremendous value in his estimation. Just as the Trinity is a mystery, he pointed out, so is the marital union. And misunderstanding roles can lead to conflict and marital breakdown:

> [It] points back to God and to how things are even within the Trinity . . . there's no loss of worth or value of the Son, I mean, He is just as [much] God as God the Father. Even though they're different. And so people have lost that understanding. . . . And so when the roles, the distinction between roles and worth is lost, and people think that there has to be equality of roles, and it is not [equal], then you are going to see that conflict, that battle of the sexes happen. . . . Women are going to want to try to take on the man's role, and then the man is going to want to try to put her in her place, and so the marriage is, you know, going to get nasty. Because instinctively, we weren't designed for that. . . . The loss of gender distinction and all that kind of stuff is definitely playing a part in the decline of marriage, for sure.

The Exchange Philosophy—Not Dead but Different

In general, our interviewees saw merit in the exchange model of marriage, though most stopped well short of voicing active support for the model's claims about distinctive sex roles—as Geoff did. Why? Because this is not how most Christians anticipate the marital division of labor anymore. Talk of distinctive roles seems to them out of step with modern norms and with their plans—whether intentional or involuntary—to have dual (though not dueling) careers.

However, our fundamental commitments are best discerned in actions rather than attitudes. In their behavior, a type of complementary exchange still appears common among the globe's Christians—if more in the form of the second shift mentioned earlier than in any radical distinction in roles.

Jasmine is a 28-year-old Filipino American who works in marketing for an American university's extension college in Japan. She completed a systems engineering degree in Wisconsin, is currently pursuing an MBA, and recently became engaged to an officer in the U.S. Air Force. Jasmine is Catholic and comes from a family that actively practices more traditional sex roles.

She wants to continue working, even if children come, but she doesn't expect that work will bring the sense of purpose and meaning that family does:

> I don't think there's enough out there career-wise that could give me the fulfillment that I would want, you know, that I could feel as I could in being in a happy marriage—and be that support for someone else, too, who I also know is on that track. And then us being able to work together, too, you know? It's kind of like the sum of the parts is greater than each individually.

Jasmine not only acknowledges that she will someday work the second shift, she endorses it: "Even if I do like working—I want that career—I also want to be home with dinner ready when he comes home."

Jasmine is heavily influenced by her mother's example. "She has played the motherly role in the home—the housekeeper, homebuilder role—very well," Jasmine explained. "And that's something I want to echo from what I've seen." She considers her homemaking duties to be one way to safeguard a marriage: "Because it's like, you know, just support for your husband that he can't get from anyone else. You wouldn't want him to get it from anyone else." It is unlikely, however, that Jasmine's mother was much of a career woman. The reality of what it takes to work outside the home and still run a household with all the comforts Jasmine envisions providing to her husband might not live up to Jasmine's imaginings.

This state of women who "simultaneously work and take care of the house" (as described by Magdalena earlier) is hardly the feminist mutiny so many of my peers have envisioned. In fact, it's a gender revolutionary's nightmare—to have come close, by way of dual careers, but feel so far away from the goal of truly egalitarian households. In reality, Jasmine and Magdalena are simply worried—concerned that career will best family. And they're willing to give way for marriage and family matters.

Ander is a 25-year-old from San Sebastian, Spain—in the Basque country. He was interviewed in Pamplona, where he is studying to be a doctor. I met his fiancée as well. (It's worth mentioning that she was "out of his league," as the saying goes. Becker's theory accounts for this, since Ander brings other valued qualities to the union.) Ander was particularly blunt in his criticism of what he called "these ideologies about gender that have emerged with the intention of denying [sex] differences."[52] In fact, he's convinced, these differences "clearly affect the way that matrimony works." He finds marriage dynamics that are "pretending we're the same" a farce:

When I talk to friends, they say there are no differences in the way that men and women are. This point of view makes things difficult in marriage. When the other person reacts very differently, you don't know what to think. You think she should react in the same way you do, but in reality she reacts differently, has different sensibilities and empathies.

Ander thinks this sort of androgynous attitude is both empirically inaccurate and—for him as a Christian—morally deceitful:

It's like pretending we're the same, that there are no differences, instead of acknowledging that and making it compatible. . . . If we're supposed to be the same, which is not true, we're not going to understand difference. In society, it is pretended that we are the same, and in reality, that is contrary to the complementary nature of men and women.

The reasons Ander offers here are not, however, distinctly Christian or even sentimentally conservative. They are simply self-obvious to him. He's not against women in the workforce, and he doesn't think their "place" is in the home. In fact, Ander's fiancée is also studying to be a doctor.

Pyotr, a 34-year-old unmarried molecular biologist from Moscow, navigates the gender revolution in a manner similar to many in Russia. Women's extensive labor force penetration was accomplished there long ago, and yet sex distinctions not only remain visible but are now increasingly esteemed in a type of neotraditionalist revival. (This is a far cry from the state-enforced public egalitarianism of the Soviet era.) Pyotr was asked about how he thought the distribution of household tasks should work in a marriage. While perceiving his own (future) role as being "responsible for the family, for making strategic decisions," and for protection and help, his wife "would be dealing more with tactical decisions." But at the level of everyday living, Pyotr thinks a blend of expectations and talents should guide couples—and that without so much angst. Neither party should keep score:

Of course, we are living in the twenty-first century, and it would be anachronous to think in patriarchal family terms. Normally, both husband and wife have jobs, so the one who has the ability and capacity to do something does it. Again, taking into account gender differences.

Sociologists of gender often equate discussing sex differences with brooking patriarchy. Pyotr doesn't, obviously. What does he have in mind?

> For instance, the husband should replace an electric socket, fix or hang something, or take out the garbage. The wife should do the cooking, even though the husband can also do it sometimes—if he comes home earlier than his wife does, then why not? The issue of washing clothes is irrelevant now; you just put your laundry into the washing machine and it does all the work. Cleaning—I regret to say that I am not very fond of it. But I will probably have to learn how to do it.

Hardly revolutionary stuff. Notice two related themes in the accounts offered by Jasmine, Ander, and Pyotr. First, they demonstrated appreciation for what sociologist Kathleen Gerson calls "gender flexibility"—flexible approaches to who earns money and who cares for children.[53] Second, there is no evidence that such gender flexibility has become a means to make men and women interchangeable or "equal" or to contest patriarchy. It's not an end in itself, but a tool used to help couples overcome practical obstacles.

There is hard data to back up the perspectives of Jasmine, Ander, and Pyotr. In 2000, University of North Carolina demographer J. Richard Udry created a firestorm among sociologists of gender when he documented how prenatal hormone levels in mothers subsequently predicted the "gendered" (in this case, traditionally feminine) behavior of their adult female children, even after controlling for "socialization." The same, however, didn't affect men. Biology, he concluded, "sets limits" on the social construction of gender as well as the possible effects of gender socialization:

> Humans form their social structures around gender because males and females have different and biologically influenced behavioral predispositions. Gendered social structure is a universal accommodation to this biological fact. Societies demonstrate wide latitude in this accommodation—they can accentuate gender, minimize it, or leave it alone. If they ignore it, it doesn't go away. If they depart too far from the underlying sex-dimorphism of biological predispositions, they will generate social malaise and social pressures to drift back toward closer alignment with biology.[54]

It's fair to say we are experiencing some of those social pressures and malaise today.

An Observed Model of Marriage

When I went about trying to figure out what Christian marriage might be, I kept learning more about what marriage more broadly actually *is*. At its core, marriage demonstrates an exchange relationship. Becker saw it. Many of the interviewees either see it, too, or else practice it without realizing it. The differences between men and women are not fixed or rigid. But nor are they arbitrary. They tend to build on nature—as Udry observed. Husbands are more likely to teach the kids how to play a sport, while wives often more carefully oversee health and schooling.

Christian marriage can be thought of as a set of (tradition-specific) expectations added to the baseline observation of marriage (in general) as the formal/legal bond and context for the generation and transfer of resources between a man and a woman in support of their union. I use the term *observation* rather than *definition* because I don't see my role as defining marriage, nor am I implying that the "male breadwinner" model exemplifies marriage best. But observe something long enough, and widely enough, and you will discern what is at its core. This is actually easier to do with marriage today than in the past, since fewer people are marrying, making the contrast between marriage and other types of relationships clearer.

Love as an emotion is not the core of marriage. Couples don't marry in order to experience love; they marry because they love already and want to add to that love what marriage *is*. There are seasons in marriage when love is rather difficult. But a marriage is a relationship of interdependence and is meant to be a load-bearing structure, strong enough to withstand difficulty. Part of marriage is, of course, the sexual union intended to reflect and recreate love (as well as generate children).[55] But sex is also not its organizing principle. Marriage, at its core, has to do with interdependence—the generation and transfer of valued and necessary resources between husband and wife. A healthy sexual relationship exemplifies this exchange by its very nature of mutual giving.

My baseline observation of the core of marriage and its four key supporting expectations are portrayed in Figure 3.1. I call these expectations *key*, not

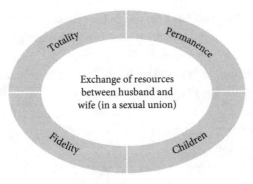

Figure 3.1. An observed model of marriage and its four key supporting expectations.

because all marriages exhibit them, but because nearly all marriages anticipate or expect them, and because exhibiting or bolstering them strengthens the core of marriage itself. This is the case whether we're talking about Christian marriage or not. Like the core of marriage, these supporting expectations are not utter social constructions, meaning they are not arbitrary and prone to change. A brief examination of each will demonstrate what I mean.

First, marriage is generally understood as a comprehensive union, exhibiting totality. It involves a sharing of life together—a linking of minds, wills, actions, and resources. It means not holding back. Theologian Dietrich von Hildebrand aptly describes this trait in relation to the core of marriage: "The beloved person is the object of our thoughts, sentiments, will, hope, and longing. She becomes the center of our life (as far as created goods are concerned)."[56] Graciela is a 29-year-old unmarried Catholic graduate student from Ecuador studying in Pamplona. Marriage, in her mind, "always implies commitment. It's saying to the other person, 'I love you for life.' " Anything short of that, she holds, is dubious and conditional—a trial run. Marriage, on the other hand, is comprehensive:

> [Marriage] implies a much deeper commitment. By that I mean that this person has been given to me to take full responsibility for him or her in every way, and that means every aspect, including on a Christian level . . . both his natural life and spiritual life. This has great implications for my life. And it's not just out of good will, but it's a commitment that you take on with the other person.

We don't simply live with our beloved, but for them. That's what is meant by totality. It is why prenuptial agreements prompt misgivings; they suggest a debt or an asset that one spouse brings to a marriage ought not be the concern of the other spouse. It's holding back. And we treat "sham" marriages— those entered into for the purposes of gaining a particular benefit—as not just deceitful but illegal.[57] People certainly do not celebrate them, because such marriages suggest a calculated, utilitarian agreement, not a comprehensive union.

Second, most marrying couples anticipate having children (if they are able to). This is the case even though contraception is widely practiced. They differ on how many children they hope to have, and when, but almost all of our interviewees equate marriage with offspring. Almost all couples struggling with infertility considered it a source for profound sadness and disappointment. The skyrocketing popularity of in vitro fertilization (IVF) and surrogacy attests to this (as well as to the rising age at marriage).

Third, people expect marriage to be permanent—a lifelong union. Who would celebrate a wedding in which the couple openly admits their union won't last? Talk of two-year or five-year rolling contracts, in which a marrying couple must opt in to remain married, are widely ridiculed.[58] Divorces are seldom celebrated, except in an ironic manner, and far more often lamented (and in plenty of cases, unwanted). Even when the separation brings relief, there is a sense of the loss of what could have been. It's not what the couple intended for their marriage; it is the death of a dream.

Note, too, the profound resentment of an ex-husband who is ordered to pay child support even though his ex-wife filed for a divorce he did not want; this is a central complaint of the "Red Pill" or men's rights movement. But the reason for a man's ire here is not simply because his wife has left him against his will. Rather, it's because he is still "married," in the sense of having to generate and transfer resources to her for the care of their common children.[59] But it's no longer an exchange, and he receives none of the benefits of the union in return. New York University sociologist Dalton Conley refers to this increasingly common pattern as "dynamic polygamy," because even while spouses split and move on to new partners, some terms of the original union's obligations can linger for years, or decades.[60]

Finally, sexual fidelity is expected in marriage.[61] Christians may take pains to portray violations of the union's terms as sinful—that would be fitting— but expectations of fidelity are widely shared outside the faith. Even atheists often recognize the value of fidelity and expect monogamy (even while they increasingly endorse others' rights to do as they please).

But there are more consequences to cheating than the emotional pain it can bring. Infidelity has long threatened marriage by a twofold paternity risk—first, that he would father other children for which he would then be responsible, or second, that she would bear children discreetly fathered by another man, obligating her husband to unwittingly provide resources to support another man's offspring.[62] Stepfathers may heroically choose to do the latter, but it seldom feels natural or easy, and it isn't consistently successful.

Idealists, including not a few supporters of the gender revolution, balk at such notions and suggest, instead, that any distinctions in how the sexes understand and practice fidelity (or family) are socialized—cultural artifacts that could be quite different.[63] I would disagree. Joao, a 25-year-old Catholic law student from Lagos, reflected on open marriage, an uncommon phenomenon in Nigeria. He finds it a good example of how attempts to bend the institution of marriage to the whims of a couple eventually collapse when their actions are fundamentally incompatible with marriage:

> I even know of a couple that comes together to share their exploits of what they do and . . . they will still actually have sexual intercourse [with each other]. . . . They will still live under the tenet of marriage, and they do things that are against [it]. You can't merge the antithesis of something and the positive aspect of something together and hope that it will work. You can only manage it for so long. You can try, but there will be a breakdown at a point.

Infidelity, even if agreed upon, always carries an expiration date.

For another example, consider marriage among gay men—the very existence of which many hold up as evidence of the radical malleability of marriage.[64] Since as many as half of gay men's marriages are believed to be nonmonogamous, explanations are deemed necessary to account for the discrepancy.[65] There is no parallel paternity risk, of course. And gay men have a different perspective on the meaning of fidelity, we are told.[66] That means their unions are not often held to the same standard.

But in his 2015 book *Just Married*, Princeton professor Stephen Macedo worried that gay men's penchant for nonmonogamy will undermine the general norm of sexual fidelity in marriage.[67] I used to wonder that myself. However, while I appreciate Macedo's concern, we will not widely observe what he fears. Instead, where sexual variety is privileged within popular culture, marriage will simply recede, since fidelity is close to the heart of marriage. The masses will bag marriage before they separate it from fidelity.

Even polygamy, or plural marriage, sheds light both on the kernel of marriage and on Christianity's influence on it. Why do some men in some societies marry more than one wife? Typically, it has been because they could afford to. That is, they have ample resources to transfer to more than one woman in order to support her and the children she bears to him. It really doesn't work the other way around; polyandrous societies are by comparison extremely rare—constituting no more than 1.1 percent of all societies, and probably closer to three tenths of 1 percent (and no sizable ones).[68] Polyandry is not how men roll, and no amount of social construction will change that. Polygamy can appeal, but it is incommensurate with Christian marriage, thanks to the first-century biblical prohibition of it. Much of the West (sensibly) still balks at polygamy.[69]

But Isn't Marriage a Social Construction?

Make no mistake—the core of marriage and its four key supports (Figure 3.1) may be socially reinforced, but they are not arbitrary. Marriage is not ours for the remaking, as marriage critic Clare Chambers advocates.[70] Turn-of-the-century social theorist Georg Simmel wrote extensively about the nature of the dyad, including the structure of marriage, and noted this very thing:

> Although each of the two spouses is confronted by only the other, at least partially he also feels as he does when confronted by a collectivity; as the mere bearer of a super-individual structure whose nature and norms are independent of him, although he is an organic part of it. [71]

Mateusz, a 26-year-old newlywed businessman from Krakow, knows what Simmel was talking about. He lived with his wife for about a year before marrying her. When asked whether living together was comparable to marriage, Mateusz made reference to an "internal sense" of responsibility: "I must admit that it [marriage] is something completely different. I think that there are some advantages and disadvantages, but it's something incomparable." What's the difference?

I think that now when we are married, I can feel much more responsibility for what I'm doing [when I'm] completely alone, not strictly connected with my wife. I feel some commitment. I wouldn't call it a burden, but some internal sense that when I do something, it will influence the two of us more than when we lived together or when we were just a couple earlier.

This is not a specifically Christian perspective. Nor is it American, or strictly Western. It's not a matter of race or ethnicity, and certainly not language.

Nevertheless, to its modern critics, marriage is a pure social construction, meaning it can be changed by political or popular will to suit new needs, interests, values, definitions. Think the exchange model of marriage is odious, a relic of patriarchy in need of unmasking? Deride it. Undermine it. Strip it of its unique legal benefits, so that marriage is no more beneficial than living alone or with friends. After all, today's adults "have the opportunity to live radically liberating lives," writes psychologist and marriage critic Bella DePaulo. We have what she calls "the Great Unraveling" to thank:

> Once upon a time, many of the big, important components of adult life came all rolled up in the ball of marriage. Now, the threads have been pulled and are left scattered haphazardly on the ground. Each of us as individuals gets to reassemble them any way we want—or leave them behind and come up with entirely different threads for stitching together just the right life.[72]

DePaulo's "any way we want" remark suggests that the structure and functions of marriage could be radically different or not exist at all. Sociologist Christian Smith calls such naivety "social constructionism," something scholars ought to avoid rather than uncritically embrace.[73] As he notes, social constructionism cuts both ways. There is no way to pursue the unraveling of marriage as a mere social construction, to be rebuilt in a more "just" and "equal" manner for instance, without having to admit that justice and equality would themselves be social constructions, open to radical revision. In that case, there would be no "reality" from which to put down roots and foster social change. It then becomes not a question of justice but of power—power to get what you want. So there is an important distinction to be made, Smith holds, between people's beliefs about reality and reality itself.[74] DePaulo is enmeshed in a reality of her own making.

DePaulo is not wrong about one thing: There are new narratives about relationships being told today—about the virtues of solitude or childlessness, the wisdom of cohabiting first, the importance of sexual chemistry, even the possible pleasures of "ethical polyamory."[75] But what marriage constitutes legally or culturally is not the same as what we will observe in practice—in social reality—over the long run. Undermine any of its four central supports, and marriage will recede, regardless of marriage law and any political or economic stimuli. Why? Because such cultural, political, and legal moves are the only obvious social constructions here. The core of marriage is a stable reality.[76] Even the Finnish philosopher and sociologist Edvard Westermarck—who openly criticized Christianity and was an early champion of feminism—couldn't dream of a marriageless world. It won't happen, he said in 1936:

> The unity of sensual and spiritual elements in sexual love, leading to a more or less durable community of life in a common home, and the desire for and love of offspring are factors which will remain lasting obstacles to the extinction of marriage and the collapse of the family because they are too deeply rooted in human nature to fade away.[77]

Those who wear marriage uncomfortably are better off trying to market a new form of union than trying to make marriage something it isn't.

This is not to say that there are no socially constructed aspects of marriage. The number of Christian variations in what marriage ought to look like and how it should function (noted in Chapter 2) bears witness to this. For example, the expectation that a husband will be the spiritual "head" of his wife is a social construction—valued in some Christian marriages and not others. The same can be said for the Catholic emphasis on marriage as concerned with the salvation of one's spouse. Many Christians aren't even aware of this principle. However, variations should not prompt a claim that Christian marriage itself is entirely malleable. Instead, they highlight the core of what marriage has long comprised. Christian marriage affirms, expects, and reinforces marriage's key traits: fidelity, permanence, totality, and children. But there is more to Christian marriage than these basics—hence the variations valued by different Christian traditions and denominations.

In their own behavior, Christians no doubt vary in attentiveness to and competence in any of the four key marital expectations. The sacredness of the enduring covenant can be forgotten amid the doldrums of daily existence. Decisions about children get revisited, or suitable mates may not materialize until well after the fertile years. Addictions can erode totality. But what Christians tend to display (and share) in lived reality, so far as I can tell, is above-average commitment to the baseline observation of marriage as being about the formal, committed union within which differential resources are secured and offered between the couple and among their children (as described earlier and in Figure 3.1).

Although it would be anachronistic to suggest what Westermarck or Simmel would have thought about the institution of marriage today, the latter wrote over a century ago that "marriage, essentially, allows only acceptance or rejection, but not modification."[78] Marriage either works on its own terms, or it recedes.[79] Alternate visions of marriage may be buttressed for a time—decades even—but the energy and resources it takes to prop up public opinion (that marriage is something other than what it is) will wane eventually. Insofar as Christians' understanding of marriage drifts away from the model of Figure 3.1, their interest in marrying diminishes, but at a slower pace than in their surrounding societies.

That slower pace of diminishing interest is associated with a kind of sex role distinction that is still more apt to characterize Christians' marriages. Harper, a 24-year-old psychotherapist living in suburban Detroit, plans to marry her boyfriend, and she anticipates clearer distinctions in their marital roles than she sees around her. To her, exchanging differences is a marriage saver. It's when roles are identical that everyone suffers, because then, "the wife can't be home":

> And then the kids are at daycare from six in the morning when the parents head to work until six in the evening when the parents get off work. There is just like no bonding in the marriage. You're always tired—you're exhausted—whereas before, you know, if you're a stay-at-home mom you can be there and like serve dinner and make your husband fall in love with you every evening, just by doing those little things.

I know. It sounds so throwback. It's certainly not required, of course. (And it's no longer the norm in Christian marriages in any of the seven research sites.) But Harper sees conflict in the marriages around her that she would attribute to a lack of traditional homemaking:

> I mean now [husbands] are like, "Well, I'd rather eat at a restaurant, because if I go home, there's not going to be food on the table, so why would I want

to go home?" . . . They don't want to be home, and the wives are like, "Why aren't you at home? Are you cheating on me? What's going on?"

"I'm all for stay-at-home moms," Harper leveled. The couple worries about money, naturally, but Harper has glimpsed the constant upward economic climbing of other kinds of families around her, and she doesn't think it's worth the sacrifices. "It's hard these days," she acknowledged, but "God will provide." Interestingly, Harper didn't reference her faith as the *reason* for her sex role preferences. Rather, she's "all for stay-at-home moms" because she thinks it's asking for trouble to live otherwise.

Conclusion

Men's earnings—long a linchpin of sociological explanations for rising marriage age and falling marriage rates—seem less pivotal to the formation of marriages today in a world where women are thriving educationally and economically. The marital impulse is waning, but this should not be mistaken for evidence of a gender revolution going on among young adult Christians. Rather, Christians are merely typical; they have high expectations for marriage and material well-being and they often sculpt their employment behavior to meet those ends rather than nebulous goals of liberation. Christians around the globe exhibit sex role flexibility but are not gender revolutionaries. Their behavior reveals no interest in overhauling longstanding relationship norms.

When marriage has less to do with the movement of resources between spouses and more to do with joint consumption of resources, marriage should recede, because marriage is not simply about a loving relationship. Observation reveals a relationship of interdependence. Insofar as spouses are functionally similar, marriage becomes less necessary, and so less popular.

Marriage will not disappear, however, and its core and central traits are not subject to social construction. Public relations campaigns can win ballot initiatives, but they cannot overhaul marriage. There is a reason that marriages that end in divorce or suffer unfaithfulness are widely considered around the globe as having fallen short of the ideal: fidelity and permanence are expectations close to the heart of marriage. Even more central are the generation and transfer of income and other resources for the sustenance and protection of family, including children. There will be no wide future of intentionally childless marriages. There may be a future of intentionally childless *unions*, but the marrying part would come to seem superfluous.[80] Marriage rates are shrinking, then, because of increasing disinterest in what marriage actually *is*.

4

Sex

Moscow today feels more like New York City or Paris than most other former Soviet and "satellite" cities, like Vilnius, Bratislava, or even Warsaw. It is most definitely not the Moscow image of my youth. Nor is it the Moscow of the 1990s—the challenging post-Soviet decade in which the future of Russia was wrestled over in government offices and in the streets. With inflation, shifting political norms, rapid privatization, and interpersonal and organized crime and corruption, it was an era to be endured, suffered, or exploited. Alcoholism, spousal abandonment, and divorce rates surged, creating a generation of Russian youth apt to be raised by their grandparents. The legacy of fatherlessness is palpable—but difficult to document, given poor record keeping.

The Moscow of today sports a construction boom, high-rise apartments, and scores of Western businesses. Economic sanctions imposed by Western nations have unwittingly fostered a surge in domestic production and exports, as well as bolstered ties with Asian neighbors.[1] The culture and spirit of the place, however, is still very much Russian. Among the most obvious resurgent forces in the post-communist era is the Orthodox Church. It is now the foundation of Russia's cultural and national identity.[2] The Kremlin officially favors Orthodox Christianity; President Vladimir Putin and Kirill, the patriarch of Moscow, appear together with some regularity. Putin visibly participates in holy days, and Orthodox symbols permeate public culture.[3] Nevertheless, a church-state distinction remains, and a general agnostic (if not atheistic) consciousness pervades the public sphere and regularly divides family members. A significant minority of my Russian interviewees were converts of a sort, having been raised in secular or religiously antagonistic households. Boris, 34, a mathematician and weekly attender, described the tension:

> My mom is totally against me becoming an Orthodox. She would constantly tell me off for doing my morning and evening prayers, buying religious books. [She] was totally against talking about religion. Now she's

gotten used to it and does not openly oppose it, but of course she doesn't welcome it. I am trying not to touch religious topics in conversations, in order to avoid unpleasant and unnecessary talks.

Soviet-era Russia was a unique example of forced secularization, a process very few nations have experienced and few English-speaking sociologists of religion have adequately documented or understood.[4] Its experience is quite unlike secularization in the United States and much of Europe, where drift away from religion has been uneven. In Russia, churches were closed, destroyed, or repurposed; seminaries and monasteries were shuttered, and priests were imprisoned or killed. The cosmos under Lenin and Stalin was emptied of the divine. The Orthodox Church was either barely tolerated or actively suppressed, in repetitive cycles. To be a professing Christian after 1917 was to deliberately choose a life of profound difficulty on top of normal, shared miseries. Even speaking of Christianity to your own children was a crime meriting imprisonment during the 1920s.[5] As a result of such massive political and social engineering, multiple generations of Russians had no understanding of what many Western Christians take for granted—an internalized, personal experience of Christian faith. Only since the collapse of the Soviet Union have a minority of Russians been encouraged by a resurgent priesthood to make their faith their own. It's a tall challenge. Although as many as 80 percent of Russians self-identify as Orthodox, only 3 to 5 percent of Muscovites—and more old than young—attend Divine Liturgy on a monthly basis.[6]

Russia's Cheap Sex Experiment

Secularization wasn't the only Soviet social experiment. The Bolsheviks ended the Church's oversight of matrimony in favor of civil marriage at the outset of the 1917 Russian Revolution, subsequently moved to ease limits on divorce in the name of "freedom" and "dignity" shortly thereafter (1921), and reinforced these changes by the 1926 Family Code. The first sixteen years following the revolution offered a natural experiment about what happens when a nation seeks to unravel not just marriage, but a host of sexual norms. The czarist era was replete not only with clear social class differences and high inequality but also traditional norms about family and marriage. The marriage and family laws of 1921 aimed at fostering egalitarian unions that would better welcome socialist thought. The legislation, according to government officials at the time, "frees her and enables her the more readily to accept the principles of socialism which will ultimately free her."[7] Unburdened by "obsolete" social norms and gendered expectations, writes historian Wendy Z. Goldman, "men and women would come together and separate as they wished" in free unions.[8] The "economic foundations of monogamy would disappear," wrote communist visionary Friedrich Engels.[9] Russian-born Harvard sociologist Pitirim Sorokin noted that official Soviet theory in the early days of the revolution regarded sex as a "glass of water." That is, "If a person is thirsty, so went the Party line, it is immaterial what glass he uses when satisfying his thirst."[10]

Many Russians were skeptical, asserting that the new laws would put women "in a vulnerable position by encouraging men to abandon family relationships."[11] In advance of the enactment of the 1926 Code, a wide listening tour took place, enabling normal people to register their sentiments. It was perhaps the last time a Soviet state policy was so freely and democratically discussed, Goldman notes.[12] She captures the drama:

> Peasants and women boldly testified about their experiences; snide jokes and sexual banter competed with scholarly legal polemics on the meaning of marriage. The discussion was open and forthright, marked by little ideological obeisance. . . . The draft Code's proposal to provide the same legal rights to people living together in de facto unions as to those in registered marriages provoked the greatest controversy. De facto marriage was happily hailed by some as the new wave of the socialist future. . . . Yet others argued that de facto marriage was not a sign of the socialist future, but rather of . . . chaos, disruption, and dislocation . . ."[13]

Protests went largely unheeded. The Family Code further simplified divorce, made cohabitation the equivalent of civil marriage, and authorized the state to assign paternity in unclear cases. Vestiges of the old order—marriage ensuring communal property and the distinction between nonmarital and marital fertility (i.e., legitimacy)—disappeared by fiat. New religious marriages were not banned, just ignored. Only civil marriage mattered. If one spouse moved, the other was under no obligation to follow. Divorce could be pursued by both parties or just one. Abortion laws were liberalized, and cohabitation was encouraged, orchestrating a sexual revolution a full

half-century before the West's.[14] The Code did, however, expand and sim-
plify adoption—a necessary measure given the rampant child homelessness
that followed the Bolshevik sexual revolution.

It turns out that cheap sex and free unions didn't work out well. University
of Pennsylvania ethnographer Kristen Ghodsee, lauding the sexual benefits
of socialism in the *New York Times* in August 2017, attempted to paint a portrait of Bolshevik marriage laws as having guaranteed women's reproductive rights and freed them from their economic tether to men.[15] The reality
was far less picturesque. Life turned sour for women in a way that most of
Lenin's advisers had not predicted (some had forewarned him). When sex
was cheap, men's interest in strong commitments waned, and many abandoned their families. Disillusionment with the sweeping changes eventually
reached the revolutionaries themselves.[16]

The grand Soviet project of massive economic reform, it seemed, was
going to have to hinge on stability in relationships and a more circumscribed
sexuality among the masses. The permissive laws were not just abandoned
but reversed by Stalin in 1936, due to the social and relational chaos that had
emerged in the form of homeless children, abortions, envy fostered by poly-
amorous mates, and even problems in the workplace.[17] By 1944, divorce had
become complicated and beyond the capacity of most couples. The rights of
children born out of wedlock were curbed. Material advantages were provided to mothers who had at least five children.[18]

It's hard to imagine such profound upheaval legally foisted upon the
family—one of the oldest and most primal of institutions—only to be
reversed in a decade's time. (And this is to say nothing of the famines, wars,
political repressions, and extreme economic cycles that plagued the nation.)
It's no wonder the Russian people were thirsty for God, after so many decades
of seeing what godlessness yielded.

Nonetheless, there is not a deep freedom of religion in Russia today. The
American evangelicals who swarmed the country after 1990 have largely
returned home, often not by choice. Islam is tolerated—there are Muslim
regions of the country, after all—but it's understood that Orthodoxy is the
national faith. Still it can hardly be accused of being a shallow Christian tradition, and a recent explosion in priests and parish buildings in metropolitan
Moscow attests to genuine growth. Father Stefan, a young priest with five
children, spoke at length with me about the sacrifices—that is, the costs—
that marriage entails, alternately quoting from C. S. Lewis, the Gospels, and

Immanuel Kant. His perspective could not be more different from that of Lenin's advisers:

> [Marriage] is a giving love, while *eros* [romantic love] is often perceived as a consuming love. . . . In his book *Screwtape Letters*, C.S. Lewis relays this episode wherein Screwtape, the elder demon, writes to Wormwood, "Wormwood, I love you so much that I would eat you." This is spoiled *eros*, the desire to possess, to dominate. . . . In the case of *agape* [godly love], love becomes a willingness to sacrifice . . . seeing a partner not as a source of energy, possession, or satisfaction, but as a person. Kant wrote that a person should not be a means, but rather the goal. Here, a person becomes a goal. . . . Love in this case is understood as help, as a sacrifice, as a willingness to give oneself up for the sake of another person, for the sake of another person's happiness. When Christ said, "There is no greater love than to lay down one's soul for one's friends," he meant himself on the cross, of course. We sometimes wrongly relate these words to war. But in fact, this can also be related to any real marriage.

This is certainly not a shallow understanding of Christian marriage. When I sat down with Father Stefan at his parish for what I thought would be a private conversation, several of his congregation gathered to listen (I can understand why):

> When a person is married and suddenly he falls in love with someone else, then the demonstration of a true love would be to tell yourself that this erotic love is not love, that I have a wife whom I love not only in the erotic sense, but also as a friend, as a relative. I love her with sacrificial love. Even when there is no *eros*, there is a desire for salvation, which means loving the person whom God sent you.

Orthodox priests with whom I interacted expressed an obvious grasp of the purposes, joys, struggles, and sacrifices of marriage. Now if only the masses would follow suit. Russia displays one of the highest rates of early divorce in the West. As noted in Chapter 1, 5 percent of marriages—most of them civil, involving no religious rite—are over before the end of their first year, and over 40 percent do not last five years. These are astounding numbers. The Orthodox Church has its work cut out for it, and the clergy know it.

The Cost of Sex among Christians

What exactly is meant by the term *cheap sex*? I wrote a book with that title, published in 2017.[19] I won't rehash it all here, but a brief introduction to the concept is in order. Economically speaking, women *have* what men *want*. Thus, they possess something of considerable value to men, something that conceivably "costs" men to access. Historically, men have had to give something in exchange, most typically significant (economic and relational) commitments or promises, to gain access to her body.[20] I affirm that men appreciate women for other reasons, but that fact doesn't make this claim less true. Sex is "cheap" if women expect little from men in return for sex, and if men do not have to supply much time, attention, resources, recognition, or fidelity in order to experience sex. Cheap sex is characterized not only by *personal* ease of sexual access but also *social* perceptions of the same.

The "cost" of sex can be measured by the speed at which a new sexual partner can be found, or in the frequency with which one has sex. The key lies in the *ease of access*. If it's easy, it's cheap. Moreover, cheap sex is not just about access to sexual intercourse. Pornography-fueled masturbation is arguably the cheapest form of sex and more closely mimics the real thing today than it did, say, thirty years ago. Do Christian young adults think sex is easy to get? We asked them. "Yes," the vast majority replied, whether male or female. Here is a short sample of their responses:

- Charbel, 28, unmarried, Beirut: "Yes, very easy. As a matter of fact, it is harder not to have sex, or to commit to not having sex."
- Bernadette, 28, unmarried, Beirut: "I think it is very easy, unfortunately. You easily fall into it. It affects the couple, because they feel they can have everything without marriage."
- Bethany, 30, unmarried, Austin: "It definitely is something that like, if you want to, it's very easy and very possible [laughs]. . . . I've seen more Christian women maybe not necessarily getting attention from Christian guys, but they start getting attention from non-Christian guys, and they start dating them, and then . . ."
- Thomas, 30, recently married, Austin: "Girls are just so easy to access, and then they want to access you too. It's a two-way street. They're the ones putting themselves out there by messaging you back; no one's forcing them to talk to you back, because they're interested in what you're selling too, you know?"

- Kingsley, 29, unmarried, Lagos: "[Sex] might be very easy for me, and some guys are struggling. We still have male virgins in their forties that just masturbate or watch pornography. For me, it is easier for me, but it might not be easier for the next person. But on the average, I will say it is easy."
- Joao, 25, unmarried, Lagos: "It's too easy these days, because of the fact that casual sex is practiced worldwide. It is no more even a thing tradition or custom can hinder you from. It is too easy these days. People are flaunting the sacredness of sexual intercourse as easy as they drink water, as easy as they wake up in the morning."
- Ndidi, 26, unmarried, Lagos: "It is easy. Everybody is having sex except me."
- Julia, 24, unmarried, Lublin: "Yes, it is very easy. People lose the meaning of sex. It is being reduced to a physiological need which has to be satisfied."
- Aleksandra, 40, unmarried, Warsaw: "I think that it's too easy. It's socially acceptable or even advisable to first try having sex and then decide if this person is the right one or not."
- Pablo, 32, married, Mexico City: "It's the easiest thing that you can find today [laughs]. Everything is eroticized! Everything!"
- Ana, 21, unmarried, Mexico City: "I think that it's super easy."

It's not just the sexually experienced who think sex is easy. Estella, a 28-year-old from Guadalajara, has never been in a sexual relationship. She nevertheless considers sex "super easy" to find today: "You go to a party, you meet someone, and that same night you have sex. . . . At least, people in a relationship, I would say 90 percent of them have sex."

A tally revealed that 32 percent of our unmarried young adult Christian interviewees said they were currently in a sexual relationship.[21] That doesn't mean that the remaining 68 percent had never been in one—some had, some had not. Those numbers also don't include marrieds, who might have been in a premarital sexual relationship, including with their spouse.

Some critics have recently chided me for my claim that sex today is cheap.[22] They point to the declining frequency of sexual intercourse in the United States as well as to rising rates of virginity as well as sexless unions and the increasing age at which Americans first have sex—for evidence that sex is not cheap.[23] They're wrong. None of these offer indication of elevated chastity and "expensive" sex.[24] Rather, it means more men and women are delaying marriage—hence limiting their access to a stable partner—and more are finding satiation in the dopamine hits that come from social media consumption or from masturbation. In 2018, 60 percent of never-married men in the United States reported having masturbated, and 54 percent had used pornography, in the past six days. The same was true of 33 percent and 19 percent, respectively, of never-married women.[25]

Some think I shouldn't speak of sex in this manner—that doing so trivializes the sexual act. I understand and even empathize. There are other ways of talking about this most intimate of behaviors, ways that are certainly more sensitive and theologically attuned. But no matter what the vocabulary used, what I am asserting here is still true.

Men are, on average, more sexually permissive than women and, hence, they provide more of the social support for cheap sex, while women provide—on average, but far less today than in previous generations—the social control against it.[26] The double standard around sex has weakened but not disappeared.[27] Basically, women do not readily gravitate toward cheap sex but can learn to accommodate it. It becomes a patterned expectation, affecting how both men and women come to perceive subsequent encounters and even the purpose of sex. As far back as the early 1980s, economists were suspecting that sex had become cheaper as contraception began to infuse relationships. Marriage rates, in turn, began to drop. Why? The price of sex had declined: "Whereas in the past most men had been obliged to offer the benefits of marriage in exchange for sexual favors, increasingly, in the 1960–1975 period, more of them were able to offer something less."[28]

The ready availability of sex in the wider mating market permeates the interviewees' social settings, from conservative Krakow to liberal Austin. It didn't matter whether they chose to engage or abstain; sex was still considered cheap. Chastity, meanwhile, is rarer—not among the interviewees per se but in their social settings. Abstinence felt costly. (It's raising the price on sex—by yourself or among friends—and hoping someone will be willing to pay it.) A Russian Orthodox priest we interviewed in Moscow expressed his frustrations about the situation, words that could just as well have come from the mouth of a Catholic priest in Mexico or an evangelical pastor in the United States. Note his reference to the kind of narrative I describe, which communicates an unquestioned "truth" about dating and sex. Note also the subtle expressions of power to coax the other into desired behavior, and men and women's concern about what's going on in the surrounding market—what others are doing and how these others would react to countercultural behavior:

> I can say that the big problem for these young men and women is to be chaste before marriage. Because nowadays, girls approach me and say that they have met a young man, but there is a problem—he drags her to bed. He says that this is how it is done, and if they don't sleep with each other, no one will talk to them. Young men also approach me. They say that everything is heading toward a sexual relationship—that this is how girls are nowadays, and if you don't do this, no one would talk to you. Even girls and guys who attend church are convinced that this is some necessary step that must be taken, despite the fact that the church is against it, simply because now you cannot marry without it. [*How do you respond to this?*] As a clergyman, I try to communicate with them in the spirit of the Gospel. It is clear that we cannot welcome such a relationship. This relationship is illegal, whatever one may say, for the simple reason that this is theft. One must bear the responsibility for another person.

Unfortunately, men and women seldom perceive how the marriage market—that invisible social structure in which the search for a spouse occurs—works. They witness the dynamics I have described, but they're often too caught up in it themselves to see things clearly. Instead, what they discern is a narrative—a set of what sociologists call *scripts*—about sexual relationships. Sadly, the scripts are largely devoid of Christian meaning. The Western narrative has far more to do with novelty, spontaneity, and lust or raw attraction than it does with familiarity, patience, mature love, mutual gift, or even that long-standing proof of sex—pregnancy. Sex is far more about Hollywood than Holy Matrimony. Estella (mentioned earlier, from Mexico) perceives this narrative when she observes her peers' premarital behavior: "There are people who are convinced that [sex] is part of a [romantic] relationship; it is like holding hands or kissing." What's at stake, Estella maintains, is nothing less than marital stability: "I think [premarital sex] affects the marriage emotionally." A premature sexual relationship can blind one to significant warning signs of a union primed to go south after marriage, when the blinders always come off. (More about this later in the chapter.)

How Cheap Sex Slows Marriage

Klara, a 25-year-old hairdresser from Lublin, Poland, is engaged to be married and articulates a discernibly Christian perspective on marriage. And yet she's been in a sexual relationship with her fiancé for an unclear amount of time. (She didn't want to answer when asked how long.) Her parents don't know about it and wouldn't approve, she suspects. However, when Klara looks around her, she perceives limited options: "I think that [sex] is easy. Let's not fool each other. You can find a partner for sex everywhere. And now most girls don't limit themselves. They are in such relationships." Whether Klara is right or not about "most girls" in Poland today doesn't matter as much as the fact that she *thinks* this is true. (It is our interpretation of situations that shape our behavior, not whether we are discerning the situation correctly.)

Klara also believes in sexual chemistry, a concept that many judge helpful in choosing a marriage partner. Klara and her fiancé aren't cohabiting, though she believes cohabitation reduces rather than elevates risk:[29] "I think that it's a good idea to see how you live with each other before you make that final decision. It's a good idea to see if you match each other." Matching of this sort is a new phenomenon, stimulated by surging interest in online dating algorithms. It would seem to replace "social learning," the more sensible notion that couples figure out (that is, learn) how to relate to their beloved as they go along.

Valentina, a 30-year-old married Muscovite, thinks cheap sex privileges the interests of men far more than women:

In my opinion, [sex] involves negative consequences, because from the men's point of view, the man gets everything he wants and bears no responsibility for that. I mean it motivates the man to stay irresponsible. It even strengthens this position in him. From the woman's position, she gives everything, and no one takes on responsibility for her. . . . Actually, to a large extent, it gets in the way of people getting married. Because the man does not see the point to hurry. For what purpose, if he gets everything and is not supposed to bear any sort of responsibility? The woman suffers, because she wants to have a man nearby who takes on responsibility, while it turns out that there is someone by her side who gets everything and in return just spends some time with her.[30]

Strip her discourse to its foundations, and Valentina is lamenting that the terms of the exchange relationship become, when sex is easy, lopsided and unfair.

Sofia a 22-year-old, fourth-year university student with whom I spoke in Guadalajara, has defied the odds here (sort of). The second of three children of middle-class parents, whose marriage she wishes to imitate, Sofia is studying to be a schoolteacher while working part-time doing data analysis and alumni tracking for the university. And she is also in a precarious spot, as an unmarried mother. Her 1-year-old daughter was conceived, unexpectedly, the first and only time she has ever had sex—a reminder that sex can turn out to be profoundly expensive. She was on a date with her boyfriend. The entire experience could have soured Sofia on Church teaching. However, it only reinforced how congruent Catholic teaching on marriage was with her own convictions. Sofia doesn't disparage sex. Quite the contrary. What she despises is the degrading reduction "to a material object" that she witnesses in her peers' sexual habits. Sex isn't meant to be cheap:

> They reduce everything to that—the sexual act. Whether they like [the sex] or not, or [would it be] better . . . with other people. . . . Testing that is like going from flower to flower—trying everything. And at the end, you don't like anything. . . . In fact, you reduce yourself to a material object. You do it with someone and you didn't like it, and you'll do it with another person, and with another one after that. Then I ask, "Where is your dignity?" But also, "Where is your self-love? Your respect for your body?"

This might seem ironic, especially from a young woman who deeply disappointed her parents—her mother in particular—with her premarital pregnancy at the age of 21 and has endured the awkward stares and conversations with stunned friends. But the recognition of dignity in ourselves and others is at risk, Sofia fears. Hers is a different, older meaning of *dignity* than what has become popular today, dignity as something of a synonym for freedom.[31] Sofia is one of the few interviewees who connected sex with dignity. It's a long-standing link, however. Chastity, writes theologian Reinhard Hütter, is "the virtue that both expresses and preserves the dignity of what is a genuine and surpassing good: the dignity of the human person in sexual matters."[32] "Outrages upon personal dignity" is key to the Geneva Conventions' condemnation of sexual violence and degradation as a tool of domination in wartime.[33] Sofia is onto something.

A Salesian (Catholic) priest in Bratislava, Slovakia—who has observed relationships and marriages since the communist era—perceived a consistent problem at work in many relationships: "[Men] don't have a problem accessing sex, so they don't have a reason to change the status of the relationship." Why do women go along with this? "They do have power, but they are not active in [wielding it]," he said. If the women leave their current partner or insist on marriage, "there is a fear that nobody will want them." Sofia risked her relationship with her boyfriend by choosing to retreat from subsequent sex. But she was confident it was the right thing to do. He responded by pursuing marriage. At the time of the interview, the two were engaged.

The Power Wielded by Men

Women's unwielded power is an astute observation, because power in this case is a pivotal element. Power differences within premarital romantic relationships typically reflect inequalities between the two people—the most obvious being a difference in physical attractiveness. There are other inequalities: wealth, debt, social status, personality, religious commitment, educational achievement, social class background, and job prestige, to name several. Men and women tend to weigh or value these differently, however, so inequality is common and not a problem per se.[34] While Christians may value a vibrant faith in a mate, as they ought, that seldom means these other traits don't matter.

When Christian Women Outnumber Men

But a bigger hurdle to marriage—one voiced by numerous interviewees—is the inequality of options in the surrounding market—that is, the availability of potential partners. Women now outnumber same-age men in terms of their interest in marriage. This sex ratio problem tends to be far worse inside Christian churches, though the gap will vary by country, denomination, and (most importantly) congregations. Here is a short selection of remarks from interviewees about their own churches:

- If there are men, they are already married and come with their families.

- There are a lot of unmarried women. Very beautiful, incredible, remarkable girls.
- He knows that he is [only] one, and there are thirty girls ready.
- There are a lot of girls, and few guys.

Twenty-nine-year-old Viktor, an Orthodox Christian and clinical psychologist working in a psychiatric hospital just northwest of Moscow, knows the odds are in his favor. He can sense it: "I socialize in the Orthodox milieu, where girls have quite direct interests. Even in the way they look at you, you can quite guess something like a proposal to be together." As the women in his orbit grow older, his own power becomes even more obvious. He doesn't mind:

> Especially if these are girls above 25—for them it's already a painful feeling; they are ready to consider me, a decent (more or less) young man, [as] a groom. So I mark the boundary, like, "You should not consider me [as a possible husband]," though I realize that I am a good bridegroom.

For Paweł, the 24-year-old Cracovian we met in Chapter 3, this opportunity for power play is all behind him. He had thought about becoming a priest but decided against it. He didn't turn out to be "fireproof," his wife, Marta, said. She described the process whereby Catholic men considering the priesthood spend considerable time together with (and outnumbered by) marriage-minded young women in Christian groups. Those men who eventually navigate the process and still choose to enter the priesthood are dubbed "fireproof." But the process also demonstrates how selective such men, in general, arc able to be.

Those who have more options simply have more power than those who have fewer options, and that power translates into the ability to mold a nascent relationship into what you prefer. As a result, obtaining sex from a woman gets easier when marriageable men are outnumbered by marriage-minded women—and obtaining commitment from a man gets harder. Veronica, the 28-year-old schoolteacher from Guadalajara, knows this firsthand:

> I think we women are doing something wrong; we're making things too easy for men. Well, intimacy is starting very young in girls. We don't know how to make them give us our due. At least I see this with my friends. We

don't demand anything. We do everything to make them choose us for marriage, for someone to decide to be with you.

Note how Veronica perceives the situation as women "doing something wrong." What they are doing is reacting to their weakened position in the marriage market. They're attempting to woo men, rather than the other way around. And the way to capture his heart is through sex, many erroneously believe. Paweł, however, was different. He used his power to pursue and marry Marta. Why? Maturity:

I grew up a bit faster. I liked older people. I left home at 18, living on my own. I traveled when I was 15—hitchhiked to France, didn't tell my parents. Maybe this is a key to interpret some things. I experienced some relationships a bit earlier. I knew I wanted to do something serious. I was fed up with quick relationships, for one night or one week.

Other men use their power in far different ways than Paweł did. They string women along, feign genuine interest, accrue sexual experiences. Because they can. There's no way around the conclusion that unmarried Christian men who are committed to chastity are in a far better position to realize it in a relationship than Christian women who are committed to the same. Thomas, a 30-year-old recently married Catholic from Austin, works as a project manager for a major telecommunications company. He reflected on the effortlessness of finding potential marriage partners:

It's just a lot of fun being single, especially if you are outgoing and extroverted. You can meet a lot of great girls out there, going on a lot of great dates, especially if you're using some of these apps to meet girls, and especially if you're in a community.

When Thomas refers to being "in a community," he means a group of Christian friends rooted in a congregation, parachurch organization, or Bible study. He's also making veiled reference to the kind of sex ratio imbalance therein, like Paweł experienced in Krakow, where the numbers tend to play to the man's advantage. Thomas also discussed the mating market using rather blunt language that conveyed a clear sense of controlling what happens:

I always like to joke with my secular friends like, so it's all about the cost of admission, right? So, if [women] have a low cost of admission, [they] are going to get [their] heart broken a lot. But if [they] have a high cost of admission, [they] might actually get to meaningful relationships. And I ultimately feel like if your relationships have intimacy outside of marriage, don't be shocked when . . . you make it to like, the tenth or fifteenth date or whatever, and [the man is] done with you, and it's like, "Oh, I guess that's it."

At the same time, remember that women's standards are higher than in the past, as noted in Chapter 3, because they don't need to marry in order to live an economically independent, rewarding life. Hence, the greater selectivity displayed by women is running headlong into the numbers problem just explained. Demographer Gavin Jones documented a similar shift in women's perceptions of men's marriageability—in his case among educated women in Asia—noting that the "problem of the marriage market is not so much the lack of available males as the shortage of men who share [the females'] values and expectations."[35] The result is greater trouble than ever in making a match happen (and then making it work). To be fair, some congregations don't have such a sex ratio problem, or they have it in the other direction.[36] But not many.

The "Crime" of Unequal Exchange

I confess I was surprised when the Orthodox priest quoted earlier described premarital sex as theft. Objectionable. Immoral. Premature. Tempting. I'm familiar with all those descriptors. But theft? That was new, or so I thought. But then I remembered that an economist (and evangelical Christian) at the University of San Francisco had made a similar claim. Bruce Wydick had been struggling—in today's climate of easy sex—to articulate why people ought to favor marriage over cohabitation when the latter seems increasingly popular. Writing in *Christianity Today* in 2016, Wydick returned to the "biological asymmetry" between men and women, something most Christians still agree upon. (Most of my colleagues, on the other hand, privilege what Wydick calls a "psychological androgyny.") Speaking economically in a way that fits the history of marriage, Wydick leveled with his readers:

A sexual relationship between a man and a woman involves, among other things, an exchange of sex for commitment, commitment on behalf of the man to the welfare of the woman and any resulting children. Seen in this light, the commitment of a man to a woman with whom he has a sexual relationship is not prudery; it is social justice. From a biological standpoint, sex devoid of genuine male-female commitment is a form of stealing. And a widespread social acceptance of sex without commitment represents an injustice against women and their deepest biological interests. The tragic irony is that the "sexual liberation" espoused by some secular feminists couldn't play more perfectly into the short-term, selfish interests of men. Limiting sex to the confines of a lifetime commitment between a man and a woman is God's intention because, at least on the biological level, marriage as an institution promotes a fair exchange between the sometimes competing interests of men, women, and children.[37]

That last sentence is understated. Marriage typically features many moments of "competing interests." It's called conflict. But Wydick is right—marriage is meant to be a safe haven wherein competing interests are negotiated, and where sex is a seal as well as a salve to conflict. And yet we see marriage rates plummeting. Why? In part because of men's greater power in the mating market.

Cohabitation is a less just arrangement than marriage. It plays to a man's advantage more than a woman's, since men retain (for far longer than women) the option to stay and form a family or leave to pair off with someone new. Women seldom actively desire cohabitation over marriage, unless they perceive the former as (1) a beneficial, reliable stepping stone to the latter or (2) less risky than marriage, given ambivalence about the man with whom they are in a sexual relationship. Esteban, the 27-year-old from Guadalajara quoted in Chapter 3, articulates how this works. Recall that he owns his own ad agency. Hence, like many marketers, he is keenly aware of sex differences as well as the demographics of marriage. And he knows they matter. In fact, it's why Esteban could methodically explain why his ex-girlfriend broke up with him after five years of being sexually active but going nowhere in terms of commitment:

She was 26, and she felt like her time was passing. I would tell her that she was only 26, and she would say something about her biological clock. I would tell her that it was going to last until 37. My mom had my sister when she was 34. My aunt got married when she was 32, and she had my cousin at 38. So she shouldn't get all worked up about it.

Esteban certainly isn't getting "worked up." He knows the data favors his side of the argument: "Everybody gets married in their 30s, and it is normal. That is becoming a trend." He thinks that this particular trend is part of a considerably larger shift in priorities and expectations, wherein people want to explore all their options and experience previously inaccessible knowledge. And he sees no downsides to it:

> I think that it is beneficial. There are a lot of things happening in the world that have never happened before. It is simply so much information [now], so many things to see, so many things to decide. . . . It's what is called "big data" times. . . . It's like a child in a candy store.

Would he consider sex easy to get? "It depends on how you look [laughs]. Yes, I think it is much easier than before." Predictably, Esteban's outlook and behavior pull him away from active participation in congregational life. He attends Mass only occasionally now, about once a month.

Emmanuel, a 26-year-old Catholic architecture student in Lagos, operates with a similar approach to Esteban. He, too, wants to marry—in his case by around age 30. When asked about whether sex was easy or not, Emmanuel responded, "It depends on how you see it. I won't say it is easy; it becomes much more a reward that guys look for." What does he mean by reward? "Like, I do this for you and you give me that. . . . Ladies, that is how they pay back. . . . It is something you can get in exchange for what you give as a guy." Emmanuel, however, is more unhappy than Esteban about the bluntly material calibration of relationships that he perceives around him:

> The ladies try to look at the guy for what he has. Not because of his potential, not because of what he could be in the future. They cannot wait, so it is what he is now. And it is "for better or better." No one is ready to go for the "worse." That is why marriage has become materialistic: it is what he has now, not the future. [*So you think before now that marriage was not materialistic?*] It was more about love, much more about togetherness compared to now, let me put it that way.

The Gamble of Premarital Sex

Sociologist Jay Teachman, evaluating nationally representative data from 1995, noted that the 55 percent of women who had had more than one premarital sexual relationship exhibited increased risk of eventual divorce, when compared with married women who had had no such relationships or with the 27 percent who did so only with their eventual husband. But that was twenty-five years ago. What do today's data show? The exact same pattern. In fact, in a study of American men under age 50, 32 percent of respondents who reported premarital sex had subsequently divorced or separated, well above the 12 percent rate among men who did not report premarital sex.[38]

Still, it is untrue that premarital sex dooms a marriage. Indeed, most new marriages are characterized by it. Rachel from Chapter 3, for instance, is happily married to her husband in spite of the fact that she slept with him after their third date. (I say "in spite of" because they have literally beaten the odds.) While sexual experiences do tend to slow down the maturation of premarital relationships, and in so doing diminish the odds of eventual marriage, they do not entirely squash the probability. Maria, a 23-year-old devoutly Catholic woman from Guadalajara began having sex with her fiancé about six months before marrying him. She admitted it wasn't her ideal timeline but asserted, "It's something you can't explain. When you love a person, it's something natural." She does not think that it has had an effect on her marriage, and she "never feared" that her fiancé would break up with her. Rachel had displayed similar confidence in her (future) husband.

What distinguishes premarital sexual relationships that will flame out in a painful breakup from those that will turn into marriages? Other than engagements with set wedding dates, which are an obvious signal of marital intention, no easily measured pattern characterizes them. The key variable is the marriage mindedness of the men involved. If they are serious and mature enough to truly consider marriage, and they display sacrificial actions toward their girlfriend, marriage is more apt to happen for them in the near future. If these things aren't true about them, then marriage is unlikely.

When premarital sex is involved, there is also the risk that the shift from a relationship in which sex plays more of a lead role among two independent adults to one in which sex plays a supporting role in an interdependent union of marital intimacy and commitment is too much of a jolt to overcome. Rachel has felt this shift, and she seems to have navigated it so far: "I can say for me, sex is not a part of my life like it was before I got married and in past relationships. I don't necessarily know if that has to do with the Christian thing or some other factors." Rachel's remarks here are not about the disappearance of sex in her marriage, but about the right appearance of it. "Certainly sex is more meaningful," she continued, "if it's between two people who sincerely love each other. Especially for women." Rachel observed, "Women can talk all day long about how they don't really care, don't get attached, and it's no big thing." But having once lived that life, she has tired of all the messages claiming that it is healthy and empowering for women to have multiple partners: " 'If men can do it, you can do it.' I truly believe we're not wired for that, and it's destructive." She reflected on the commonly shared confusion surrounding marriage today: "I never had a fear of marriage, but I think that I didn't know what a truly healthy relationship looks like." And, "I think it affects everybody," she said, Christians as much as non-Christians.

Rachel's words reinforce the vulnerability of women to what research psychologist Scott Stanley calls "premature entanglements," relationships wherein romantic and sexual connections fuel emotional attachments without leading to the development and clarification of commitment.[39] Premature entanglements are apt to lead to ambiguity, frustration, anxiety, and power plays—not fertile soil for commitment. Relationships that display levels of commitment insufficient to support sexual intimacy are prone to collapse. A sure sign of low commitment can be measured by his prioritizing his relational interests over hers. This was clearly not the case with Rachel and her husband. She knew from the first date that he was the one, and the feeling was mutual; they felt like a team from the start, and they wed ten months later.

But much more common is a story like Noor's, a 30-year-old Catholic woman from Beirut, where she is a judge. She's in a relationship with a man about whom she remains ambivalent, due largely to his passive manner and intense self-focus. He had sort of asked her to marry him once, she told me. Sort of: "He said, 'I wouldn't mind spending the rest of my life with you,' " a remark that bespoke his profound insouciance. And yet Noor loves him: "He has a great heart. He's a great guy. He loves Jesus—top of my list. He's forgiving and accepting in so many ways. He's a deep person." She admits, though, that sometimes he spends too much time in his own head and doesn't pursue interaction with her on a personal level: "Sometimes it bothers me—always talking about philosophy and theology."

The day before we spoke, Noor had had a heart-to-heart talk with him about his tendency toward self-absorption: "It's important that he asks me about what's going on with me." She longs for a take-charge leader, rather than the high-maintenance man she is with.[40] As with many Christian relationships—spanning the globe—Noor's, too, became sexual while dating. And that, she believes, tends to slow relationships down.

Interestingly, Noor and her boyfriend ceased sexual involvement: "We stopped, because we both know it's not what we'd like to live, religiously not good for us." This cooling off of sexual activity has neither led to the termination of the relationship nor sped up her boyfriend's interest in marrying her. She's in relationship limbo:

> Sometimes I think I've already made my decision, that I don't want to be in this relationship. But I also see his good qualities. So I reconsider. But I'm fed up with not knowing. [How are you going to figure this out?] Maybe if he leads more. If I feel secure and safe . . . [Do you see signs of that or not?] Not really. That's why I had this talk with him yesterday.

How Contraception Split the Mating Market, and Why It Matters

Look around, and you will see myriad supposed reasons why marriage should be flourishing: Poverty is receding. Populous middle classes are sprouting up in the Global South. Gender pay distinctions are shrinking. And yet, marriage is lagging far more today than it was as recently as 1980. An alternative—or at least accompanying—account seems warranted for explaining what has happened. That account should consider the disappearance of impending fertility as a chief producer of marriage. Babies are becoming rarer today, and so also is the "shotgun wedding," courtesy of a mating market saturated by the expected use of contraception and the resulting introduction of sex early in relationships.[41]

Artificial contraception is certainly no social construction. It's quite tangible. The births it prevents are real, too. Less easy to understand, but still very real, is the influence of contraceptive use on the marital impulse. It is a key, I hold, to understanding modern relationship dynamics. Over time, the wide uptake of effective contraception—which took a major leap forward with the advent of the Pill in the early 1960s—unwittingly split the "mating pool" into two overlapping but distinctive markets—one for sex (or short-term relationships) and one for marriage, with a rather large territory in between composed of significant relationships of varying commitment and duration (for example, cohabitation).[42] Prior to that time, there was a relatively unified mating pool, since sex implied commitment because it risked pregnancy. Laura, a 24-year-old Baptist woman from Austin married to a Christian convert from Islam, characterized the pre-Pill mating market bluntly: "If you tried to satisfy your sexual desires outside of marriage, there were hard consequences."

Not so today. The average woman who could previously count on seeing clear evidence of commitment before sex now faces the reverse—sex is expected before commitment. In an era of everyday contraception, sex is considered less risky and, hence, harder to avoid earlier in relationships. Men's and women's preferences haven't radically changed; women have always been more interested than men in marriage (on average), and they have long tended to prefer more time and commitment in relationships before having sex. Yet with the rise in popularity of the Pill, and the drop in the "price" of sex in relationships, women's bargaining position in the marriage market has deteriorated.[43] Nowadays, relationships tend to develop more readily in ways that fit his preferences than hers.

Diego, a 27-year-old engineer working for a marketing company in Barcelona, could be a poster child for this phenomenon. A self-described traditionalist from Pamplona, living in an increasingly secular Spain, Diego thinks of himself as a conservative because, in contrast to other Spaniards, he still idealizes commitment: "Nowadays, people get together and then split up in a casual way, which isn't the same as in the past." Not Diego. He and his girlfriend "have been together for six years and we were [living] apart for four of those. I think that says a lot about the commitment that we both have." The two have been sexually active for five of their six years together, and he slept with other women as well, prior to meeting her. When pressed about how this lifestyle fits with his Catholic faith, Diego confessed, "I'm a practicing Christian but obviously there are things about the Church that I don't share, and this could be one of them."

Marriage, for Diego, would constitute a capstone in more ways than one: "I can't conceive of marrying someone without really getting to know her, without living with her, having a sexual relationship with her, everything." He wants to be "completely sure about it," since divorce would constitute "a total failure" of judgment. Marriage is "something that I want to do in the right way with the person I really love, but I'm not anxious to do it right now." First they have to move in together: "I think it's very important to live together before you take the step. When you live with someone you find out their nuances, which may act as a warning." It's the "small things," he's convinced, that "could lead you to the conclusion that this isn't the right person for you." Six years in, Diego reckons he still has five or six years more to go before marrying: "I'm not in any hurry."

On the other hand, Genevieve, a 25-year-old from Lagos, was brief in her response to questions about her own romantic relationship. She offered little color commentary but left the distinct impression that the future of the relationship is out of her hands. Her boyfriend calls the shots:

INTERVIEWER: Are you currently in a sexual relationship?
GENEVIEVE: Yes, I am.
INTERVIEWER: Would you call that person a boyfriend?
GENEVIEVE: Yes.
INTERVIEWER: So how long have you been in this relationship?
GENEVIEVE: Like, six months now.
INTERVIEWER: Do you think you will be with this person a year from now?
GENEVIEVE: I should.
INTERVIEWER: Ten years, five years . . .?
GENEVIEVE: I don't know.
INTERVIEWER: Do you think you will marry the person?
GENEVIEVE: I don't know.
INTERVIEWER: Does he want to get married soon or not?
GENEVIEVE: No.
INTERVIEWER: Do you feel any pressure to get married?
GENEVIEVE: No, I don't.
INTERVIEWER: About how long was it before you started having sex?
GENEVIEVE: Like two to three months ago.
INTERVIEWER: Do your parents know?
GENEVIEVE: No.

Peter, a 26-year-old from Lagos in a sexual relationship with his girlfriend of one year, seems far more confident about what happens next. He was not only confident that he would marry his girlfriend, but he felt he could do so at any time: "Yes, she wants to get married. Like, if tomorrow I [ask] her to get married, she is okay with that." But he's in no rush. Marrying around age 30 would be just fine with him. Without cheap sex, the capstone vision of marriage would collapse.

Combine women's diminished power in the marriage market with the congregational sex ratio disparity discussed earlier in this chapter—that is, more women than men active in church—and the lopsidedness gets even worse. This is how power flows away from young Christian women and toward men. Many women find themselves in a bind under these circumstances: either chemically alter their own natural processes (when it comes to the Pill at least) or be blamed for negligence when an unintended pregnancy happens. In addition, wide contraceptive use incentivizes women to act against their own interests and sleep with men sooner than they prefer, rather than collectively reinforce a "higher price" for sex among their peers. Such a shift in power would require a concerted, organized effort on women's part that frankly seems impossible on a wide scale today.[44]

This situation yields a marriage market experience in which some women seem to "have it all," having found a good husband after a short search. More succeed after a long search, with years of dating and failed relationships, and still others keep trying—some using sex as a lure, while others refuse to do so, convinced it's not a smart strategy. Many find themselves in relationship limbo, having fallen in love but sensing they're nowhere near marriage.

Resistance to premarital sex is now rare and almost entirely moral/religious or psychological in its sources.[45] Abstinence is no longer considered a rational reflection of anticipated pregnancy risk. What has emerged is what the late Pope John Paul II called the "contraceptive mentality," or the assumption of sterile sex.[46] (It is, however, just that—a mentality. It's not reality. Contraceptive failure rates remain well above zero.) As a result, relationships become sexual earlier—why, after all, should one abstain if pregnancy won't happen? Indeed, 28 percent of Americans who've ever had sex said they first did so in their current or most recent relationship before the partners even agreed that they were *in* a relationship.[47] (An additional 32 percent had done so by the end of the relationship's first month.) I am hardly unique in noting this. Nobel laureates and a recent Federal Reserve chair saw it coming.[48] British social theorist Anthony Giddens predicted it nearly thirty years ago in *The Transformation of Intimacy*.[49] Even Pope Paul VI discerned it, back in 1968. He understood something of the economics of sexual exchange, and he worried about the Pill's effect on relationships and sexual decision-making. He received considerable flak for what he wrote in *Humanae Vitae*:

> Let [people] first consider how easily this course of action could open wide the way for marital infidelity and a general lowering of moral standards.

Not much experience is needed to be fully aware of human weakness and to understand that human beings—and especially the young, who are so exposed to temptation—need incentives to keep the moral law.[50]

Note his choice of words about how obvious this is to human observation: "Not much experience is needed to be fully aware. . . ." He's saying that it doesn't take a rocket scientist to see how this works. The pope's logic here could be taken a step further, though. In the era of the Pill, men and women increasingly need incentives not only to keep the moral law, but also now even to marry. *Humanae Vitae*, though modern secular feminists would decry the claim, had women's interests at heart:

Another effect that gives cause for alarm is that a man who grows accustomed to the use of contraceptive methods may forget the reverence due to a woman . . . reduce her to being a mere instrument for the satisfaction of his own desires, no longer considering her as his partner whom he should surround with care and affection.[51]

In fact, the effect has become mutual over time; both men and women have become more adept at using each other. Rachel lends a Baptist voice to the realization of Paul VI's fears of utilitarian relationships:

I'm not sure that women know how they want to be treated. There's just a lack of respect generally between the sexes. Which is why the kind of respectful relationship has just kind of turned into "How can you please me?" It's really tragic and sad. And sex. Everything is about sex.

Of course, as discussed before, Rachel is one of the lucky ones. She finally met a man who was marriage minded.

It seems scandalous to talk like this today. On the one hand, Christian leaders don't like such blunt (and irreligious) language about sex and marriage. On the other extreme, my academic peers are apt to insist on strict equality when discussing men's and women's interests. Critics tend to become unhinged when I outline contraception's influence on modern mating dynamics, as if the grand project of fertility control were fragile and prone to crumbling just by describing it.[52] This fierce impulse to protect and defend has to do with the conviction among scholars that something so popular and helpful to women's economic flourishing must not be perceived as having any problematic downstream consequences. In other words, they want to prevent a devastating public relations problem for the Pill. I happen to believe that women can handle social scientific information without it being filtered for them by professional gatekeepers.

"Planned" Parenthood

Planned parenthood—the concept, not the organization—is an assumption evident in the interviews. By that I mean that churchgoing Christians employ language about marriage that not only implies the likelihood and desirability of having children but also includes a timetable that necessitates and assumes stable control over fertility. Some interviewees responded with a "whatever God wills" when asked about the number of children they would like to have, but they were uncommon. Even lots of Catholic interviewees—more women than men—expect to have small families, in spite of the Catholic Church's well-known objection to chemical and barrier forms of birth control.[53] Contraception, the Church holds, demeans women rather than empowers them, encourages men to view women as objects of pleasure, discourages responsibility, fosters a utilitarian approach to human relationships, and understands children as problems to be avoided rather than gifts to be valued.

Beirut's Maronite Catholics, in particular, wrestle with the Church's teachings against artificial forms of contraception. That's to be anticipated in a Catholic rite in which most of the priests are married—and can empathize rather than just sympathize on the topic—and in a country where the cost of living continues to surge. Few interviewees there spoke of wanting a large family. "Two or three" was the norm. Given social expectations about elevated material standards and private education—combined with comparatively modest salaries among the middle classes—it is understandable why many prefer smaller families. (In the United States, on the other hand, conservative Catholics and many evangelicals exhibit notably greater average family size.) Larger families seem impossible among Lebanese Christians for all but the wealthiest or the most abandoned to providence, as one interviewee there described it:

> People don't trust anymore that God will provide and help; they don't believe that he will open new horizons so that things work out. This "absence"

of God makes young people feel they have to arrange everything, from all sides and aspects, before they commit. All this delays things and makes them harder.

It is a rare scholar who admits that contraception has been a key shaper of the modern unraveling or deinstitutionalization of marriage.[54] The late sociologist of gender Janet Chafetz, however, did so. Chafetz was prescient in her 1995 prediction of marital and fertility delay and decline:

> Once college-educated women enter the labor force and begin to accrue experience, skills, promotions, and pay increases, the potential "opportunity costs" of marriage, and especially of children, increase. The energy and commitment required by a family are seen as significantly reducing such women's career opportunities, *given that traditional definitions of women's obligations to husbands and children persist*. Likewise, as women earn more money, the attractiveness of marriage as a means of support decreases. Able to be more selective in their search for a spouse, women are likely to take a longer time before making such a commitment.[55]

Chafetz was right on target. She predicted that fewer marriages would result but that they would be happier, on average, than when marriage was nearly universal. Expectations for marital satisfaction would soar, and failure to meet those expectations would prompt more divorcing. This is social reality for Christians and non-Christians alike today.

There may be additional unforeseen costs of widely used contraception, including the cognitive presumption that a woman is infertile. This could make the sexual violation of women by men seem less risky to the perpetrator, who assumes he need not fear the evidence of a pregnancy. The #MeToo movement of 2017–2018 highlighted just how widely women experience sexual violation.

In one sense, contraception leveled the playing field between men and women. Women could not only have casual sex like men—should they wish—but they could have uninterrupted careers like them, too. They could be peers in the bedroom as well as in the boardroom. But instead of greater respect between the sexes, what has resulted is a mixed bag, together with a more urgent need to clearly signal one's preferences about sex very early in relationships, since the default expectation is easy, early sex.

For Christians, Competing Realities

Christina, a 25-year-old graphic designer in Guadalajara, observed, "Men are going to take everything you want to give. They won't say no, and they won't say stop. I think that this is where women must set limits." But limits are not easy to set when power is flowing away from you. It is a difficult conversation to have, not just because it may be awkward, but because she fears his disappointment and so frets about whether he'll stay or leave. These are legitimate concerns. While in her mid-30s, a marriage-minded friend of mine dated what she described as three quality men. None of them, however, would brook her terms (i.e., no premarital sex). They each admired and "respected" her values, but they all walked away. Now in her late 40s, she has not married.

It is a frustrating position in which to find oneself—forced to choose between one's religious commitments and what is seen by many as the next important step in adulthood. Tanya, a 28-year-old journalist and Orthodox Christian living in Moscow, recently married an irreligious man she had met at the library.[56] We talked one-on-one after an informal focus group of Orthodox couples, which was convened to discuss how men and women meet today. Her husband, she said, had pursued her. Unlike many of the men Tanya had interacted with—including some Orthodox—he was not "infantile," in her words: "Good God! How come I am 23, and they [the men] are 33, they are so much older, but I happen to feel older than them?"[57] Even the infantile men, however, seemed to get their way in her wider social circle. When discussing the challenges of moving a relationship forward in terms of commitment, she relays the helpless position that many women feel they occupy. They simply cannot bring themselves to press men on the matter of marrying, while Tanya cannot understand their reticence to speak bluntly:

> I have never understood [women's silence]. For me, it's incomprehensible. I don't know why. When they [her friends] tell me, like: "Are you crazy? I can't. You can't be that pushy. He will just leave me!" Why do you need such a partner, with whom you can't share what's on your mind?

Tanya had moved her own relationship forward without the introduction of sex. But trying to renegotiate the sexual terms of a relationship after a couple has already been sexually intimate? That is difficult. Few relationships survive the withdrawal of sex, as Duke University economist Peter Arcidiacano has demonstrated among teens.[58] Another Orthodox woman put it this way: "Despite all the promises that you may give, if it has happened once, it will happen again." How did Tanya manage to stick to her guns to postpone physical intimacy? By being up front.

> With my future husband I said, "Come on, I'm not going to date you for years. Let's set a certain period during which we will be evaluating each other. Let it be half a year. If during this period we realize that we are not the ones to spend the rest of life with, we simply break up and do not get in the way [of] each other looking for love. Or we get married. There are no other ways. This period may be shortened, but it cannot be prolonged. Six months is enough to understand." In the end we got married after four months.

Compared to Farah, the daughter of the Lebanese Maronite priest who thought four years was a minimum amount of time to get to know a suitor, Tanya's four months is profoundly rapid. I'm not sure I would recommend it. But to Tanya, it made rational sense. And look at what resulted: both she and Farah wanted to marry, but only Tanya has done so.

But what if Tanya and her husband are not sexually "compatible"? Many men and women wonder this today. It's what I call "exogenous" sexual chemistry—the idea that compatibility in the bedroom is either present or absent at the outset of the relationship, and there's nothing to be done about it except figure out whether it exists or not. (Several interviewees mentioned the idea.) But it's a myth. In reality, sexual chemistry is learned, not foreordained. You figure it out when you're in the relationship. And Tanya knows it:

> I believe this matter [sex] should necessarily be discussed before the marriage. But I believe that, in principle, you can understand what he will be like in bed when he is courting you, without getting undressed. It's in the way he helps you put on your coat, the way you talk—it shows quite clearly what he will be like in bed. Always, as I believe. The rest are technical issues—if you can talk with this person, say "Touch me here" and stuff.

For Tanya, it's about communication, not chemistry. While the mating market favors men's preferences over women's, her story reveals that it's not necessary to simply play along. There are other options. They entail risk—that he will leave. But to Tanya, that would be a clear signal that he was not the right man.

Half a world away, Kara, a 27-year-old Catholic from Austin, would agree with Tanya. Kara is hardly averse to the idea of giving herself to a man, but the thought of hooking up strikes her as odd: "Not as a Catholic. Just as a person. It's very, very strange to me . . . the idea of like, giving every single part of yourself, including sex, including everything, to a person who hasn't committed their whole life to you." Then why do people do it? "Good question. I don't know. I think that they imagine themselves—these two people specifically—imagine themselves getting married someday." This certainly isn't true of every woman. Plenty of young adults in any country would balk at Kara's befuddlement.

Kara, however, is not only unmarried; she hasn't been in a serious relationship yet. An accomplished violinist and teacher, Kara represents a nascent form of American Catholic—conservative, observant, and far more versed in Church teachings than scores of her Catholic peers, even plenty of those who still make their way to Mass most Sundays. To Kara, marriage is a sacrament, "a commitment to spend your whole life putting the needs of the other first and before your own." She was homeschooled for much of her early education—something utterly foreign to Christians in most other countries but increasingly popular in the United States. Hardly naïve—something many suspect of homeschoolers—Kara graduated from a secular university where she had full freedom to engage in or refrain from the myriad activities. She senses a vocation to marriage, to use the formal Catholic term, but it became quickly apparent to her that most of her fellow university students weren't thinking that far ahead. If you met someone, fell in love, and married, you were unusual. Kara knew several students who did just that. She was not one of them, but it doesn't bother her.

Jenna, a 24-year-old globetrotter, moved to Austin to be near her boyfriend, Stephen, who has made her rethink her long-term antagonism toward marriage. She was raised by a stable parental marriage in a military family, yet she is in no hurry herself to marry: "Minimum, we both want to be 30." She and Stephen are cohabiting, but age 30 is six years away. Still, she is so enamored of Stephen that she moved for him—a big deal among millennials. After experiencing the uncertainties inherent in sex devoid of any commitment, Jenna much prefers her current cohabitation arrangement. She values her wider exposure to sexual experience than what her Catholic faith and family might prefer for her, yet even cohabitation hasn't quieted her fears: "In my personal situation, I get very, very nervous and anxious, and doubtful sometimes about whether or not Stephen and I can make it work."

Jenna's decisions—especially given her genuine anxieties and misgivings—would simply not make sense to Kara. What is it that people are seeking in marriage? Kara didn't have to think long about her answer, which tapped into both Christian and secular sources of inspiration and idealism: "There is something in the heart of every person that longs to be intimately known for who you are and loved anyway. Like to have someone look at you in the face and see everything that you are and still choose to love you."

Because Sex Is Cheap, Marriage Is Getting Expensive

People apply mathematics to lots of questions about marriage. They think about by what age they should marry, how long is too long to date before marrying, how many children they would like to have, how much the wedding will cost. But beyond the ways that most people understand, there is additional math that shapes the marriage markets in which they are participating. Marriage, one could say, has a price—a cost that men pay in order to marry a woman. In *Cheap Sex*, I talk at length about the price of sex, that is, what it costs a man—in terms of commitments, time, and sacrifices—in order to have a sexual relationship with a woman. Not a whole lot, I deduced. What about marriage? Is marriage more "expensive" for Christians? Yes, but Christians are also notably more willing to pay the price. Why?

Brian Hollar, an economist at Marymount University, explores the costs of marriage for devout Christians in the United States, using data from the biennial General Social Survey.[59] Whereas I argued that the price of sex is best measured by how much time it takes before a couple becomes sexually involved—after one date, three dates, months and months of devoted courtship, or in the most expensive case, marriage—Hollar gauges the cost of *marriage* in a more resolutely economic fashion. The price of marriage, he argues, represents the expected income transferred from men to women in marriage. While that's not exactly how I would have expressed it, Hollar's observation of marriage is not unrelated to the one I describe in Chapter 3. Economists have long understood marriage in this way, as the socially accepted arrangement by which a man transfers his present (and pledges his future) financial resources to a woman and the children she has or will bear and raise for him. It's not a Christian definition of marriage, of course. And it sounds old fashioned. It is, however, the same idea that is embedded in sociological and demographic research on men's earnings as key to understanding declining marriage rates.

Hollar defends his logic well. He holds that supply and demand affect marriage markets. (Definitely.) He notes that women are more selective today because they are able to be unmarried and still prosperous. (Agreed.) And he observes that sexual alternatives—think cohabitation, sleeping around, even pornography and masturbation—function as substitutes to marriage for some men. (True.)

A helpful distinction to make here is between what economists call normal and inferior goods.[60] Normal goods are those for which demand increases when income improves. It pays to think of marriage as long having been a normal good, one that young men—under adequate financial circumstances—angled toward. Historically, the responsibilities and routines of work, marriage, and fatherhood have afforded men an important sense of masculine identity, not to mention the optimal benefits of help, children, and a socially acceptable sexual relationship.[61] But several things are occurring now that prompt men to settle for inferior goods. What sort of inferior goods am I talking about? Like the marital alternatives Hollar notes, I mean cohabitation, temporary sexual companions, porn, or even the virtual intimacy some exhibit in online conversations. Each falls well short of a genuine and total gift of self.

Today, cultural and marketing efforts are boosting the demand for inferior goods, lowering the "price" of these marital substitutes. Marriage is hardly esteemed in popular music or on film. Governments may—in a roundabout way—penalize dependent mothers for marrying, an act that often pushes women out of reach of more generous social welfare support. High rates of nonmarital fertility reinforce the idea that men and women don't actually get and stay married. Pornography delivers a virtual sexual experience without having to navigate risk or a relationship.[62] Elites, often beneficiaries of marriage in their parents' and their own lives, increasingly scorn marriage publicly in order to appear sufficiently progressive. As a result, marriage looks less and less like the normal good that it actually is. It should be no surprise, then, when inferior goods become preferred by increasing numbers of men. But *Christians*?

Hollar claims that being active in your faith increases the cost of these (otherwise cheaper) marital substitutes. How? By problematizing marriage substitutes as morally suspect, that is, wrong or sinful. In that way, devout Christians feel far more social pressure than the less religious to avoid sexual alternatives.

Let's not overreach here. Congregations don't throw people out of church services for their moral failures. At worst, there are whispering campaigns or subtle shunning. At best, concerned intervention. Why would they do anything at all? Because marital substitutes have a way of corroding one's spiritual life, and tolerance of marital alternatives poses a threat to the group. It seldom comes to this, however, since those who pursue marital alternatives tend to self-select away from active participation in the life of the local church, as will be discussed in detail in Chapter 5. The pivotal idea here, however, is that sexual alternatives are considered immoral. That's what raises the cost of marriage, by delegitimizing marriage's "competition."

Other forces are at work that have nothing to do with morality concerns. For example, women's increasing choosiness about a spouse, a byproduct of education and career opportunity, has also raised the price of marriage. He has to offer more than he otherwise would have. It's not just financial, of course. Other qualities in both men and women—personality and politics, for example—matter more than they once did when it comes to matching. Christians are among the most interested in marrying, but the bar for them is not lowered just because they are more apt to esteem the institution in the first place.

The devout, Hollar concludes, are paying the highest price for marriage today. (That doesn't mean they pay more for their weddings, though.) In return, they are also benefitting from the decision. Devout married men make 11 percent more money per year than do married men who attend church less often. And religious or not, married men with children earn more than single men without children. Whether such men were more attractive as mates or worked harder and earned more once they were married is unknown here, but the point is that since devout Christians are more likely to marry, they more often benefit from the role differentiation of husband and wife.[63] There is a large and statistically significant difference, Hollar notes, between the incomes of married, devout men and married, devout women; the latter are more likely to be financially dependent on the former (when compared with less devout couples). This is partly due to their greater sex role traditionalism. Many Christians and non-Christians alike perceive this scenario as risky and/or unattractive today. But frankly, what they're also conveying is their low confidence in marriage and men, and the need for an exit strategy before even entering matrimony.

Pilar is a 28-year-old who works in a medical complex in Pamplona, and her story illuminates the rising cost of marriage and the attractiveness of marital substitutes, as well as women's elevated thresholds for marrying. Pilar thwarted Christian sentiment about cohabitation when she moved to Pamplona to be closer to her agnostic boyfriend, with whom she cohabited for the next three years. In Hollar's words, Pilar settled for a marital substitute, believing that she was still on the pathway to marriage. Her modest faith wasn't enough to discourage her. Pilar described her faith to us as "more Christian than Catholic." The former "is the essence." The Catholicism so familiar to her "is just a pathway." She opines further about the Catholic Church:

> Sometimes it makes sense, and sometimes it doesn't. Now that we have Francis as pope, I see myself more connected to his views and the way he wants to spread the faith—a more humble perspective, more involved in the world's needs, taking into account ecological disaster. I like the way he's doing things. He's more inclusive, to be concise, closer to people's needs. He's translating the Church into a more community concept.

When we asked what Catholic teachings she disagrees with, Pilar's remarks focused on marriage and sexuality, namely, contraception. It's arguably the most popular doctrinal squabble among young adult Catholics. Given the human penchant for bringing one's belief system and personal practice into harmony, I'm not surprised that Pilar cited it. She wants the Church to change. Other related concerns, like the permanence of marriage, accompanied Pilar's problem with contraception:

> There are sections of Catholicism that see matrimony as something that must be for your whole life, and I don't agree. Of course, that should be the intention, but not if it's a case of putting up with it regardless—no. And for example, I don't agree with him [the priest] as regards planning a family if it's not done in a responsible way. Taking precautions if you don't want to have more than two or three children, or indeed the number you believe to be reasonable, is responsible. There are circles that don't accept this, and I don't agree with that.

The remark about "for your whole life" makes sense, not because Pilar isn't interested in lifelong marriage—she is—but because her parents' marriage was nothing to emulate. Pilar and her boyfriend, who had been together for eight years, broke up three months before I spoke with her. Pilar was cognizant of the loss—she had begun the relationship before she turned 20—and of the challenges facing her in finding someone else. Why didn't it work out? After so many years, she said, "the relationship was demanding a change from us." Pilar wanted to finish her degree first before getting married, and she was beginning to think about working abroad, while her boyfriend "wanted to settle down, have a family." In the end, she initiated the breakup, "but we were on the same page. We had talked about it several times."

Here is a clear example of what Brian Hollar (as well as Janet Chafetz) calls the "opportunity cost of marriage" for women. Pilar sees marriage as costing her something personally and professionally. This phenomenon, Hollar argues, has an inverse relationship to the supply of marriage, meaning—as Pilar demonstrates—that it takes women out of the marriage market. To make matters more complicated, Pilar had been diagnosed with multiple sclerosis within the past year. The close encounter with mortality made her want to embrace life—taking up dancing—and reconnect with friends and family, to "stop spending energy on things that didn't matter." Meanwhile, her boyfriend, who she admits supported and loved her unconditionally, was trapped in the mundane world of job-related stresses. He was marriageable, but they had grown apart. There was a spiritual side of the decision to split, too:

> My health problems made me reconnect with an essential part of myself, rethink life. As a believer, it helped me a lot to approach my problem. I didn't feel alone, that God was helping me with strength to face the situation, to see the positive aspects of this time. I recovered the spiritual dimension of health.

At this point, her boyfriend's agnosticism became an issue in a way that it had not been before. He had tried to understand her: "It made me think about how different our values actually were. He didn't have that transcendental approach to life, to see that your life was part of something bigger. He wasn't able to understand the ways I was seeing my life." In the end, they were no longer a good fit. And since Pilar felt advantaged by professional opportunities and disadvantaged as a future mother, marriage and "settling down" soon didn't make sense anymore. Her Catholic faith, while stirred by her illness, was not so traditional as to rule out future participation in marriage alternatives. But people change, as Pilar has demonstrated. It's worth checking in on her in five years to see where things stand.

The High Cost of Marrying

Technically, starting a marriage—the getting married part—is not expensive. Even Christian marriage can be done inexpensively: a member of the clergy to preside, some family and friends, and a church or chapel (or not). The reality, of course, is something quite different. Costly weddings are common, and they are certainly social constructions. For some interviewees, weddings are so cost-prohibitive as to create real financial barriers to marrying. But the barriers aren't often erected by churches, ministers, or priests. In Beirut and Guadalajara, for example, weddings are a very big deal, laden with social expectations and the expenses that follow in their train. A priest with whom I spoke in Guadalajara noted the high cost of what ought to be religious events: "First Communions are celebrated like aristocratic weddings, and weddings themselves are celebrated like royal weddings." The costs vary only by degree among rich and poor, both of whom are expected to put on a display: "Instead of French wine, you have Coca-Cola, and instead of seven hundred people present, 80 to 120."

I wondered aloud whether such big events help coalesce a community, creating social solidarity that can pay downstream benefits for the marrying couple in terms of support and social control—helping them weather future external or internal crises. The priest recognized the social value of community solidarity, but he wasn't convinced. He made a habit of not encouraging the show: "I never go to the parties. I tell them, 'We need a priest who prays, not a priest who parties.'"

Ignacio, a 27-year-old computer programmer from Pamplona, thinks people are discouraged from marriage primarily because of economic hardship in general. While some financial challenges face entire nations, as has been the case in Spain, some of it is self-inflicted: "The truth is that in Spain, we have created a huge business surrounding weddings." Ignacio described the process by which good intentions are overrun by the structure of the wedding industry and social expectations:

Initially, you say "Right, we're going to keep everything simple." But then you get drawn into the whole thing. [It begins with] "It's going to be an intimate affair in a small church with just close family and a simple meal." But if you decide to invite just one of your friends or a slightly more distant relative too, this opens the floodgates, and that's what has happened to us. At first, we decided that financially it was overwhelming, but on the other hand, it's a big celebration and we're going to invite a few friends, too. But one thing leads to another, and you end up organizing a huge wedding whether you like it or not, and that's expensive. I think that this is one of the main things that scares people [away from marriage].

Across town, Diego, the 27-year-old working in a marketing company, feels the same way. Marriage is just out of reach financially. "People who do get married want to do it properly, in the same way that it's always been done." That is, inviting around two hundred guests, complete "with a good wedding reception, with a stag [and] hen [bachelor and bachelorette] party." And so marriage waits until the wedding can happen "properly."

Mariana, a 25-year-old Catholic from Guadalajara who anticipates marrying her boyfriend of five years, pines for something smaller—like her own parents experienced: "My mother said to me, 'When I married, there was no such thing as a honeymoon, nor did we have a super apartment all furnished. You had the bed and with that, you [managed].'" Strangely, Mariana's humble tastes are going unappreciated: "I said to my family that I wanted to have a small wedding and a not-so-ostentatious honeymoon and that I also wanted children. They thought that it was odd." The pull of the cultural event of the wedding is strong, and Mariana's parents still desire for her to go over the top with her plans.

Cohabitation has surged at all socioeconomic levels for several reasons, and the cost of putting on a wedding is certainly one of them. In the United States, a small wedding is considered a respectable and feasible option, but in other sites—as just described—it is much more difficult to accomplish. Marta and Paweł—the married couple from Krakow—are among those couples who have successfully pulled it off. She's a full-time mother to their 1-year-old daughter, while he is in the middle of graduate studies. Paweł, in particular, flouted the emergent logic that advises patience and the completion of degrees and the purchase of a flat or apartment before getting serious about marriage. It helps, of course, that they live in a more religious city in a comparatively Catholic country. So there is social support for marriage in general.

But that doesn't mean they didn't have to buck some old and new trends. By having a more modest wedding, one that didn't feature invitations to numerous people their parents had suggested, they saved money. But in doing so, they frayed some social ties. Marta is from a smaller town in the hills south of Krakow, where weddings are a big deal. "It was a bit of a scandal,"

Paweł relayed, "because we didn't have a big reception. Marta's mother had trouble with an aunt for a time because of it." While the tensions have diminished, they could fire up again. Marta anticipated that the next family wedding would invariably raise contrasts with theirs. But Marta and Paweł seem confident enough to handle it with aplomb. In other locales, flouting such norms is even more difficult.

The elevated cost of a wedding means that some Christian young adults— particularly in countries where average wages are notably lower—face unfortunate, high barriers to doing something that (1) their faith endorses, (2) they may wish to do, and (3) is becoming rarer for all the reasons already described. What is uniquely pernicious in the case of Beirut's Christians, for example, is the explosion in housing prices without a concomitant climb in earning power or the ability that many American young adults have of moving to other prosperous states or cities that have a lower cost of living.[64] A couple from Boston or northern Virginia could marry and move to South Carolina and find good jobs and far more affordable housing. Lebanon's Christians cannot do likewise. They can move out to the periphery of Beirut but in so doing face commute times like those of New Yorkers, but sans the trains, subways, and boats that make moving toward and around Manhattan feasible. Frustrated Lebanese could, and plenty do, consider immigrating to Europe or the Gulf states.

It's easy to conclude that Lebanon is exhibiting a combination toxic to the formation and success of Christian marriage. Malek, a 27-year-old pharmacist and Maronite Catholic from Beirut, relayed the story of his cousin's wedding the previous Saturday. It had been underwritten at "a minimal level," he said, the least that would be expected. "How much do you think that was?" he asked me. I guessed $10,000. "Three times that," he clarified. How could that be? He listed some of the expenses:

> The bride's dress will cost $3,000 to rent. The cameraman, $3,000. The zaffa dancers, $2,000. The restaurant? Five to six thousand. You can't just rent one car, either. You have to rent several cars. That costs $1,000. Flowers are $2,000. Other decorations, $2,000. Chocolate, $2,000. [*Chocolate costs $2,000?*] Including the cake. Everything is another $2,000. It's crazy!

A local diocesan premarital counselor concurred when I asked him about this. But he signaled religious leaders' powerlessness to do anything about it.

"It's not just about weddings" that the Lebanese feel social pressure to display wealth few actually have, he asserted.

Malek has six years of university education and works as a pharmacist for under $30,000 per year. He wants to marry one day, but how could he possibly afford a wedding? One option is borrowing the money. In fact, a drive up the Jounieh-Beirut coastal highway reveals multiple billboards advertising loans for weddings and honeymoons. Americans are notorious for credit card debt, but American Christianity is not known for overspending on weddings. (In my hometown, a modest church wedding followed by ham sandwiches and cake downstairs in the church basement was sufficient.) Why does this drive toward conspicuous consumption seem to affect the Lebanese so?[65] Malek explained:

> Our generation is living in a conflict. They still have an impact from their parents—how they used to get married in their villages. The whole village would attend. Everyone would help you in the marriage. They would help you build your house. What we've lost, however, is this social support that followed [the wedding]. But you still have to do all the stuff. [That is, the expectation of wide attendance at weddings is still present.] In the future, this is unsustainable. Weddings will have to get more Western [i.e., smaller]. We're seeing a trend of weddings abroad, because they are cheaper. No one expects you to invite and pay for so many people to attend. This is what I plan to do.

All this means that a particular strength of traditional Lebanese life—support and mutual aid to the marriages and families among them—no longer readily accompanies the expectations that "the village" will be invited to the weddings. The benefits of social solidarity have nearly evaporated, due, in part, to the decline in village life that has accompanied urbanization. A glimmer of hope has begun to emerge in Lebanon, however: mass weddings, featuring dozens of couples exchanging vows while saving precious cash. Is it a trend? The New York Times thinks so, but it's too early to tell.[66] The pull of social desirability in plotting your own wedding is strong.

Other sites, including Lagos, Guadalajara, and Pamplona, deviate from this reality only by degree. Joseph, a 27-year-old Catholic who works as a regulatory officer in a pharmaceutical company in Lagos, is convinced many things have changed about marriage, right down to the wedding itself:

No, marriage is nothing like what it used to be during the days of our fathers. Now these days, marriage is about high status: the big hall used for the wedding, the amount of people who came in for that wedding, the amount of money spent. . . . Back in the days, it was really modest. You find someone you want to marry, you go there, tell them you want to marry this person. They organize a little thing, they get married. But these days, it is about the big people in the society.

Interviewees speculated that an average wedding in Pamplona ran around $20,000—not quite Lebanese levels but still rather high for a country whose economic position remains precarious. Unlike in Lebanon, however, one can more easily thwart the dominant paradigm there and have a small Catholic wedding. You might offend the sensibilities of friends and extended family, perhaps, and cause them to wonder about their own obligation to invite you to their weddings in the future (or regret doing so in the past). But it can be done, a priest in Pamplona assured me.

Rashid, a 24-year-old Baptist and former Muslim now living in Austin, saw the same thing happening among Muslim young adults in the United Arab Emirates. They were getting married later primarily "because of the cost":

The cost is increasing. [*So just too expensive to get a house?*] Get a house, also the way it works in the UAE is that the husband pays . . . the future wife's father some amount of money. It's decided by her dad. And that's just rising, and it's really too expensive to pay that. . . . And then doing the wedding as well is very costly. Like $30,000 at least for the wedding.

So why, in Rashid's mind, do Americans marry later, despite the fact that the average wedding in the States costs less than in many other sites, more Americans are able to afford weddings, and parents remain significant contributors to the expenses? In the United States, Rashid believes, the push factors away from marriage are different: "I don't think it's really [financial] circumstance for people in that situation. Mainly because [Americans] don't see marriage as something important, and they believe that all the marriage brings can be obtained outside of marriage, and so they don't see it as a major need."

Conclusion

While sex and marriage are still connected in the minds of most Christians, the link has certainly weakened in the twentieth century. Cheap sex has become normative throughout much of the West, a process boosted by the separation of sex from fertility by wide use of effective birth control. Hence, sex has largely lost its primary "cost," that is, the risk of pregnancy. Sex was described as easy by interviewees across the seven data collection sites, including more traditional locales like Lagos, Beirut, and Krakow. The "reverence due to a woman" that Pope Paul VI spoke of in *Humanae Vitae* is diminishing, just as he predicted it would.

Clergy and religious leaders struggle to motivate chaste behavior on the part of their young adults, a task made more difficult by the power that flows toward young men when they are outnumbered by marriage-minded women. The situation calls for creativity on the part of congregational leaders and blunt conversations between women and the men they are dating.

Meanwhile, matrimony is getting more expensive just as sex becomes cheap. Christians are more willing than others to pursue marriage, but social expectations of a big wedding are a drain on their pocketbook. Marriage waits, as Christians save up money for a ceremony that need not be so expensive. Given how tightly connected the future of Christianity is with the future of marriage and family, expensive weddings (especially when not accompanied by concomitant social support from friends and family) can be doing more harm than good—in the form of expedited sex and delayed marriage. The capstone model of marriage depends on cheap sex.

5

Uncertainty

Estella is a 28-year-old living in Guadalajara, the second-most populous metropolitan area in Mexico—home to just over five million people. Despite being situated in Jalisco, a state that is currently wrestling with more drug-related violence than most other regions of Mexico, Guadalajara remains popular with tourists and is considered the source of such quintessentially Mexican traditions as tequila and the mariachi band.

Like many global cities, Guadalajara is coming to terms with the collision of free-market growth and long-standing socialist-style inefficiencies. Attractive new apartments and condominiums are rising without ample investment in transportation infrastructure. So, new occupants can't move around the city easily, and traffic is getting worse by the year. Meanwhile, laborers staff positions that Americans have long since automated. But it's economically explicable: unskilled or semiskilled workers in Guadalajara—and much of Mexico—are paid too little to consider automation worth the costs. The ironic result is greater employability among the poor and working class. (For example, private security jobs abound.) In that way, it is not unlike Moscow. On the other hand, whereas Moscow's secular past remains palpable today, the cultural legacy of Guadalajara is decidedly one of Catholic-infused "family values" traditionalism. As in all seven research sites, standards of living are rising, and expectations about sex roles are shifting.

Estella works in her family's (modest) real-estate business, and she saves money by living with her parents (as do many unmarried adults in Mexico). She's able to keep what she earns, but it still isn't very much. Estella is hoping to become engaged soon to her boyfriend, a man different in many ways from the men who previously interested her. The turn toward him had been intentional. When we spoke, Estella revealed a strategy in seeking a mate that had finally worked: stop eyeing only the men whom other women want and, instead, expand your field of vision to those overlooked, all the while prioritizing a discernible Christian faith:

He's not like a cute guy, like, "OMG, he's cute!" But he has a big heart, and he's smart. When I met him, I felt like I was failing in relationships, because I don't fall in love with important things. . . . So I realized that I have to start looking for something more.

There were other facets of the relationship that wooed her:

I am attracted to being able to share everything that happens to you with someone. For example, when I have had relationships, I love telling that person what excites me, sharing who I am, feeling safe, and being certain that that person knows me with flaws and all. The fact that he loves you anyway, and he helps you grow as a person, and you are happy for his success, just seeing him happy. Also, when one of his friends tells you that since he has been with you, he seems happier, more hard-working, that sort of thing. One more thing that I am excited about is having a family, having children, seeing them happy and healthy.

Estella isn't misled into thinking that marriage is all sweetness and light; she spoke just as fluently about her fears of what could go wrong. But the fears are manageable, she believes. Her boyfriend respects Estella's values, including her sexual conservatism. He attends Mass weekly, though "it's not that important to him" (a common refrain).

If he asks Estella to marry him, she will say yes. In fact, she has told him she would be content to marry now, even while he wrestles over the instability of his own family's business—commercial electrical contracting—which is currently in good shape, given the boom in building in western Guadalajara and its neighbor Zapopan. But competition is stiff, and the uncertainty that accompanies the industry seems to be slowing down his plans for starting a family.

Men sense they have to have it all together—the capstone model of marriage—before they can feel confident enough to move forward. It is a secular mentality that is no respecter of creed or country. Estella told me she wishes this were not so: "I kind of understand why, but I feel like we are losing the path. We're thinking it's more important to *have* than to *be*." Estella thinks she'll be engaged within a year, and then married a year after that. By then, she'll be nearing 31. She had hoped it would be sooner.

A blend of uncertainty, ambiguity, individualism, and materialism characterized many of our interviewees. Some struck me as purveyors of this mixture—more men than women. Others seemed victims of it, themselves at risk of perpetuating it in their next relationship. Still others appear to have emerged from it, wounded but enlightened, determined to do things differently next time. Katerina is one of those. A 28-year-old unmarried and unattached schoolteacher we spoke with in a Moscow restaurant, Katerina emits the kind of energy that can be both attractive and intimidating. Orthodox and practicing now, Katerina divides her relational life into two—the part before she became a Christian and the part after. "It's just two completely different stories," she leveled. What came before was "this sort of brainwashing," with consistent anxiety about all things material and a drive to avoid any sort of unpleasantness. She found herself saturated with questions: "Where are we going to live? How will we live? How are we going to make a living? We don't have our own home. We don't have enough money to give birth to a child." Katerina is different now, more willing to abandon herself to the providence of God: "You realize that if you start a family, everything will be as it should be. The Lord will arrange it. . . . If you are given some difficulties, that is as well." She has found in her new faith a contentment that had long eluded her. Marriage, however, eludes her still.

It was easy for my Russian interviewees to declare that marriage had changed profoundly, given the monumental social overhaul that Russia endured with the collapse of the Soviet Union in 1991, shortly after Katerina was born. That it was not a militarily violent transition remains astonishing to those of us who remember it. It just didn't seem possible. (A wave of interpersonal violent crime, however, did ensue.)[1] What the swift transition from communism to a form of capitalism did do, however, was multiply *uncertainty*—a social psychological phenomenon that diminishes rather than boosts marital confidence. And yet well after post-Soviet economies have begun to recover and adjust, uncertainty still seems endemic. Uncertainty thrives when material and emotional expectations of relationships become elevated, but there remain wide and consistent difficulties in achieving them. Too many new options at once—such as other jobs, more education, new romantic possibilities—also tend to foster uncertainty, which, in turn, undermines the quest for the kind of relational settledness that culminates in marriage.

In Moscow, the result of all this uncertainty has been an increase in relational turnover. Fear of missing out on sex and maybe love, yet lacking the material requirements to commit, creates a seeming inability to stay with one person for long. Relational pathology has stalked the country in a manner not unlike the 1920s (described in Chapter 4). Katerina knows something of that and wants no part of it anymore. Her last relationship before her spiritual awakening "was a big mistake." "I realize that I hurt him," she lamented. "Of course, I am very ashamed. Probably I will have to meet him [someday] and ask him to forgive me." Katerina yearned for her hometown, where she felt family life was easier to realize—a theme repeated by numerous Russian interviewees:

> Nowadays, it's all different. We have a very large choice—not exactly choice, but I would say great freedom. And when you are given a lot of freedom, immediately there appear a lot of temptations. If a person is not involved with the Church, he or she sways from side to side. Today you are with this person, tomorrow with someone else, and so on. Well, not everyone does it, of course. There are close-knit families. For example, I come from Volgograd. There, families seem to be stronger or something. Everything is like more real, because there are fewer trends, less influence as in Moscow. Because in Moscow there's a lot of everything, a huge lot of people, a huge lot of temptations, a huge lot of money. And it all affects you.

"The brain becomes littered here in Moscow with seductions," she told me. Katerina isn't alone in sensing a distinction between that city and the rest of Russia.[2] Everyone knows it. A 30-year-old divorcée from Moscow put it plainly: "Life [in Russia] takes place in the cities now. Villages as such, country settlements, are sort of fading away." That can be tough for those anticipating families. Viktor, the 29-year-old clinical psychologist from Moscow, believes so:

> It's very problematic to create a family in the conditions of a modern metropolis. It implies pushing yourself into a box of an apartment, with a garden[-size] common children's playground. . . . All those processes inherent to large cities, those environmental, urban, and cultural processes, in general, create insecurity for the family.

Viktor wonders what he would do if his wife became psychologically unstable or difficult. What if he struggled to support his children? The very concepts to which he is attracted—having a wife and children—create uncertainty in his mind. Samara, a 20-something unmarried Orthodox transplant to Moscow, worries, too:

When I lived in Siberia, everyone got married early there. Here everything is more difficult, because probably you don't feel much help. Everything around is not yours; there's no security. Even if you have a job, it's enough just to cover food, transport, and maybe some housing, you know. And if you get married, it's such a responsibility. Your own family!

New options. More choices. Greater temptations. High expectations. Consistent anxiety. Urban density. These aren't problems limited to Russia. Versions of each were verbalized by Christians in every country. Ander, the 25-year-old engaged physician-in-training whom we first met in Chapter 3, is marrying soon, comparatively young for Spain, but after six full years of dating his girlfriend. One might think that he of all men, a doctor marrying another doctor, would exhibit greater confidence as he approaches marriage. But when originally interviewed by a member of my team, he brought up the matters of insecurity, fear of commitment, "completely unpredictable situations with your partner":

> It's logical that people are afraid, [given] the uncertainty we're faced with, but the fact that people are delaying [marriage] to such an extent suggests to me that this fear is now pathological and is stopping us in some way from doing a good thing, and impeding us from facing up to it, or causing us to delay it.

Later, when I got a chance to meet Ander, I pressed him about this particular remark, and he had more to say:

> I feel included in that fear. I understand that fear. [*What is the fear of?*] Not to be free. Tied to someone. Compromised. Things you don't know that you don't know. Maybe we're okay now, but not later. [*Okay. How?*] Differences arise in a couple. The other person is different than you thought they were. [*You dated for six years. Isn't that long enough?*] I feel like I don't know her that well after six years. There are for sure things that I don't know, not having lived together. And then we will have a child, and she responds in one way and I in another. [*Are her parents a window into her?*] In part. It helps with some things. We are all educated by our parents, marked by the mistakes they make.

Our conversation continued. I asked if his fears made him wonder if he's made the right decision—to marry her: "Yes, I've thought about that. But I don't think I should be moved by fear. Because if I have doubts that come from fear, I shouldn't pay attention to it." "Are they particularized fears, with her?" I asked him. "Or would you be afraid no matter who it is?" He admitted that he "would have fear with any woman" but that with his fiancée, he has "particular things" that concern him.

Ander is not alone in expressing uncertainty and its accompanying anxieties, as well as premarital jitters. Nor is he unusual in expressing only modest Christian resources to deal with the issue, even though his faith is strong and he's embedded within a supportive community of believers. He recognized that understanding marriage as a sacrament "gives you a certain amount of tranquility," but it didn't seem like very much. I asked him whether there was any security in the idea of the permanence of Catholic marriage, or whether that makes him all the more afraid—that he could be stuck:

> The fear isn't about religion. It's about human nature. When man bonds his life to a woman, it doesn't matter if you're Catholic or not, or an atheist. [*So marriage has a permanence to it, no matter who you are?*] Yes. The breaking of that relationship involves a lot of suffering, regardless of whether you both are Catholic or not.

In theory, uncertainty could just as well press couples forward toward commitment as stall them. After all, two together can accomplish more than one, following the logical advice of the author of Ecclesiastes 4:9–12. As articulated at length in Chapter 3, men and women bring their differences—their strengths and weaknesses, distinctive skills and needs—into a marriage and, hence, benefit from the "gain in trade," not to mention sharing living expenses while commonly boosting shared income.[3] Committing should diminish uncertainty. But this is not how most men and women perceive marriage anymore. Delay is a far more common response to uncertainty than acceleration, and it is happening, notwithstanding the dramatic, sustained reduction in extreme poverty worldwide, diminishing family size, and an enduring longing to know and be known.[4] Why?

Is the Gig Economy to Blame?

Unemployment rates have been trending lower over the past decade—at least until early 2020—and yet still marriage rates tumble. Maybe the story is found in the disappearance of the *kind* of jobs you could once have depended upon, whether you lived in a capitalist or communist society. It's possible the new "gig" economy we inhabit is more toxic to marital intentions than the older economy was. This is a common refrain. Enrique, the 28-year-old industrial engineer working for a construction company in Guadalajara, notes both opportunities and hazards for families in the gig economy:

> Companies now are subcontracting. Companies only look for freelancers, and the trend is what young people are seeking, too. Not to have a boss, not to have an owner, but at the end of the day, we earn less than our parents. There are studies about this; it's a reality. If we are free to do what we want, I think that that gives us "freedom," but I think that in regards to remuneration, it's a bit lower.

Peter, from Chapters 2 and 3, would be considered middle class in Nigeria. And he appears to be an obvious case for the economic instability argument:

> The money I have been making from my job is not even enough for me to think of engaging in marriage. And I know what is inherent in marriage takes a lot of things; you have to consider aspects such as having a child, paying bills, settling for allowances for your children. . . . Things have not really been easy, unlike [earlier] days where things were a bit less stressful and many people wanted to get married. And these days we have to have made a certain amount of money before considering having a partner. [*Okay so why do you think it is that people are marrying later today?*] I would say a significant factor for that is stability of income. By that I mean that I notice that people do not have steady amount of income and any means of generating wealth, and if you cannot have a steady amount of income you cannot be thinking of anything relating to marriage.

Peter went on to explain that even if your income was rather modest—18,000 naira, or around $50 per month—so long as it was stable, you could think about marrying. But if it fluctuated wildly, rising to 100,000 naira ($275) one month and plunging to 10,000 naira ($28) the next month, such uncertainty was apt to get into your head and prevent you from pursuing marriage.

Justyna, a 24-year-old engaged woman, is working as an insurance adviser for a car dealership in Lublin. She described the differences between her generation and that of her parents, who grew up in General Jaruzelski's communist Poland:

> It was easier [then] to get a flat [i.e., apartment]. When my mother was 22, she was already married a year and had a baby. I didn't imagine having a baby when I was 22. When they got married, they first lived with my mother's parents. But they moved out quickly, after two years, because their employer provided them with a flat. There was such a possibility. So, it was different. They could afford to get married. If I get married now, nothing will change. I won't move anywhere, have a different flat. Nobody will pay for my wedding. Now, parents don't pay for that. The young couple has to cover the expenses on their own. Now, it's more difficult to find a job, a flat. We often change workplaces. In the past, you used to work in one place for twenty years.

To be absolutely clear, no interviewee openly professed a desire to abandon market-based economies. They simply observed its costs—in terms of stability—while remaining enamored of its benefits.

And yet recent economic research suggests that the gig economy "has scarcely changed" the overall labor market, at least in the United States.[5] The share of workers who are considered "independent contractors" has changed little since 2005, save for those working in transportation (think Uber). More than 90 percent of American workers have "traditional" jobs, meaning they are on the payroll of the company for which they labor. (It doesn't mean that people aren't also working a second freelance job; it just means that their primary job is not contractual in nature.) A pair of Harvard and Princeton economists revised their estimate of past growth in gig economy work, asserting that there has been "a 1–2 percentage point increase in the share of workers in alternative work from 2005 to 2015, instead of the 5 percentage point increase originally reported."[6] The gig economy provides additional sources of work for people struggling to get by. In that way it can be helpful for attaining greater financial security.

Can more stable jobs prompt a new surge in marriage? I'm not convinced. At best, we're talking about how stable work could yield a modestly greater likelihood of doing something (getting married) that fewer and fewer people are doing every year anyway. While it is no doubt optimal for marital happiness, employment stability may have less to do with getting married than in the past. There is more to the story.

Is Capitalism to Blame?

One of the attractions of (government) central planning, at least in theory, is the supposition of a more predictable life than is the case in a free-market economy. Interviewees who mentioned life in the communist era noted that the reliability of a stable job seemed to help couples plan for their future together, even if (or perhaps because) that future together would be lean and challenging. Today's capitalism, some hold, is too dynamic and uneven to allow for stable planning for the future—prompting elevated expectations without the means to meet them. This is how the free market indirectly fosters uncertainty. But instability by itself does not undermine marriage per se, as marriage is actually built to weather it.

When I spoke with a Salesian (Catholic) priest about the marriage situation in Slovakia, I heard how economic uncertainty—even in a scenario of general improvement—is nevertheless undermining the marital impulse. But the process, he held, is less a rational one than an emotional or social psychological one.[7] I asked this 60-something priest about differences he perceived in the marital impulse before and after the communist era in Slovakia:

> There is some economic aspect to it, but I think it's more mental. [*Was it easier to envision a large family in the communist era?*] It was easier to find housing, and there was the guarantee of a job, and perhaps society valued family a little more. Now, not so much. Education is feminized. [That is, very few men are schoolteachers.] Fathers sometimes travel all week for work. Salaries are low.

One female focus group participant in Moscow summarized it this way:

> In the Soviet times, you could marry anyone, and he could get a job, any kind of job, and he will have a job and support a family, and the country will help. And we don't have that with our state now. It supports the families, but people in large cities expect from their spouses a more serious income.

More predictability and fewer options made for more marriages in the past.

When I asked Jerzy, the head of a Warsaw-based think tank, about marriage seeming more stable in Poland's communist era than today's consumer era, he did not disagree. But he suggested it had much less to do with effective family policy than with a shared experience of deprivation. "It was a communism of poverty," Jerzy contended, an era that forced people to depend upon each other.[8] And it was not only marriage that thrived—out of necessity— under such conditions. Friendships and neighborly relations did as well.

None of these interlocutors wished for an earlier era, but each perceived something corrosive to marriage and family in the current economic age. What is it? I submit that it is the intrusion of a *market mentality* into our homes, marriages, and bedrooms. The West has allowed economic considerations to co-opt, colonize, and direct our most intimate relationships— husband to wife and parent to child. How so? Here are a few ways I see it happening in the United States:

- The notion of a sabbath day of rest is a distant memory. It cuts into corporate profits.
- We have fewer children so we can "invest" more in them.
- In the context of small families, children naturally learn to be served rather than to serve.
- We work too many hours, convinced we're doing it for our families.
- We are strategic about providing opportunities for our children to get ahead of others.
- We have become suckers for (ad-driven) social media, which fosters dissatisfaction.
- With few friends, we have to pay lots of money in order to be listened to.
- We've created a lucrative industry by outsourcing the care of our own parents.

These are not shocking observations. (I'm guilty of most of them.) Each reflects, however, the logic of a modern capitalism corrosive to both anticipating and enjoying marriage as well as valuing and caring for children and parents. "The sanctity of the home is a sham," Christopher Lasch wrote in *Haven in a Heartless World*, "in a world dominated by giant corporations." And that was in 1977. Fast-forward, and now even our leisure time is organized by new industrial titans like Facebook, Instagram, and Twitter.[9] Christians have been complicit in this, and co-opted by it. And while each of the examples listed here may constitute an economic stimulus, each of them is ultimately harmful to our communities. Cherlin notes that progrowth economic priorities thrive when they are not tied down by institutions, including marriage and family.[10] Indeed, progrowth forces often prefer whatever relationship forms and norms will serve their economic priorities most efficiently. The free market is agnostic about sex, marriage, and family.[11]

Some Christians may be surprised to learn that famed apologist and journalist G. K. Chesterton, lamenting the state of marriage and family in the 1930s, pointed his finger at capitalism:

> What has broken up households and encouraged divorces, and treated the old domestic virtues with more and more open contempt, is the epoch and power of Capitalism. It is Capitalism that has forced a moral feud and a commercial competition between the sexes; that has destroyed the influence of the parent in favor of the influence of the employer; that has driven men from their homes to look for jobs; that has forced them to live near their factories or their firms instead of near their families.[12]

Chesterton's complaint didn't add anything that Pope Leo XIII hadn't already lamented in *Rerum Novarum*. In that 1891 encyclical, Leo sought to challenge the injustices of industrial-age capitalism without endorsing socialism. He safeguarded the common man's natural pursuit of private property, by which parents are (partly) empowered to provide for their children "all that is needful to enable them to keep themselves decently from want and misery amid the uncertainties of this mortal life."[13] Or, as a friend put it, the point of Leo's encyclical is to "keep the mess manageable," that is, to facilitate the better aspects of free markets and rein in or compensate for the worse ones.

Similarly, Chesterton's words should *not* be perceived as an endorsement of communism or a critique of private property but, instead, as a blunt reminder that Adam Smith's "invisible hand" is agnostic about marriage, family dynamics, and sexual relationships.[14] If your husband leaves you for a younger woman, you may call it immoral, but in the free market of relationships, it's not illogical. Elzbieta, a 31-year-old analyst working for a marketing firm in Warsaw, has no trouble at all perceiving this logic:

There are many things now which you can . . . withdraw from if they don't work. Buy new ones. We have so many stimuli from all sides—that something can be different, even better. "Why do I have to be with that boyfriend if I can have a better one?" . . . Everyone wants to be free in a weird sense.

As relationships become commodified, they are far more apt to be considered disposable, an idea utterly toxic to marriage, given that matrimony requires consistent sacrifices and higher commitments than what we may wish for at any given time. "It's very difficult nowadays to say what you want and stick to it," Elzbieta confessed.

Less than one hundred years ago, "alienation of affections" laws in most American states enabled a spouse to pursue (civil) justice against a third party believed to be responsible for breaking up a marriage. These statutes have nearly disappeared from the books and are widely ridiculed.[15] We now let the market in affection run its course freely—so freely that one spouse can leave a marriage without any reason whatsoever, and the other has no choice but to comply and adapt.

Contrary to what might seem obvious at first blush, it does not logically follow that Christian marriage benefits from Western forms of capitalism just because communist states, indeed, have repeatedly and harshly suppressed Christian expression.[16] Some conservative Christians blame "socialism" in a generic way for the shifts in marital norms. I'm not advocating for socialism here, but the story is more complex than is typically implied. Every economic permutation exhibits both opportunities and challenges for families. The vagaries of capitalist economies for marriage and family are, I hold, more the result of unintended consequences and dubious moral norms than of deliberate intention. But they sure can be corrosive.

Problems are what we should expect when we fail to remember that the state and the economy are ontologically subordinate to the family and exist to serve households, rather than the other way around. (Aristotle was right: the family is the foundation of all other societies.) We are, I fear, jeopardizing this most necessary of societies—marriage and family—in part by treating them not as a foundation, but as a feeder system. Our most intimate relationships are being treated as a means, often discarded, to attain those personal ends and acquisitions that have been most effectively marketed to us.

Managing Uncertainty by Considering Cohabitation

Growing up, Alejandra—a 26-year-old part-time student, part-time nanny, and movie theater employee living in Guadalajara—had witnessed a destructive household featuring a temperamental father. But she still believed in marriage. Slowly, that confidence began to erode after a series of failed relationships. (She described the world to us as "chaotic.") But unlike her parents' marriage, Alejandra's relationships have not been violent. They just meander, going nowhere. She is now convinced that cohabiting before marrying is a must, the Church's teaching notwithstanding. "If you marry without knowing the person," that is, having experienced a sexual relationship with him or her, "you will get a divorce," she said.

At the same time, a vision of the kind of marriage she wants remains portrayed on her iPhone background—a photo she took of a couple of 70-somethings embracing on a beach at sunset. Why them? "They represented a life together, of tenderness, of loving each other every day for the rest of their lives, that is, forever. I want to find someone with whom I can do the same."

Content for now to be unattached, Alejandra does not dispute that marriage is a sacrament to which some, even most, have a vocation (or calling). But she now thinks the Catholic Church's vision of family is too narrow, a conclusion she began to draw not because of surging identity politics in Mexico but after her relationship with her first love (and first sexual partner). It collapsed when he moved away for work, and this loss convinced her that things just tend to fall apart. People "find different paths," she concluded, including living together. Phantoms from her parents' rancorous marriage haunt her: "Maybe someone is too aggressive, or not aggressive enough. Or they worry only about pleasing themselves, and not about pleasing you." Enrique, the 28-year-old industrial engineer working for a construction company in the same city, knows exactly what Alejandra is talking about: "We are in a generation where everything is disposable. Everything. Absolutely everything," he explained. "Everything is easy; everything is fast. It's so fast to find someone. Well, before, there were certain kinds of dates. Now it's called Tinder."

This frenetic, self-absorbed state of dating affairs is not entirely lost on leaders. Pope Francis laments "the speed with which people move from one affective relationship to another." Love, they think, "can be connected or disconnected at the whim of the consumer, and the relationship quickly 'blocked.'" In this way, the pope observes, we are treating "relationships the way we treat material objects and the environment: everything is disposable; everyone uses and throws away, takes and breaks, exploits and squeezes to the last drop. Then, goodbye."[17]

Alejandra has lived this nightmare. And yet she (and many like her) continues looking for her rock—a stable someone who will love her unconditionally and never leave her. She now attends Mass on a monthly basis, depending on if she "wakes up early enough," in a city where Mass is available all day on Sunday. It's fair to conclude that her spiritual desire has waned.[18]

As should be obvious by now: my study's interviewees know there's something amiss about marriage today. This something harbors nervousness, uncertainty, and confusion. When something's a problem, people think about how they can react as individuals. One increasingly popular reaction is to give thought to cohabitation as a way of managing uncertainty.

When asked if she would be interested in marrying [again], Veronica, the 28-year-old preschool teacher and divorcée from Guadalajara, was silent. She was reminded that she didn't have to answer the question if she didn't want to, but then she did: "Certainly, yes. I will probably do it again." Living together first, however, is now a necessary requirement for her: "That would be my condition." Cohabitation is popularly believed to lower the risks of making a tragic mistake—being deceived, getting married, and then finding oneself stuck. Tatiana, a 27-year-old from Moscow, exhibits a similar logic as Veronica (as well as a similarly modest religious practice), without actually having cohabited. She accepts cohabitation as normative and perceives disadvantages in marrying, but her sense of morality still shapes her decisions:

> Earlier it was shameful. You could not [cohabit]; you would encounter quite serious disfavor. And now, not anymore. You can just live together. Also marriage is, frankly speaking, a pain in the ass, you know. Because if you divorce, you need to divide the property, no matter how awful it may sound. . . . It is much easier just to live together. Many cohabit for five or ten years. I have never lived with my boyfriend, and I'm against it, because you can live together only in the context of being married, right?

Tatiana's, Alejandra's, and Veronica's pessimism about commitment is a learned emotion, reflecting the realities of men's behavior. Ignacio, the 27-year-old computer programmer from Pamplona, has been sexually active with his fiancée for three years, and living together for one. While he considers himself religious, Ignacio has become selective about the teachings to which he adheres: "I have worked it out well in my head," regardless of what his priest or parents think. He didn't initiate the talk of marriage; his fiancée had to ask him. "In a subtle and amusing way," he recalled. "She said, 'I want to marry you. I'll leave it with you, and you can ask me when you are ready.'" Ignacio eventually got around to it several months later. That was about four years ago, with no wedding yet. He doesn't really fear marriage, but he doesn't think getting married will change much on the human level, because he sees it as "a way of introducing a spiritual component to the relationship."

Esteban, the 28-year-old owner of a failing advertising agency in Guadalajara, is also practicing his faith less frequently these days, attending Mass perhaps once a month. But he does Ignacio one better. He recently split from a five-year-long relationship because his girlfriend would no longer settle for his lack of commitment. Most importantly, he assured me he is not alone: "A lot of men I know have been splitting up with their girlfriends and getting a younger girl who won't pressure them to get married." What's going on here? "Marriage is being perceived as a cage" by men, Veronica maintains, even while machismo is in retreat. (Both Ignacio and Esteban praised the new turn toward egalitarian relationships.)

An additional concern weighs upon Guadalajara's interviewees: Catholics get one shot at marriage; the Church does not recognize the legitimacy of civil divorce. But, it does permit an annulment—that is, a Church-granted declaration that a marriage thought to be valid was in fact invalid (from the beginning) due to some impediment (for example, if one or both spouses is found to intend to have no children, or if the marriage was not consummated by sexual intercourse, or if consent was impaired by parental pressure or mental defect). Typically, an annulment is not pursued until an ex-spouse has someone new in mind. Americans were responsible for 41 percent of the world's 41,255 annulment cases introduced in 2015.[19] Next in frequency was Poland, which accounted for 7 percent of the world's total. And despite there being far more baptized Catholics in Mexico than in the United States, there are eleven American annulment cases introduced for every one case pursued south of the border.

Despite a solid case for annulment,[20] Veronica is not interested. She's done, at least for now, with perceived social, cultural, and ecclesial obligations. And annulments are complicated. The process takes time, requires awkward interaction between estranged spouses, and is not culturally normal in Mexico. Wanting to avoid all this on top of potential divorce, many Mexican Catholic couples choose to cohabit, perceiving it as a strategy to avoid disaster. (A similar lesser-of-two-evils logic leads many young adult Catholics to use hormonal or barrier contraception in their premarital relationships. Better that, they hold, than face a difficult decision about abortion.)

Cohabitation is not, at least not yet, a secure alternative to marriage. Steven Ruggles, a renowned demographic historian, notes that despite how common the arrangement has become, "we see no systematic increase in the stability of cohabiting unions."[21] Cohabitation remains more fragile than marriage, even in Europe: children born to cohabiting couples there are twice as likely to experience a household breakup by age 12 than are children born to married couples.[22]

Whereas the social science used to be clear about the heightened probability of subsequent divorce among those who had previously cohabited, that effect has diminished some with time. Of positive influence are factors like definite plans to marry, marital commitment prior to cohabitation, and older age at cohabitation.[23] Today, those who cohabit with their eventual spouse—especially closer to the date of marriage—only exhibit a modest elevated risk of subsequent divorce. What bodes more ill, family scholars say, is the experience of multiple stints of cohabitation. Among American women, serial cohabiters' subsequent divorce rates are more than twice as high as those who cohabited only with their eventual husbands.[24] Sadly, serial cohabitation is no longer the practice of a tiny minority.[25]

When Christians Cohabit

Now far less affected by organized Christianity than in the past, relationship systems in the contemporary West continue to encroach further East and South. Forms once deemed immoral and illicit have come to be envisioned and practiced with varying degrees of acceptance. Still, living together is never considered, by Christians, as an alternative to marriage. It's a step in marriage's direction. (That's how it started in the wider population a few decades ago.) And Christians are certainly more likely to *slide into* cohabitation than *decide* to do so, finding themselves caught up in a more-or-less stable sexual relationship in which so many nights are spent together that a shared domicile just happens.[26] That was the case for Mateusz, a 26-year-old newlywed businessman from Krakow. He slid into cohabitation, and then into marriage. Mateusz made no reference to the uncertainty so common elsewhere but, instead, spoke as if his marriage relationship's trajectory had been established whether they cohabited or not. It wasn't his own faith that convinced him to marry. He is, by his own admission, "very passive" about his faith, though he attends Mass regularly. It was his parents who pushed him to marry, reinforced by Polish Catholic culture:

> If my parents hadn't told me and my wife that marriage is an institution, and [if] they hadn't been married, we would probably not have done that. We wouldn't have gotten married. Everything depends on the influence of our parents or people close to us. . . . Do they make us get married? Definitely. My parents definitely did.

In Mateusz's case, any uncertainty he might have felt was mediated by his parents' confidence in marriage and family ties. It's hard to imagine such parental assertiveness in the United States.[27] Mateusz went on to describe his extended family, "with many children for generations, tightly connected by religion, in which there have always been weddings." Because matrimony is what adults in Krakow do, marriage is arguably further away from the capstone model there than in any of the other interview sites. (It is, however, moving in that direction.)

For others, including those who experienced tumultuous relationships—either their own or their parents'—cohabitation seems a calculated way to reduce risk and manage uncertainty. They don't really expect their congregations, parishes, priests, or ministers to support them (but they often wish for it). Justyna, a 24-year-old working in insurance for an automobile dealership in Lublin, had been dating the same person for several years, cohabiting for the last two. She is engaged and wants to get married soon. In fact, she wishes she were already married. Why isn't she? "Financial reasons," she asserts:

> If I had had financial stability earlier, I would be married now. This is the main factor—not getting married itself. The wedding reception and elegant clothes cost a lot. Some of my friends decided to have a very modest ceremony, just dinner for the family and wedding gown for 1,000 zł ($260 USD), so at the most modest price. But for me it's important. I'd like to look beautiful and the way I want to. It's the one and only day in my life [that] I won't experience again. My fiancé and I would like a ceremony, maybe not a lavish one for two hundred people, but just the way we imagined it.

We need money to organize it. Some people say that you can get married in a small church, then go for dinner to a restaurant, and it will be fine. They keep persuading us to do it like this. But this isn't how we want to arrange it.

She's no activist—Justyna is not seeking to rewrite the story of Christian marriage. And she holds, as most Catholics in Poland do, that marriage is categorically distinctive from living together:

> I believe that it's completely different. . . . Let me put it like this: I've already lived with my fiancé for two years, and I feel the need to get married. It's good. We've made the decision to get married. We both work, lead a normal life. It's similar to a marriage, but it's not marriage. Thanks to getting married, we'll be even closer with each other. I have a need to be a wife. . . . Some would say that a wedding is just a document. It's difficult to say, but I think that it brings people closer. We show more respect toward the other person because we decide to get married, [to make a] vow. And, there's some anxiety that it'll be forever. I don't accept divorce. There's no divorce in [the] Church.

But living together before marriage has become part of the architecture of Western relationship systems. Notice Justyna's claim that she and her fiancé "lead a normal life." Cohabitation patterns tend to be more pronounced among Catholics than evangelicals, since the former have to wrestle with the Church's stronger claims about divorce (as well as artificial contraception). Evangelical Protestants, on the other hand, are less apt to consider divorce or birth control problematic.

Justyna describes the logic and process by which a young woman comes to validate both cohabitation and marriage, while still privileging the latter. When asked about the *purpose* of marriage—something she very much wants—Justyna struggled. Rather than focus on marriage itself, she seemed only to be able to compare it to cohabitation, defending the merits of each:

> It's difficult to say, because cohabitation also means that people decide to be together. I don't sneer at it. I think that it's also positive. I'm not saying that people who live together without getting married are worse than married couples. I think that they'll also make it, be together, and not cheat on each other. Therefore, it's difficult to determine the purpose of marriage for me.

I believe that those who live with each other without getting married are equal to married couples.

She did finally settle on marriage as the superior situation, however, owing to some difficult-to-define protective bonding agent of matrimonial vows:

I believe that marriage bonds. It seems to me that in some cases, it can prevent couples who have some problems from having love affairs. It seems to me that they struggle harder to make it through together, and it'll turn out better for them than couples who aren't married and can split up easier. They don't make a marriage vow. This vow motivates you to abide by marriage: "We made this decision and have to fight to remain together." It drives you to struggle, even despite some obstacles. As for love affairs, marriage motivates you to remain faithful. It's easier than in the case of those who aren't married.

In other words, Justyna is arguing that marriage reflects and reinforces fidelity and expectations of permanence in a relationship of totality (see Figure 3.1).

We asked Justyna what her priest thinks about cohabitation. He had been clear with her: "Of course, such relationships as mine are sinful. They shouldn't exist," she relayed. "Marriage is right, consistent with God's will. . . . It's the only proper relationship." Does she agree with the priest?

As for marriage, I agree with everything. I believe that it's a good choice. . . . However, I believe that you shouldn't condemn other people who don't decide to get married. [*Do you think that the Church condemns such people?*] It seems to me that it does. Because if you live together without getting married, you don't receive absolution. I don't take the Holy Communion. So I'm not fully a member of the congregation. This is what the Church aims at. Such people back out themselves then.

What does Justyna mean by condemnation, given that the Catholic Church makes no claims to determining damnability? It's hard to say. But she is right that cohabiters are scarce in church. In the United States, only 2 percent of active Christians are themselves currently cohabiting. (The estimate is 5 percent among the ones under age 30). And yet a stint of cohabitation is certainly becoming more common among churchgoing Christians. In the United States, for example, 29 percent of all current weekly church attenders say they have cohabited at some point in the past.[28] In Lebanon, on the other hand, cohabitation is extremely rare and socially suspect. Among the seven countries of focus in this book, cohabitation is most common in Mexico, Spain, and the United States. Nigerians and Polish both cohabit at lower rates. (Those two countries also have not exhibited the same pattern of secularization as displayed in much of the West.) But Mateusz and Justyna's accounts suggest that living together is hardly absent in Poland.

Why Marry? Cues about Marriage in the Resistance to Cohabitation

In the relational system—or mating market—in which young adults are embedded, cohabitation simply does not afford a sense of legal and emotional security comparable to that of marriage. Some prefer it that way, if only temporarily, but most cohabiting Christians are angling to make their status more permanent. They tend to defend their decisions, as Justyna did, referencing examples of couples who have successfully transitioned from cohabitants to spouses.

Even as science has shown that moving in together still raises the risk of breakup before marriage ever happens, it's hard to convince cohabiters of the hazards. University of Denver psychologist and relationships expert Scott Stanley explains how it works. Cohabitation increases constraints—things like shared rent, pets, debts, furniture, and sometimes children—before having ensured greater commitment to each other. And some poorly matched couples marry who otherwise might have broken up, he holds, because cohabitation constrained them, making it difficult to move on.[29] It's a sequence that is riskier than formal marriage, even though cohabiters commonly believe themselves to be reducing risk by moving in together.

Harper, a 24-year-old Catholic therapist living in suburban Detroit, would attest to Stanley's observations. Although she has a boyfriend, Harper isn't living with him. She contrasts their relationship with that of her cousin, who has been with her boyfriend for nine years already. Stanley's two warning signs—constraints and lack of commitment—were obvious when Harper described her cousin's situation:

He just doesn't want to marry her. . . . He just doesn't. "What's the differ-ence?" he thinks. "I will have to give you an expensive ring." [*Do you think she's happy in that situation?*] No! She hates it! She wants to get married. You know this is what happens. You're already like a married couple. Without being married you have everything you need.

Monika is a 25-year-old Polish woman who recently married. She's more cul-turally religious than actively so, and she's ambivalent about the prospect of children: "I don't have a maternal instinct," she explained. Her husband feels differently, so they may have one child. "But if so, I would like to get pregnant late." Monika cohabited with her husband for several months before their wedding, yet she, like Justyna, is hardly a cheerleader for cohabitation:

I don't regret [cohabiting]. But I'm happy that it was for a short time. I think that there are more positive emotions when you move in together after getting married. You feel that it's new. We aren't as happy as if we'd just moved in together. Had I lived longer with my husband before the wedding, then we would have more problems.

Monika has felt the constraints observed by Dr. Stanley that cohabitation can create, despite popular narratives to the contrary:

It seems to me that there is some strange Western thinking that you can live together without getting married, that it's cool. Or people are afraid and want to have this option that they can always leave. But this is not true. Sometimes it's more difficult to leave than when you're married, because there are some bigger expectations, commitments. . . .You think, "There is nothing which keeps us together" [when cohabiting], but there is a lot. Besides, we think that there are so many things which we would like to do before getting married, because marriage will change a lot in our life—that we won't be able to do many things. It's not true. We can do many things after getting married.

José, a recently married 32-year-old university student living in Mexico City, gave words to the unforeseen bonds that Stanley describes when he was asked whether marriage and cohabitation—something long common in Mexico—are the same: "No," he answered. Marriage "implies commitment and security. And [cohabitation] also means commitment, but it doesn't give you full security." He continued, clarifying that cohabitation's commitment is inherently unstable. "There is the question if you're going to stay or if you won't. Because there's nothing, no commitment . . . more than the emotional one. And because it's emotional, it's volatile." Jillian, a 28-year-old married Catholic and new mother from Austin, would agree: "No matter how much you do together, there is still a separation between the two of you, because you haven't made the total commitment."

Thirty-year-old Oksana, from Moscow, has already experienced marriage—a year-long stint. (Russia—as noted in Chapter 1—is known for brief first marriages.) She has since matured rapidly and was emphatic with us about the disparity between cohabitation and religious marriage: "For an Orthodox person, it's a huge difference." We asked her what marriage is about. "Responsibility. Security, especially for a woman. Responsibility of the man, security of the woman." When asked about cohabitation, she emphasized a distinct concept that differentiated it from marriage: *family*. For Oksana, this word meant a type of unity that couldn't be contrived:

> Cohabitation is not something that can be called family. You can call it whatever you like: we are friends, we are partners, we live, we like it, everything is super. And when the word "family" comes about [by marrying], there comes unity, a sort of common feeling of such unity. You can buy a TV together, you can give birth to children, you can do everything together. But in the case of just cohabitation, there is a fear: what if we now buy this TV and tomorrow we decide to break up? Who will get the TV then? Things of this kind. There is no unity.

Oksana is convinced that men and women are meant to marry, not to wander through life having a series of relationships that never threaten their core independence. Her years alone, solving her own challenges, have bred a lack of "softness" that she worries will prevent her from marrying again. This new era of independence could be considered a feminist utopia, but all Oksana sees in it is the makings of a dystopian solitude. Her yearning to marry again is replete with imagery of sexual union:

> It is a sort of constant craving. You may be of any views; you may say, "I'm so very cool, and I can be on my own." But still, at one point you'll be there, crying from the fact that you're unhappy and lonely. So there is this thrust toward each other; it is there anyway. Accordingly, the purpose is to reunite.

To the probable disappointment of their religious leaders, the majority of interviewees articulated objections to cohabitation that were not religious in nature. Instead, misgivings were more often about a lack of commitment and clarity, rationales that many of their secular counterparts could theoretically share (but decreasingly do). In fact, objections tended to be about how cohabitation purported to mimic marriage but still fell short—especially on marriage's four key supports (see Figure 3.1). Oksana discerns that cohabitation lacks the permanence she seeks. Enrique senses a lack of totality in cohabitation: "If you want her completely, then make a complete commitment." Justyna perceives cohabitation as more vulnerable to infidelity: "Marriage motivates you to remain faithful. It's easier than in the case of those who aren't married." And while some of our married interviewees may have experienced premarital pregnancies, there were no nonmarital births.

Distinctively Christian arguments against living together were rarer, but not entirely missing. Malek, the 27-year-old pharmacist from Beirut quoted in Chapter 4, lamented at length the challenges of making it in Beirut on a mediocre salary, saddled with expensive educational debt and the prospect of a costly wedding. Despite obvious barriers to marrying, he was nevertheless adamant that cohabitation was not an option (and not just for cultural reasons, either):

> As a believer and a committed Christian, and according to my vision of life, cohabitation and marriage have nothing to do one with the other. In cohabitation, you live with the person and you're just going for the benefits, sexual and financial, where there would be a sexual relationship with sharing of life and house expenses. But there is no commitment with the person. This means that at any moment, one can decide to kick the other person [out or] leave. . . . Marriage, on the other hand, is about two people who commit to love each other, living the sacrament of the project of God. . . . The purposes of the two persons meet, and they live together and love each other. They start a family. They might get kids or might not be able to, but the important thing is that they are living a certain desire to be together through this way. This does not exist in cohabitation, where someone has narcissistic reasons and might get bored with the other person.

Cohabitation, Malek maintained, was less about willing the good of the other and more about protecting the self and hedging one's bets. That order of priority, he held, was not anywhere near the heart of Christian love and practice. Of course, since living together remains socially unacceptable in Lebanon, Malek's resistance is not particularly difficult for him to actualize.

Parental Divorce Creates Uncertainty

As should be evident by now, sociologists seem enamored of the role that money plays in marriageability. (It certainly does play a role, but it's decreasingly influential.) What about the question of how to make marriageable people in the first place? How do we fashion young adults who not only want to marry but are prepared to do so in more ways than financial? One neglected story here is about how parents show children the way to get and stay married. That is, parents provide their own children a narrative, typically either how to seek marriage or how to avoid or escape it. Using data from the 2013–2015 National Survey of Family Growth, my own analyses reveal that the stable marriage of an American man's parents predicts his own stable marriage, even after controlling for decisions to cohabit, religiousness, income, education, and premarital sexual behavior. (Results not shown.) When Mom and Dad marry and then stay together, their son is much more likely to do so as an adult—no matter how much money he makes.

Here again, survey data doesn't really do justice to this intimate topic. We learn how to get and stay married by watching it happen successfully around us. Timoteusz, a 28-year-old recently married freelance copywriter and student in Lublin, didn't mince words about the role of parents in how children understand marriage: "It's a damn big role. They are the first image. Their marriage really determines the concept of marriage that their children will have. So, parents' example at every stage of raising children is very important." Tomas, a 34-year-old school counselor from Guadalajara who is getting married in two months, agreed:

> Young people that live at home, their first reference of marriage is their parents. So, I think that how parents live their marriage will make a strong impression. And I imagine that if the relationship is sweet, if there is really love, I think that generates enthusiasm in a young person to say, "I want something like my parents have." And if not, I think there can be a rejection: "I don't want to live with someone and be fighting all day long."

The breakup of parents' marriages can be overcome, but we're fools if we think it doesn't matter to a child's future. It does. Tomas's words suggest that even a stable marriage can foster uncertainty if it's an unattractive one. As one Russian interviewee remarked, bad examples are "a sort of vaccine against marriage."

I don't often insert my own stories into my writing, but this is one time it seems to fit well. I got married when I was 22. There really was no honeymoon period. It was unanticipated tough slogging early. After a couple years, I gave some thought to leaving. Some, but not much. Why not? I attribute it less to my religious commitments than to the utter absence of exemplars. I had no "how to leave your wife" narrative to follow. My parents and in-laws were still married. My grandparents had remained married. Their troubles had been overcome or else endured. Those friends of ours who had already tied the knot were still married.[30] Within my social orbit in the mid-1990s, there was simply none of the "infectiousness" of divorce that sociologists would later describe.[31] I didn't know how to leave my wife, and there was no one to show me. I'm glad for that. She and I slowly solved our problems, and the marriage improved. We built something together, including three remarkable children. I occasionally look back on those early years and wonder about what would have happened if I had left. I shudder to think of it. I know not everyone's difficult marriages will improve, and for many, the ceiling of marital happiness is not very high. I'm just grateful that I didn't hit the eject button on my marriage—in no small part because I didn't know how.

Many of my study's interviewees did not have such luxury of ignorance. Their parents had split, or in some cases never married, and they were left to figure out how to improve upon their own family of origin. Alena, a 24-year-old teacher (of English and French), was born in Barnaul (Siberia) but moved west with her parents to Moscow, where she now lives. Like many Russian Orthodox today, she converted, having come from an irreligious family. But faith may be easier to catch, or teach, than how to be a spouse:

All the men who've courted me came from divorced families. . . . Maybe that's why I'm not yet married, because those people . . . they did not understand what they wanted in a relationship, in the aspect of marriage. . . . They had no role model. . . . They were "going by touch" [as if they were blind]. They had some guess about how it should be, and they started to impose it on me, the way they saw it. But as for me, I see it every day; my parents are together. And when [the men] begin to tell me how it should be, I'm like, "Guys! This is not how it works."

Alena has lost at least one chance at love because of the divorce legacy of previous generations. Her last suitor, whom she referred to as "an Orthodox believer," had proposed to her. "But it didn't work," she explained, "because he had never seen what it should be like in a family."

There are few more obvious and solid conclusions I could draw in this seven-country study than that of the long reach of divorce. Divorce is the gift that keeps on taking, echoing down through generations. I realize that divorce can improve upon a desperate situation, but it's never without pain and negative consequences. Even judicious decisions to leave never bear only good fruit. It's a mixed bag. My late colleague and family sociologist Norval Glenn found that even so-called good divorces are consequential. Amicable divorces, he noted, foster disorientation in children, who feel at a loss to explain what they've witnessed, much less improve upon it themselves someday. Such divorces, he concluded, are worse than maintaining a mediocre marriage.[32] This falls largely on deaf ears today, even among Christians.

Esteban, quoted earlier in this chapter about how he and his friends have taken to finding younger girlfriends who won't pressure them into marrying soon, reflected clinically on the divorce statistics he estimated within his own family and friendship orbit: "Ninety percent of my friends' parents are separated or divorced. . . . Ninety percent of my friends' grandparents are together. So that indicates that there was something in my parents' generation that caused an outbreak of divorces." Esteban's discourse revealed much more of his childhood experience, however, during our follow-up conversation: "I was around 13 or 14 at the time, when my parents got a divorce." He wasn't surprised when it happened. "There was a very clear circle of infidelity—all my uncles on my father's side had girlfriends, and they bragged about it to their kids." Courtesy of his father's philandering, Esteban was never taught how to uphold fidelity, a key expectation of marriage. He was only taught how to use and lie to women:

[My father] wanted me to be the same. [For example?] The words quite literally came out of him: "You know, son, you have to do as many women as you can. Please don't tell your mom." I asked, "Dad, why do you do it?" "I just want to," he said. At the same time, he protected my mom a lot. He was a very jealous man, a double-standard person. In public, he'd talk about family values. But I always knew what was going on there. . . . My father didn't see [the divorce] coming. . . . My mom felt liberated; my father took it worse. My dad still dates a lot, but in a nomadic fashion—he moves on after a few months.

It's not hard to see why Esteban's mother left his father. What's more surprising is that Esteban still desires—in spite of his childhood experiences— a loyal, lifelong relationship: "a relationship based on equality. I would like a marriage, but one based on trust and similar long-term goals." Our conversation was replete with the expression of noble intentions together with more sobering realities about his habits. Given his insensitive remarks (see Chapter 4) about his ex-girlfriend's fertility concerns, his keen awareness of how the marriage market favors men like him, and the absence of stable— let alone egalitarian—marriage in his family history, the union he wishes for seems more like a fantasy than a plausible reality.

By contrast, Alvaro's parents are still together, and it seems to have made all the difference. Alvaro is a 31-year-old married nurse living and working in Pamplona, and by most standards, he seems rather conventional. He lived with his wife for the better part of eight months prior to marrying. They were engaged for four years, revealing the common pattern of delayed marriage for which Spain is now well known. He wouldn't think to judge others for waiting: "That's a personal matter, as it depends upon each individual's beliefs, so my view is that everything is respectable." He's fine with new sex roles in relationships, too: "Obviously, things have changed enormously, and I think that this is very positive."

And yet two things distinguish Alvaro from many of his peers in Spain when it comes to having navigated relationships and now marriage. First, he's still engaged with his church. He perceives this as a core piece of why marriage is lagging: "I think that people have changed. They consider themselves to be a Catholic or a Christian but they are not practicing. . . . They don't go to Mass, they don't know the essence of matrimony, so they don't place the importance on [marriage] that it really holds." Second, his parents are still married—happily so. This matters for his own marriage, since "the first mirror that you look in is the one that's nearest to you." He displayed none of the uncertainty that characterizes many he knows. No second thoughts, no crippling anxiety. Alvaro's faith and his family showed him a positive path to follow. "[Marriage] is beautiful," Alvaro raved. "It's obviously not paradise nor absolute happiness, because these don't exist, but if you go into it with conviction and knowing what you are doing, it is so worth it, and it's very happy." His interviewer was taken aback at his words, and asked, "You're delighted [with marriage]?" His reply: "I'm enchanted."

Social Media and Online Dating Foster Uncertainty

Charbel is a 28-year-old Maronite Catholic from Beirut. He's middle class, as many Christians in Lebanon are, and works in a small family business. He and his family live in a house, unlike the apartments of many those living in his close-in Beirut suburb. Charbel is, like his namesake saint, a simple man, devoted Christian, and one of a small group of men—alumni of a local university—who still get together for socialization and prayer. In an unusual scenario, Charbel's income stems from a shared pool among family members, all of whom work at the same venture. The money is shared somewhat evenly, but life stages are taken into account; his married older brother is given more. For a time, his younger brother balked at the unequal arrangement, but he has since come to terms with it.

When posed a question about how marriage had changed, Charbel—himself unmarried and not presently in a relationship—had clear thoughts about the matter:

> Love has decreased. We rarely find couples in love as before. If you look at a couple at the age of 90 and compare them to a couple at age 25, you realize the first love each other more. The young couples are on the phone, busy with technology. Whereas in the case of the old couples, you see them talking, he pokes her, she plays with him. Technology changed us a lot.

In particular, Charbel laments the influence of communications technology. He's right. It's one thing to talk about how television diverted the attention of lovers. It's another thing altogether to add smartphones, on-demand content, social media, and dating apps on top of it. We now know as much about the lives and mundane thoughts of others as about the people with whom we live, and sometimes more.

Social media usage is associated with poorer marriage quality, while greater Facebook penetration tracks with increasing divorce rates.[33] Curated, filtered images make us more prone to disaffection and unhappiness than would exposure to a more realistic lifespan frame, to which viewers are not

privy. At the same time, we become distracted from our own most important relationships—our marriages and families—with fictional intimacy
about others' lives. We don't think it will happen to us—that we have man-
aged to be "responsible" users. We may be overestimating that. At best, social media is no better than marriage neutral. Social media siphons time, and
it exposes us to desirable alternatives—competition. David, an unmarried,
25-year-old Catholic employed in logistics in Lagos, is concerned about the
capacity of electronic communication to divide marriages: "For example,
joining forums and chat sites . . . you end up pouring your emotions out to
someone you don't know . . . therefore finding solace in total strangers." This
artificial intimacy is exacerbated, too, by how men and women utilize social media differently.[34] Men use it less but are more apt to use it to seek new
relationships, while women report using it more, but for the maintenance of
ongoing connections.[35]

Not only does social media use convey perceptions of competition, it
creates yet more anxiety in a marketplace that already had plenty. Claire, a
27-year-old campus minister at an all-girls high school in suburban Detroit,
pointed out the angst of the girls with whom she works. They want to be loved
and accepted, but they are afraid of any kind of obligation:

> My high school girls . . . you know, even they love the prospect of having a
> boyfriend and being in a relationship but are so afraid of commitment—
> even if it's going to a certain college. And I think there's a huge issue with the
> idea that you have to keep your options open. . . . Part of it is we are individ-
> ualistic. Part of it is just there are so many options out there, like the media
> influence. And there's so much out there that you want, and you have all the
> information.

What is the result of this situation in the hearts and minds of her girls?
Disquiet, indecision, uncertainty, and a lack of stable identity: "When it
comes down to it," Claire observed, "it creates so much anxiety, so that you
just don't know what's right. And you *want* to change, but you *don't* want to."

"I see couples prone to Instagram marriages," observed Father Kevin, a
Catholic priest in Boston. He leaned on science to demonstrate the fragility
of this trend: "There's a pretty good study showing that couples who heavily
invest in posting happy pictures of themselves tend to be less happy in real
life, because it's compensating." Compensating for what, I wondered. "Maybe
if I can portray an abstract image of what I want to be, it'll help me eventually

get there," he surmised. "Once I have a marriage, a house, debt free, whatever the conditions are for being happy, as soon as I have those things, my feelings will be exactly the way I expect them to be."

There is yet more bad news about social media. Its "social" nature trims some demand for the relational benefits of marriage. You feel like you are in contact with lots of other people (sort of). And that scratches an itch for social interaction, all with no more effort than moving your fingers. It's why physical proximity is less compelling to young people today than thirty years ago. How much does the exploding practice of social media use matter for the future of Christian marriage? It's impossible to say. But to suggest that Christians—married or unmarried—somehow use social media in radically different ways than others makes no sense, at least on a wide scale. I see no evidence of it. However, voices of reason are certainly present among Christians, including some of those I interviewed.

Social media use isn't "natural," argued Valentina, a 30-year-old recently married Orthodox Muscovite:

> Social networks and all that stuff ... do not contribute to the natural, normal communication, natural ordinary situations in which people used to meet. Like in the earlier times, people met—I don't know—at dancing events, at some communist organizations, some other organizations, and found each other at potato dig-ups, carrot dig-ups, and created families. And now there is no such thing, and there is a sort of artificial gap.

Aside from the pivotal role of root vegetables, similar accounts could be voiced from the other side of the Iron Curtain. In fact, most of our interviewees preferred to meet in traditional ways—at church, through friends, and in school.

While networking apps such as Facebook, Instagram, and Snapchat may encourage general discontent by stimulating envy and stoking the "fear of missing out" (colloquially, FOMO), much of their interaction lacks an obvious meeting-up function.[36] "Swipe right" dating apps such as Tinder and even the newer iterations such as Coffee Meets Bagel (which promises "meaningful connections"), by contrast, encourage discontent and FOMO *by* their obvious meeting function. That is, when you have opportunity to meet additional possible romantic interests, you tend to be more idealistic about the person you are with. Have an awkward time on the second date? A petty squabble on the third? Before you bother working through it, why not check your notifications to see who else may be interested in you? The very structure of smartphone dating heightens uncertainty.

Moreover, it removes the human mediator, the (typically informal) matchmaker who introduces one person to another. There is no one to ask questions about a possible suitor, no parent or friend who knows you well and whose opinion you trust. They have been replaced by an algorithm.[37] Online dating is the gig economy applied to marriage. Its superior efficiency works against the goal of actually "clearing" the marriage market. Instead, online dating companies earn more money by recirculating people rather than by watching them exit the market for good by marrying.[38]

As a tool, online dating tools may well maximize the likelihood of locating a desirable spouse. But they are easily misused, even with the best of intentions. Their makers tend to mold the instrument in predictable, and profitable, directions, ones that foster the treatment of fellow human beings as commodities. "People suggest certain things," one Russian Orthodox woman lamented when describing her brief and dismaying foray into online dating. Kingsley, the 29-year-old evangelical from Lagos, knows that these inappropriate "suggestions" are prone to happen. When asked, he said he hasn't tried social media for dating. He hasn't even considered it:

> I haven't, because for me, I don't see social media as being the right place to find love. . . . [Guys] go on Facebook, Twitter, Instagram, to look for girls they just want to flex with, have fun with, and dump. . . . Ninety-eight [percent] of them are not there to find a real soulmate. They just need that girl that can warm their bed.

Sonny, a 28-year-old auditor from Lagos, had similarly neither tried nor thought about using an app to meet someone: "No, it doesn't make any sense trying online dating—someone I have not seen before or I don't know anything about." At face value, his words make rational sense. They just make less popular sense today than they did a decade ago.

Among Alejandra's failed relationships were several short-term ones she had commenced on Tinder. Like many Westerners, Alejandra is both attracted to and repelled by dating apps: "I deleted it for a while, but then was bored and downloaded it again. I haven't met anyone lately on Tinder. Everyone only wants one thing. [*Men wanting sex?*] Yes. And sometimes not only men: sometimes couples looking for a third." I claimed in *Cheap Sex* that Tinder—and online dating in general—did not cause cheap sex. It simply made the acquisition of it more efficient. Such tools have certainly not contributed to the flourishing of marriage, even if some marriages got their start from them. (If they are such efficient vehicles for romantic interactions, why are marriage rates continuing to decline?)

"Online dating technologies," writes Marxist feminist Solange Manche, were supposed to "enable a revolution of the female body, finally liberating us from the slut stigma and allowing us to freely shape our sexual desires. . . . That is, if only these new technologies actually meant that we were having more sex."[39] Observing trend data from the United States and the Netherlands, she concludes "The proliferation of dating applications has, instead, culled sexual desire." I'm not convinced that desire—for marriage or sex—has waned. But people are choosing against both, even as the barriers to accessing either have diminished by our own legal and technological efforts. It is a striking development.

Even for marriage-minded individuals, online dating prompts greater uncertainty. This is not a social scientific claim about causality; it's simply a logical observation that when you're talking about something as significant as marriage—a lifelong commitment to fidelity, and a comprehensive union—having more options raises the stakes. When I got married, I wasn't saying no to anyone else—just yes to one particular woman. There was no one else in the running. But with online dating services, getting serious tends to involve a more active turn away from other possibilities (however remote).

Here again, Christians mostly find themselves in the same boat as everyone else. They may show a greater reticence to use online dating services and would, of course, have fewer options for potential meet-ups, provided they make a partner's faith commitment an algorithmic deal-breaker. Growing in popularity are specifically Christian services such as Christian Mingle and Catholic Match. They try to help users avoid certain pitfalls, reminding marriage hopefuls to "be realistic," "forgive the small stuff," and post the kinds of photos that "guarantee that someone is interested in you, exactly as you are."[40] This specialized, somewhat coached online dating experience will no doubt work for some. But will they lead to marriages in a timely manner, *on average*? That would be great, but my hopes aren't high.

A total of 38 percent of our interviewees have participated in online dating at some point. Russians were the most apt to have participated, and Lebanese the least likely. Interviewees who had not used online dating services were apt to have strong opinions against them, while those who had used them typically viewed the experience with skepticism. Oksana, the 30-year-old

Orthodox divorcée quoted earlier, had dabbled in online dating after her marriage fell apart. But no more: "It was something that can be hardly called a relationship. Actually, it was a website experience. We met just several times and very quickly ran away from each other." She gave up dating websites after that.

Mateusz, the recently married 26-year-old from Krakow, had a similarly negative experience, calling his venture into online dating "one of the worst ideas in my life." He elaborated only slightly: "I had a bad experience with that. I mean, generally speaking, you never know who is on the other side." Most interviewees who had experience with online dating considered it only modestly successful at best—unless, of course, they had met their spouse that way.

The Online Turn

It is inarguable that the West is slowly but surely moving relationship development in a more wired direction.[41] Thomas, the 30-year-old Catholic from Austin quoted in Chapter 4, works as a project manager for a major telecommunications company. On the matter of online dating and social media, he holds that there is no other sensible pathway forward except to adapt to them:

> It's just where we are today, so you can't change the course of society. Society has become more technological, on-demand. Therefore, you know, people are looking for relationships on-demand. You know it used to be a thing where online dating was kind of a *faux pas*, but now you do everything else online, so why wouldn't you meet your spouse there?

It's almost hard to remember when online dating seemed a faux pas in the United States, where the practice is now firmly established. For Estella, the 27-year-old from Guadalajara we first met in Chapter 4, its prevalence seemed bizarre. She had spent a year in New Jersey as an au pair with a predominantly secular family—in their 40s with four children—a few years before our interview. It was quite an experience for her:

> I made a close relationship with the mother and she told me things about when she was younger. She was surprised when I said I'd never had sex

before. She told me I should try it. . . . One day, she told me she was worried about me, because she knew I valued relationships and marriage.

The host mother then encouraged her to try online dating, claiming it was "very common" in the States. So Estella chose a Catholic site, but she still felt uncomfortable: "I agreed to do it, but I did not love it." Estella was skeptical of the opportunities her American hosts were pressing because she simply wasn't looking for a more efficient search process by which she could more rapidly evaluate romantic, sexual, or marital possibilities. Estella simply didn't perceive the deficit in her life that her host parents did. A few years later, the host couple divorced after a series of infidelities.

Applying technology and algorithms (with a profit motive) to speed up and depersonalize the search for a mate is bound to disrespect boundaries, as well as dignity. It is the end result of a free-market mentality applied to a domain—marriage—in which efficiency and fluid networks are not helpful values. Estella sees things clearly: social embeddedness in a community, not the efficient circulation of potential partners, is what promotes stable relationships and the formation of marriage.[42] Thomas, who has a personal stake in the tech industry, sees it differently. He tries to distinguishes the good from the bad:

> There are good [dating] sites to go to, or you can make it very clear in your profile, "I'm actually looking for a relationship." Some apps have, you know, a bad reputation per se, but ultimately you can put in your profile if you are looking for the people who aren't interested in a relationship. And they'll just skip you. And same thing in life, too. So that kind of part of it doesn't make it bad.

What Thomas doesn't apprehend, however, is that what he calls "good" and "bad" sites operate with the same logic and organizing principles, even if only unintentionally. Their users are treated to a privileging of physical attractiveness. Additionally, all such sites and apps encourage the rapid evaluation of people—if for no other reason than they (often) have plenty of others to show us. This, in turn, powerfully reinforces within us the idea that other persons are there for our happiness and satisfaction. Overcoming this self-centered impulse can be done, but the method of meeting and its bent toward rapid evaluation on a modicum of qualities does little to assist people toward that noble end.

Conclusion

Uncertainty and its siblings—ambiguity, individualism, and materialism— characterize the marriage market today, giving birth to the sense that our most significant relationships may be more disposable than we thought. Uncertainty has been fostered by the job insecurities that have accompanied global free-market economic expansion, as well as the surge in options and elevated material expectations made possible by the same. A perceived smorgasbord of choices has universally raised hopes for what marriage should look and feel like, and Christians have been insufficiently skeptical of this turn. They have tended to repackage what has emerged—social media and online dating—with nothing more than a Christian overlay. The new chronic uncertainty has slowed relationship development and contributes to lagging marriage rates, even though the opposite scenario could have occurred. It happened this way because uncertainty is, in part, a conviction that you don't yet have what it takes to merit getting married—a reflection of the new dominance of the capstone mentality. Parental divorce adds to this uncertainty, fostering anxiety among many young adult children that they may not have what it takes to stay together either.

Uncertainty moves some toward a deeper Christian faith and trust in providence, but it pushes others away from their faith and toward a greater pursuit of control over relationship development. More Christians are cohabiting, but they are not seeking to rewrite the rules about Christian marriage. Living together before marriage, however, almost always contributes to a diminished life of faith, even if only temporarily.

6

Revitalizing Christian Marriage

No sooner had Katerina (from Chapter 5) concluded her lament about Moscow's temptations (and her wistful commentary about the simpler life in Volgograd) than she latched onto a person whom she claimed exemplified the meaning of marriage. "For me, it was Elizabeth Feodorovna, a saint I love very much."

I had never heard of this person, so I looked her up. Born Princess Elisabeth of Hesse (Germany), she married Grand Duke Sergei Alexandrovich of Russia, fifth son of Emperor Alexander II. So far, her story read like just another royal's, but it subsequently proved quite different. Elizabeth became renowned for her hands-on charitable acts among Moscow's poor. But as the seeds of revolution sprouted, charity would not prove enough to save her or her family. Her husband was assassinated in 1905. Elizabeth publicly forgave his killer and became a nun, selling off much of her fortune in 1909 to underwrite a convent to serve Moscow's poor. The rise of Bolshevism, however, would be satisfied with nothing less than systemic and violent overhaul. And so Elizabeth Feodorovna—this heart in a heartless world—was arrested upon order of Lenin just months after the October 1917 Revolution. She was thrown down a mine shaft by the Cheka, forerunners of the Soviet secret police. Two grenades tossed in did not kill her as she continued singing hymns from her dark prison. A pile of burning brush, however, was thrown in, and the resulting fire ended her life.

Today, Elizabeth Feodorovna is a beloved figure in the Russian Orthodox Church, which canonized her in 1992, shortly after the collapse of Communism. Katerina was not the only interviewee who mentioned her—even though we did not inquire into personal sources of inspiration about marriage. For Katerina, the saint's life story had elevated her own marital standards and expectations: "The marriage of Elizabeth Feodorovna has affected my vision. It has become a sort of example" for harmonious marriage:

I love her very much. I mean, her married life with Sergei Alexandrovich. . . .
It's just breathtaking, to the point of, I mean, such purity, such devotion,

such a way of seeing things, all for Christ. They were believers, they sought holiness, and they had such a relationship. I think that when [marriage] is in Christ the Savior, that's what it's like, probably. . . . It's such an example for me, a sort of standard. . . . It has changed my views a great deal, I mean, as to relationships [and] marriage. Probably. Actually, *not* probably! That's what a relationship *should* be like. To love each other with your soul, first of all with your soul. It's not about [sexual] passions but the connection of souls. That's what people should be together for.

Expectations for marriage are more effectively "caught" than taught—that is, they are socialized by our own experiences with our parents and others, including—like in Katerina's case—historical and religious figures. Some of these expectations are more realistic than others. Is a marriage like the one Katerina thinks Elizabeth Feodorovna enjoyed even possible today? "I don't know," she responded when asked. One thing she was confident in: "The impossible is possible for God." The saint's biography has certainly raised Katerina's expectations for what an optimal marriage is like.[1]

This chapter ventures outside the more traditionally social scientific into the prospective. I am leaping from an attempt to describe the modern marital impulse among the globe's young adult Christians to an advisory discussion of how to improve matters. I want to light a candle rather than curse the darkness—so I discuss eight general themes of advice that emerge from the interviews as well as from my own wider observations of this topic after studying it for several years:

1. Tell exemplary stories.
2. Create or recover marriage-friendly subcultures.
3. Make the home a haven (in a heartless world).
4. Effectively prepare people for marriage.
5. Help others navigate challenging marriages.
6. Parents: be mindful about the advice you give.
7. Consider allowing adult children to live at home before marrying—but only for the right reasons.
8. Experiment with prudent, targeted state investment in marriage.

Most of these themes are social in nature; that is, they're less about personal advice to individuals and more about the general circumstances that can foster success. Some of them are targeted at persons; others aim at groups or even governments. Most of the themes are a double-edged sword; they can aid the marital impulse or—played differently—make things worse. For example, we can tell stories about the beauty of marriage, as well as stories of disaster. Congregations can develop helpful tools to foster marriage, or they could end up wasting time and energy on impotent ones. Young people living with their parents—a decidedly un-American piece of advice—can help or backfire (depending very much on the culture of the parents' home). States *can* invest prudently in marriage, but it's not easy. Much government intrusion to help has been wasted money, and social policy has been far more apt to undermine than foster marriage.

Some of these ideas are personal decisions—largely under an individual's control—while others are much harder to realize because they involve collective decision-making. I'll start with the easiest one.

Tell Exemplary Stories

Whether higher moral standards will bring Katerina the husband she's looking for is unknown. And Katerina may be prone to exaggerating the past, a "way we never were," to borrow a phrase from Stephanie Coontz, the American social historian.[2] No matter. Sociologists know that "myth," or story, can both motivate action and make sense of experience. The famous Thomas theorem captures that clearly: "If people define situations as real, then they are real in their consequences," even if you or I can see the cracks in their narratives.[3] Perhaps we are lacking marital heroes and heroines.

One of the most moving stories about marriage I have ever heard was told to me on my first visit to Poland. It still gets to me whenever it comes to mind. I was in a Warsaw hotel restaurant, striking up a conversation with Gintaras Grušas, the Catholic archbishop of Vilnius, Lithuania, who had spoken at an event I had attended. I sat down next to him at breakfast and remarked to him about his exceptional American English—which had no discernible accent. I asked him how he had accomplished that, to which he quipped, "I worked at it for a long time!"

He had me there for a minute, until he let me in on his joke. This head of the Catholic Church in Lithuania explained that he had been born in Washington, D.C., and had spent his youth and young adulthood in Los Angeles, including an education at UCLA followed by management experience at IBM. He was as American as they come. How did he wind up in

Vilnius? What came next has never left me. It was an unbelievable account of marital persistence and sacrificial love in the face of the odds against it.

The archbishop explained that his father, like not a few displaced Eastern European young men, had wound up on the Western side of the Iron Curtain following the end of the Second World War. He couldn't get home to Vilnius. Nor could his wife and their daughter get to him. They didn't even know each other was still alive for over ten years. He moved to the United States, and began to try to get them out of the Soviet Union . Finally, fifteen years later, the three were reunited as part of a gift to President Nixon from Soviet premier Nikita Khrushchev, who had agreed to allow 200 separated families to reunite. Gintaras was born a year later—seventeen years younger than his only sibling. The archbishop told me that his parents and sister were all still alive and now living in Vilnius.

I'm not at all sure I have the details of this story correct. And I don't know anything about *how* the archbishop's father and mother coped with their exile from each other. I don't know how much effort his father put into their reunification (I presume plenty). Was their reunion as blissful as one could imagine, or was it marked by a profound awkwardness and the enduring sense that too much time had passed—that they had become very different persons? There are dozens of questions that the social scientist in me would want to ask. Still, the most compelling aspect of this story is one of undying patience. It is a story about honoring your marriage in spite of all the forces arrayed against it.

I return to that story every now and then. I ask myself if I have what it takes to do what the archbishop's father did. I wonder whether the West can still make men like that. (I don't know.) That the archbishop's account recirculates in my mind highlights the power of personal narrative for marriage formation (and in this case, maturation). The stories people tell, or the narratives they internalize, matter considerably for marriage. They are all anecdotal, but that doesn't weaken their influence in the least. For this reason, social media can be an effective communicator of such narratives, too. And let's be honest—survey numbers rarely move anyone.

While narratives can be exceptional motivators toward marriage, it is obvious when we look around us—and listen—that the most captivating stories circulating about marriage today are not like this one. Instead, they are horror stories about violent marriages and narrow escapes or about adulterous men poisoned by machismo. I have no interest in censoring such accounts. I just know that many, many inspirational stories are out there, privately harbored by many people. And the news crews are seldom going to interview those folks. Bernadette, a 28-year-old, unmarried bank employee from Beirut, wants to hear about more than the hardships of marriage: "I am seeing the sacrifice, the ties, the duties, but not the happy part of couples. I only feel encouraged when I go see one of my friends, a couple whom I usually visit. That's honestly the only thing that can get me encouraged for marriage." Sam, a 24-year-old Pentecostal from Lagos, relayed his memory of a couple, married over thirty years with three or four children, and how impressed he was with them: "The man is a pilot, and the woman works somewhere, I can't remember, but they are so good. While they were on stage [speaking], you could feel the understanding [between them], the energy, this understanding coming out of them as one. [Listening to them], people *felt* they were married."

For some interviewees, their inspirational story is not even a complete anecdote, let alone a story, but, rather, an image to which they have attached their own content—like Alejandra's iPhone photograph of the old couple on the beach. They simply represented ideals she was looking for. (Sadly, so many young adults today don't even have so much as an image to cling to.) Timoteusz, a 28-year-old recently married Catholic living in Lublin, feels similar encouragement from older couples. In his case, however, he gets to see them with regularity: "I've always been delighted by the fact that I could see such images, for instance, during my walks in the park when you can see a 70-year-old couple that is walking and still holding hands. For me, it's such a strong statement that [my] faith in marriage is constantly revived." (Nowhere have I ever seen men and women, young and old, holding hands in numbers comparable to that in Poland.)

Create or Recover Marriage-Friendly Subcultures

Scholars I know and respect have lamented the collapse of what might be called a "marriage culture" in the West.[4] (Many others I know have praised its downfall.) It's not just a marriage culture that has evaporated. In *Why Liberalism Failed*, political theorist Patrick Deneen documents the near "evisceration . . . of generational customs, practices, and rituals that are grounded in local and particular settings."[5] This is discernible in all of the research sites. It's not just because there's a KFC and a Starbucks in nearly every corner of the globe (though that is true). It is more about the "monoculture" that

Deneen suggests is now spreading beyond the West, one that "colonizes and destroys actual cultures rooted in experience, history, and place . . . free[ing] us from other specific people and embedded relationships, replacing custom with abstract and depersonalized law."[6] Deneen is right. Increasingly, I find that Lebanese young adult Christians sound like Mexicans and Spaniards, who sound like Russians and Americans. Even Poles and Nigerians seemed increasingly like Americans. In the end, distinctive cultures are receding, and a dominant, standardized monoculture emerging, criticism of which is framed as parochialism or nationalism. It's global, free-market atomism.

Rod Dreher articulates the challenges and possibilities for forming new subcultures in *The Benedict Option*, an exploration in localized resistance.[7] Evangelical author Andy Crouch aptly adds, "If we seek to change culture, we will have to create something new, something that will persuade our neighbors to set aside some existing set of cultural goods for our new proposal."[8] That something, Crouch asserts, invariably starts small: "Christian culture grows through networks, but it is not a matter of networking. It is a matter of community—a relatively small group of people whose common life is ordered by love."[9] Did I see any evidence of this in the field? Certainly.

For Paweł and Marta, the married couple from Krakow, two societies that aided their marriage—before and after the wedding—were a youth organization at the nearby Dominican order, and the Neocatechumenal Way, a movement noted among several interviewees in Pamplona. The former functions as a meeting place for serious young adult Catholics in Krakow, with spiritual direction (periodical religious mentoring) and subsequent marriage preparation offered by the local Dominican order. In the Neocatechumenal Way, participants are assigned to a "family," a group of a few dozen people who meet regularly to share burdens and support one another. The movement includes singles as well as married couples, and participants range widely in age; hence, it fosters intergenerational relationships. Once entered, it is not entirely voluntary; participants are expected to do the challenging work of getting along with other people rather than quitting their family group. "The Way," as members refer to it, is not easy, but it is rewarding (the same could be said for marriage). Paweł and Marta, like many members, find its balance of social support and social control—all connected to Catholic faith—a lifeline in the fragmenting social world that is rapidly characterizing Poland and even its religious heart, Krakow.

Movements like the Neocatechumenal Way cannot, of course, entirely prevent the cultural impositions they are seeking to displace. Bernadette, the 28-year-old from Beirut mentioned earlier in this chapter, is also a member, yet she struggles to establish the kind of healthy, chaste relationship that would lead to marriage. What she will not compromise on, however, is the Christian character of any future marriage.

Others elsewhere mentioned groups not unlike the Way—in which participants would live near each other and "help each other in household issues, do something together, sit with each other's children, exchange children's clothes, chip in if someone needs something and does not have enough money," according to one interviewee. The evangelical world features similar such groups.

Like many of the married or engaged Polish interviewees with whom we spoke, Maria Teresa has been similarly involved with a Christian organization on her campus and familiar with the work of similar ones in other Polish cities. (These function like InterVarsity Christian Fellowship, Cru, and other international evangelical organizations.) She finds involvement pivotal for constructing a group of friends who hold a common vision of chastity. In the final year of her university studies in Lublin, Maria Teresa is engaged to be married—a mere three weeks after the interview, in fact. She is 23 and met her fiancé when she was only 13. Their friendship "naturally" developed into a relationship, she remarked. Outside of her network of Christian friends, opinions about her impending marriage reflect what she perceives as people's own rootlessness: "My peers say that it's too early, and we should enjoy life.... They mean that I should get to know other men or get to know my fiancé [better]. I don't know—maybe I should go on a trip," she quipped. She thinks such peers haven't "found stability, a place that they could always return to." Maria Teresa learned stability in her own family and from her parents' marriage. It wasn't perfect, but "people who are married recommend marriage," she observed.

Maria Teresa can see the general shift toward the capstone vision: "[Marriage] is one of the options, and not the main path. Now the important things are career and self-development—be it at work or in terms of entertainment." Given she's only 23, Maria Teresa is arguably entering a foundational marriage, and she knows it. And yet the two cannot be accused of rushing things: "It's not that we were eager to get married immediately and dated for ten years. We just happen to know each other for so long." She's ready: "I know what I can expect from him. I know what he is capable of doing. And the same goes true for me."

Viktor, the 29-year-old (Orthodox) clinical psychologist working just outside Moscow, was one of few interviewees who actually used the term *culture* when he spoke about what would be helpful to young adult Christians today. He tried to be specific:

> I think what would help us a lot is some culture. Sounds very general, I be-lieve, so let me try to specify what I mean by culture: literature telling about values, meanings, positive family images that it would show. Maybe films, including those broadcast on television. . . . For many people it would be a sort of stimulus. . . . These values and meanings need to be broadcast, which is only possible through culture. If we saw, say, some theater plays, songs, youth TV programs about how great family is, how cool it is. Showing that there is a lot of good about it.

Father Feoktist, a 39-year-old Orthodox monk and rector of a parish in northwestern Moscow, feels similar to Viktor but was able to provide some concrete examples of how the young adults in his parish are building, or rather recovering, a promarriage culture. In the former Soviet Union, there is a good deal of such recovery going on. Father Feoktist emphasized that these participants aren't the awkward misfits of society but, rather, regular citi-zens: "They are not some girls all covered in shawls or some guys who don't look after themselves. They are normal people who live a normal life. They live secular lives, but they believe in God," he explained. "They are trying to actualize the evangelical life in the modern world."

Music and dancing play a large part in this group's get-togethers. Also im-portant is a sense of avant-gardism, even as they attempt to access more tra-ditional mores and themes:

> They are not engaged in "reenactment." Well, there is a slight hint of reenactments, but in the form of enthusiasm for folklore. . . . These meetings where they [get together], . . . they are themed according to Russian history. It's very beautiful. It's professional. They have very apt folklore bands per-forming there. Their big friends are Отава Ё [in English, *Otava Yo*], a band from St. Petersburg. The band, of course, does not associate themselves with the Church, but you can google them and see for yourself that they have wonderful music videos, and the girls from our parish take part in those videos. . . . It turned out that there is a whole layer of folklore that was forgotten during the Soviet years. There are forgotten musical instruments. Traditional Russian ditties are not necessarily obscene and monotonous. In

reality, it is all quite different. They adapt it, use numerous instruments and play very good music.

It's important to distinguish between *creating* culture—as in this example—and *mimicking* culture. Modern Christians tend to riff off or borrow from what Deneen calls the global "monoculture." They are not (currently) known for their production of distinctive culture. But the making of something new by Christians can still be found. Another example is Ladislav Hanus Fellowship, a civic association of young adults in Bratislava, Slovakia, aimed at understanding and developing the country's Christian faith and culture. Its semiannual "Hanus Days" is a week of focused activities—music and films, scholarly lectures and panels—fostering interaction among the Christian community in Bratislava. And it connects men and women: they count fifty marriages among participants over 17 years. The Hanus Fellowship is not a return to tribal nationalism but, rather, a resistance to the eternal "today" of monoculture. But it *is* political in that it is about the cultivation of a distinctly Christian society—the Church. "Memory," Robert Louis Wilken reminds us, "is a defining mark of Christian identity."[10] It's creating a future that is connected to a past, he adds. Crouch concurs: "Before we can be culture makers, we must be culture keepers."[11]

Talk of marriage-friendly subcultures reminds me of the network of young adults that formed around, and was fostered and nurtured by, Karol Wojtyła when he was a parish priest in Krakow—long before he became archbishop of that city and later Pope John Paul II. He called it *Środowisko*, which translates into "environment," though he preferred something more akin to "milieu."[12] It was about creating a subculture, a social environment in which Christian (and human) formation could develop amid state and informal opposition. Środowisko wasn't a program, like a weekly small-group Bible study. Rather, it was a web of persons that revolved around the future pope, from whom they received spiritual direction and education, and around whom they built and enjoyed friendship—doing life together. Particular groups would form around common intellectual conversations and interests—engineering and physics were two of them—to which Wojtyła then offered philosophical engagement and pastoral support. The groups took recreational excursions together, often to the mountains south of Krakow.

The friendliness and openness of Środowisko stood in contrast to the hollow nature and false freedom of communist society in postwar Poland.

(Stalin was still alive when Środowisko got its start.) This was a pocket of joyful resistance, an escape from the toxic atmosphere of the universities, where fear of informants was a constant anxiety. "We could live more freely because we were free inside," one of Środowisko's members later recalled.[13] (Given the toxicity and popularity of today's call-out culture, this idea sounds inviting.)

As with the Hanus Fellowship, fostering marriages wasn't the point of Środowisko, but for many of its young adults, it was a welcome byproduct of it. Since Father Wojtyła had a keen interest in marriage and sexuality, it's no surprise that he was a willing ear and voice—as well as long-suffering confessor and occasional challenger and critic—as these relationships developed.[14] This was "life together," as German theologian and martyr Dietrich Bonhoeffer described in his book by that name.[15] "Communities," Crouch reminds us, "are the way God intervenes to offer, within every culture, a different and better horizon."[16]

A wide shift away from monoculture—which, Deneen maintains, transcends time, place, and even nature—is not yet on the horizon. But grassroots resistance efforts matter. For Christian culture to be renewed, "habits," Wilken holds, "are more vital than revivals, rituals more edifying than spiritual highs . . ."[17] Such efforts are tenuous projects, given how enculturated many of us are in wanting, expecting, and even demanding options and choices—including about our most intimate relationships. Many Christians are more apt to dabble in than to dwell in their faith communities. Christian organizations with vibrant subcultures offer resistance, and marriage is a common byproduct of involvement in them. Remember C. S. Lewis's remark, "Aim at heaven, and you'll get earth 'thrown in.'"[18]

Make the Home a Haven (in a Heartless World)

Like nearly everyone else in the West, Christians now widely consider marriage a capstone, not the interdependent anchor of the adult life course. The entire purpose of marriage and family is subtly shifting, giving way to economic concerns and material expectations. These considerations tend to reveal what matters most to us: work. Not necessarily the money work can yield, but the work itself.

As sociologist Arlie Hochschild describes in her book *The Time Bind*, our workplaces have become our "home," and then we're somehow surprised to find that our home life becomes laborious and a drudge to us.[19] Even discussions of family-friendly policies seem always, at bottom, to be answers to the question, "How can I get more work done, given I have tall and increasing competition for my time?" Hochschild found that the corporate employees she studied didn't actually challenge the company's claims upon their time. They didn't even try very hard to retain "a life" apart from the workplace, despite references to the contrary. They ignored long-sought policies offering shorter work hours and more time at home. When the stresses of the workplace got to them, they didn't resort to excessive drinking or drug use. Instead, she found that they stole time from their children in order to get more work done. Household efficiency was a goal, so family responsibilities were outsourced. All of this despite the fact that the company didn't explicitly demand these things. Employees constrained each other by their own overweening expectations.

Nothing has changed in the twenty-five years since *The Time Bind*'s publication, save for our invention of time-saving devices so that we can . . . get more work done. This isn't somehow the accomplishment of a centralized, overbearing state. No—we ourselves have collaborated in the destruction of the home, the peaceful family dwelling, preferring the material achievements of atomism to the intangible satisfactions and goodness of family, community, and faith.

To paraphrase Paul the Apostle, I am "the worst of sinners" here.[20] I recognize the damage that has been done *because* I have allowed my home to be co-opted by work and employment concerns. Work knows no boundaries. It wants more: more of me, more of my wife, more of the time we might allocate to others—including our own children. And it wants more whether we're at our workplaces, traveling, or at home. I get that our paid work may be important. But it doesn't follow that work must colonize our homes.

Home is meant to be a haven in a heartless world, following the famous title of Christopher Lasch's book.[21] For many, it is no longer that, if it ever was. It is just another location for the overreaching claims of the market, whose logic does not belong there. Efficiency, value, speed, and demonstrative success don't make for a better home. They make for an industrialized one.

It's not that difficult to imagine some wise, humane steps to resist those forces bent on eroding the home. Linger over the dinner table, with everyone present, for an additional half hour. (No smartphones at the table: they are for consuming culture, not producing it.). Read aloud. Pray aloud. Sing more. (An ancient anonymous source claims, "He who sings prays twice.") I can think of nothing so unbridled in its unitive power as being musical together.

Grounding yourself (and your family) into your community is also crucial. Make use of local libraries. Have a conversation with your neighbors. If it's hard to strike up, bring a home-baked offering to provide food over which to have a chat, even if only briefly. Shop local, if possible. Visit coffee shops and use them for their intended conversational purposes. Hike with friends. Learn to dance, and then keep doing it. Look *around* you (more than you look down). Unmediated relationships are in no small part what make us human—persons. Alena, a 24-year-old from Moscow, lamented the industrial traits of the contemporary home: "How can one learn to love [here]? Where can one get the experience of loving your neighbor?" If all this was foreign in the home of your youth, seek it out as an adult in the homes of friends.

Not a few of us have a growing concern that the social fabric of our communities and our nations is fraying.[22] We scratch our heads at the more leisurely and humane pace that much of the world maintains, but we do little to make it happen for ourselves, worried that somehow our own productivity will suffer. But productivity cannot hug you, or keep you warm at night.

You may say that such advice is just not realistic in today's fast-moving society. I agree it's not realistic, given how penetrated we have been by market mentalities. But if you want a shot at generating sustained happiness, emotional stability, and a sense of rootedness in your children—something they'll want to pass on to their own children—you will dwell upon the gravity of our common situation. We are making our way toward the logical ends of our atomism. Loneliness is rampant in a wired world whose connectivity is unprecedented and matchless. We are fearing, and then we are experiencing, the suicidal cry of our children at levels our grandparents, on average, did not. These patterns don't just threaten to do harm to our children. They shrink us, too. The human person wasn't meant to be a cog in either state or economy. Remember your Aristotle. States and economies exist *for* the family, not vice versa. Marriage—what it is—and family—what they generate—are a foundation, not a feeder system.

Effectively Prepare People for Marriage

The narrative about what healthy marriage looks and feels like, and what you're supposed to do when it fails to meet your expectations—as it does for nearly everyone—does not just tell itself. This is why one nascent solution is better marriage preparation, ideally including ongoing mentorship in marriage. However, there is simply no culture of ongoing marital assistance in much of global Christianity, in part because the history of widespread divorce among Christians remains comparatively new. (What's 50 years in the span of 2,000? Less than 3 percent.)

University of Minnesota professor, therapist, and researcher William Doherty pulls no punches when queried about the importance of high-quality marriage preparation: "I think we need to create a marriage ethic that would say that it's irresponsible to get married without preparing for it like it would be irresponsible to get a driver's license without getting behind the wheel and learning."[23]

Jessica, the 31-year-old nonprofit manager from Austin, would concur with Doherty about the absolute imperative of good marriage prep. She contrasted the preparation required for the two vow-related Catholic sacraments of *holy orders* and *matrimony*: "Priests often receive formation that can be up till like, ten years in the seminary before they ever are ordained or make a vow, you know, before God. Then married people can complete marriage prep in like, a weekend. Which is like, terrifying." She emphasized what she views as a ridiculous double standard: "What are we doing!?"

Oksana, the 30-year-old Orthodox woman from Moscow, had married at age 27 and divorced a year later. The pressure to marry had been considerable. Her readiness to marry? Paltry. When asked about preparation for family life, she said there had been none. Worse, she emphasized, were the strangely disjointed and often conflicting expectations of what a spousal relationship means.

> I believe that young women in many families have not been tooled for a family. There are some idealistic images that may contradict each other. It's not some integral picture of a family, not like some integral picture of your [other] half, the way you imagine your spouse—a psychological portrait. It all comes in fragmented pieces; you don't see it in real life. And as a result, you keep looking for it and cannot find it.

It is truly a bizarre notion to give so little attention to a relationship that plays such a big part over the adult life course. As Doherty said, it is irresponsible to do a poor job at preparing people for marriage. And yet no preparation is even required, at least in the eyes of the state. But many of our interviewees wished that the situation were different. "The more realistic presentation [of marriage] we have, the better," held Bethany, a 30-year-old unmarried Baptist from Austin. Good personal examples are "the best propaganda of marriage that can be," maintained Dmitri, a 30-year-old divorced Orthodox Muscovite, whose early marriage ended in a manner similar to Oksana's.

Unfortunately, family dysfunction can run deep and wide, making good examples rare—as Alexander and Anya observed in Chapter 2. Jasmine, the 28-year-old Filipino engaged to the U.S. Air Force officer, echoed other interviewees in her desire to see successful marriages across the life span:

> To bring healing and that kind of like, revitalizing what marriage means, people need to see those real-life examples. And it's hard to . . . just like, read about it and that sort of thing, or to hear it from priests. But things like retreats and, umm, yeah, just like one-on-one meetings with people who are just like you, and yet what they value is not what the media values or what movies make out to be, you know, attractive. But . . . it's the real love, and the real sacrifice, and that it's not a bed of roses. But you still make it, you know. And you can be like the old-school couples, yeah.

Good marriage preparation is in high demand, but many still find it hard to come by. In our interviews, we seldom heard about specific programs, but some did come up. A Slovakian couple—Kamil and Katarína Baginová—oversees an organization in the capital city of Bratislava called Family Garden, which provides premarital preparation and marriage coaching for couples referred to them. They operate out of a municipal building that the Salesian Brothers of Don Bosco helped them acquire and renovate. (The Salesians have a particular focus on young people.) The Baginovás and a team of fellow volunteers—including a gynecologist, psychologist, lawyer, and financial adviser—are able to provide professional counseling to married couples across a spectrum of needs. Over the course of a year, Family Garden tackles—via lectures and conversations—a panoply of sensitive but pressing questions that couples face, including the following:

- We have three generations living under one roof. How do we minimize conflict?
- How do we navigate our sexuality both before marriage and within it?
- How do we really get to know each other in our marriage?
- We're in debt. How do we get out of it?

- What does it mean to be married to an introvert?
- How do we fix what we have messed up in our marriage? How do we forgive?

These aren't softball questions. And Family Garden's *pre*marital preparation is no less substantial, involving at least nine meetings over the course of two or three months. Couples address hard topics they might otherwise have avoided, including the expectations each has of the other regarding children, work, in-laws, sex, and fertility issues. Patrik, a 33-year-old Slovakian I met while in the city for a few days in 2017, leveled with me about his experience with the new marriage preparation: "Those conversations were difficult. I'd estimate that at least 10 percent of couples who enter the premarital training break up during it, after realizing the person they were engaged to saw the world far differently than they thought." One could think that such premarital prep is counterproductive, yielding as it does more broken engagements than would the standard prep course. The volunteers at Family Garden see it differently. Their vision is to prevent future problems—and civil divorces, which are easy to get in Slovakia—by building skills now (including recognizing a bad match) rather than helping people pick up the pieces later.

Other organizations are giving life to similar ideas. Communio, a private interdenominational program hoping to boost marriage rates and church attendance in the United States, as well as to lower divorce rates, is experimenting toward that end. The organization itself utilizes available data (to guide predictive models), leans on digital outreach, and guides Christian congregations with an interest in supporting the marriages in their midst. Communio recognizes—and aptly so, given the data in this book—that as marriage fares, so will the fortunes of local Christian congregations, since rising cohabitation and out-of-wedlock births are associated with declining involvement. The early evidence of Communio's efficacy in a small number of locations is promising, with a 24 percent decline in divorce in the area of Jacksonville, Florida, where they are concentrating their activities.[24]

Still other options are rooted in particular congregations. A trend of "marriage mentoring" is a great example, wherein marrying couples are paired—well before the wedding—with couples five to fifteen years older than they. Toby, a 31-year-old married Baptist seminarian from Austin, thought marriage mentors were "completely foundational and necessary" (for the record, we hadn't brought up the topic). Trusted couples could help newlyweds navigate the challenges of blending two lives into one:

> Just to have a process that people walk through where you are helping them. They may even discover some of the landmines that if you don't help them see those things ahead of time, they are going to be married and all the sudden not know what to do with these things.

Marriage mentors fit interviewees' common interest in good exemplars and compelling narratives. (Marriage is learned behavior, after all.) Matched couples meet regularly over the course of several months, and the mentors are required to engage their charges in challenging conversations on topics important to a successful marriage. If we lived in an era whose norms and priorities were not so toxic to marriage and family life, marriage mentors might be helpful but not required. But the times have changed. The premarital preparation program *Witness to Love* leans on marriage mentors and is drawing rave reviews, together with early indications of sustainable success.[25]

While marriage's critics perceive marriage as a "burden of conformity" to expectations, mentoring can remind Christians that they are participating in a natural (and material) institution, and that even marriage's mundane aspects can be the site of holiness, sanctification, and happiness. *New York* magazine's Elizabeth Wurtzel, an unlikely candidate for promoting marriage, perceives wisdom in such institutional norms: "Convention serves a purpose: It gives life meaning, and without it, one is in a constant existential crisis. If you don't have the imposition of family to remind you of what is at stake, something else will." A society that increasingly snubs marriage is inviting a lack of social structure, and with it an unheralded source of psychological unmooring, angst, anomy, and the quest for affirmation that has descended upon many young adults today.

Help Others Navigate Challenging Marriages

Amid well-intentioned efforts to rebuild marriage subcultures by singing the praises of matrimony, there remains a persistent hazard that many people already in challenging unions will feel more discouraged, not less. After all, their marriages haven't felt wonderful for a very long time.

A measure of relational trial is, of course, endemic to the human condition. And I could advise people not to compare their marriages with those of others. But this is unrealistic; it's deeply inhuman to pay no heed to those around you. This is obvious from the rapid uptake of social media, a phenomenon that—of course—risks exacerbating relationship problems. In a study in *Computers and Human Behavior*, those participants who didn't use social media sites at all reported being 11 percent happier with their marriage than were heavy users of social media.[26]

I had analyzed that same survey data a year before and documented the long-term benefits to adult children if they grew up with a mother and father who remained married, in comparison with every other combination.[27] The classic arrangement is still the best. And I didn't even take into consideration (that is, control for) the parents' marital happiness—only their marital status. So some of those stable marriages were no doubt less blissful than others. But an unsightly building can still provide shelter. Even the death of a parent proved far less consequential than a divorce.

Maria Carmen, a 26-year-old nurse in Pamplona, thinks her expectations for marriage are very realistic and that there won't be much difference between what she hopes for and what she can find in a spouse. A key reason for her realism is her parents' marital struggles; she knows "what life can be like," and as a result, she doesn't expect any surprises:

> My parents are completely different from each other, and what I admire is that they can love each other, even though they are so different, and that they are sharing that love [because of] Jesus Christ. It's surprising for me, because I see other parents or friends of mine and think, "They're ideal, perfect [for each other]." But I look at my parents, and they're a real disaster, "chalk and cheese," total opposites. My mother is neurotic and super nervous, while my father is very calm, very quiet. And I see that they are able to love each other and reconcile. They fight eighty thousand times, but they also know how to [make up], and this for me means forgetting your selfish side, which is what I find difficult [to do]. To me that is really incredible. I believe that this is possible because they are accompanied by God's support, because if not, my parents would have separated years ago. . . . If something isn't solid, it will disintegrate.

Maria's comments about her parents' recurrent reconciliation highlight the pivotal role of forgiveness—a missing element in today's call-out culture.

Without genuine forgiveness, marriage will not work. Indeed, Christians have a language—the concepts of sin, confession, and redemption—with which to understand and practice this. Moreover, it pays to remember the distinction between salvation and sanctification. The former doesn't guarantee that the latter will be an easy road. Humility is required, and it can take tremendous self-control and sacrifice. Sometimes one party carries more of the burden in this reciprocal union of assistance. But the promise of the gospel is that even this imbalance itself is sanctification, part of carrying one's cross into eternal life.[28]

Not long ago, a friend of mine left his wife after nearly thirty years of marriage. While I don't know the particulars, his exit seems to have no obvious logic. I know theirs was not an easy marriage; both spouses had maintained high expectations for it and had experienced subsequent disappointments. One twentieth-century Catholic observer lamented this human habit—which extends well beyond marital hopes to simpler ones about work, health, material goods, vacations, and even tonight's dinner:

> That happens with so many things in life. We inject them with poetry in our imaginations, we idealize them, and come to believe they are the epitome of happiness and beauty. But then when we have them in front of us, and see them just as they are, our hearts sink to our boots.[29]

A few other friends of his and I got together with him in an effort to ask him to reconsider his departure. One of us wondered aloud, "Wouldn't it be better to limp to the finish line, with the help of others, than quit the race?" After all, if marriage is a marathon, our friend was probably nearing the twenty-mile mark. The rest of us concurred, but to no avail. I still maintain that my friend was wrong about his decision to exit his "good enough" marriage. Perhaps new information would change my mind—I don't know. There are precious few scenarios in which his children would be better off for his having left. Perhaps my confidence seems to be the height of arrogance. All I know is that his wife wanted him to come home.

That and other comparable experiences prompt several suggestions. *First, be wary of taking sides.* Remember that when we offer comfort by belittling someone else's spouse, we do damage to their marriage—an entity that we did not found, and which exists independently of each spouse. The temptation to do this is very strong (and often fed by the behavior of one of the spouses). *Second, be gentle in critique.* We harm our brothers and sisters when we fail to esteem others' unions, fragile though they may be. Praise those aspects of others' marriages that merit it. A bruised reed we should not break (Matthew 12:20).

Third, be courageous. If, in fact, many mediocre marriages don't deserve the death penalty, then you should consider speaking up. Just under 20 percent of married Americans report having thought about leaving their spouse in the past year, according to the 2018 American Political and Social Behavior survey. There are a lot of people in need of marital encouragement. We can help them "keep the mess manageable." Given more time and opportunity, even a "good enough" marriage can become "better than average." And if that sounds too noble, you can just repeat the blunt advice of Bethany, a 30-year-old unmarried Baptist from Austin: "At a certain point, you just decide this is the person I'm gonna put up with [laughs]."

Parents, Be Mindful about the Advice You Give

The topic of parental counsel arose with some regularity among interviewees. Some were appreciative of their parents' advice. Others easily discerned their parents' own relational mistakes and regrets reflected in the protective—and sometimes manipulative—advice they were giving. In contrast to the old reputation for hounding adult children about marriage, parents today—many of them survivors of the divorce generation—counsel patience. And their children aren't often rebelling. It was common for us to hear from interviewees about five-, six-, and even eight-year-long dating spells before marriage. Uncertainty, documented at length in Chapter 5, stalks young adults and contributes to the delay.

Father Jose Leon, a priest who has observed three decades' worth of students on the Pamplona campus of the University of Navarra, thinks parents pressure their young adult children to unnecessarily delay marriage: "Parents prevent children from taking risks. [*What kinds of risks?*] You're too young, they say. It [marriage] is too difficult. That's the message parents give to children." This is not a new priestly observation. John Chrysostom, a fourth-century bishop esteemed in the Orthodox, Catholic, Lutheran, and Anglican traditions, maintained that parents were disregarding their duty to help assist their children toward marriage: "It's better to wait," parents told him, "until they gain prestige and shine in public activities." (Sounds familiar.) Chrysostom balked at their reasonings, discerning in their hesitance an obsession with the material and ephemeral to the neglect of the spiritual and eternal: "It's like that because the soul is considered an accessory, because the important things are neglected and effort is made with what is secondary. Everything is thus confused and disorderly."[30]

Sometimes, of course, parental advice is prudent but young adults ignore it. And then there are parents who have a world of good advice to offer, but they refrain. Viktor, the 29-year-old clinical psychologist from Moscow, feels that his parents had more guidance to offer than they chose to give, and he considers it a loss. They never intervened in his choice of girlfriends, for instance, but looking back, he wishes they had. Curiously, he connects his desire to the resurgent interest in pre-Soviet Russia, a move consonant with building marriage-friendly subcultures mentioned earlier:

> I believe that parents are somehow able to see at once if a person is suitable enough for you, if you are a child of those parents. I mean, they know you. . . . What rather appeals to me is the pattern when parents almost decide [your spouse]. Again, if we recall our history, those alliances of the nobility. It was not exactly a marriage of convenience, although there was a calculation, certainly, in the economic, political, social sense. But at the same time, they were not stupid. They realized that in the family, a certain culture would be created. And they could foresee what it would be like. . . . In this respect, modern parents are somewhat alienated from the process, I believe.

Christian young adults report a wide array of experiences with parental guidance. Sometimes Mom and Dad can be overbearing. Other parents entirely fail to offer counsel at times when it is needed most. Some parents have little insight to give, having not received much instruction themselves. Others are founts of wisdom that go unheeded. You can't go wrong, however, in keeping in mind the spiritual well-being of your children over your own pride or expectations, even if that means making countercultural choices.

Consider Allowing Adult Children to Live at Home before Marrying—but Only for the Right Reasons

The practice of young adults living with their parents until they marry is standard operating procedure in Lebanon and Mexico, and it is quite common as well in Poland, Spain, and Nigeria. I saw it. I heard about it. But to remain in your parents' household until you get married seems somehow wrong in the land of the free and the home of the brave. Living at home as a young adult can foster complacency, for sure. What begins as an innocent method of saving up for the future can lapse into a life of lethargy, self-absorption, or codependency. It need not.

If Americans are honest with themselves, they would acknowledge that creating new households by pushing 18-year-olds out of the nest comes with genuine hazards. While independence can form character, it is hardly a straight line to virtue. But we have become so accustomed to the risks and costs that we barely perceive other options. It is ironic: We push our children out of the house before they hit age 20, and then we use electronic monitoring to keep track of them because we're worried about their physical and emotional well-being.

This pattern is partly market driven. Moving young adult children out of the home clearly creates new housing starts, more construction jobs, and—downstream—more fiscal growth. In fact, sometimes I think the American economy largely runs on the production of independence—besides housing construction, think automobiles, oil and gas, and new credit accounts.

My own children won't likely live at home until they're married, and I'm okay with that. But after listening to lots of accounts from around the world, I have concluded that it can actually be positive for the formation of marriageability to live with your parents until you leave their household to marry. Here are several pros and a few cons.

First, this living arrangement enables parents to have a greater say in the conduct of their children. Pawlina, a 24-year-old engaged self-employed Catholic living in Lublin, finds living with her parents a hurdle to starting a sexual relationship with her fiancé—and she is glad for the obstacle. She wants to wait, and freedom from parental oversight no doubt makes a sexual relationship easier to pursue. Mariana, the 25-year-old from Guadalajara quoted in Chapter 4, had a similar living situation as Pawlina—she lived with her parents before she married. But her fiancé lived on his own. Despite her stated wishes to the contrary, the two carried on an occasional sexual relationship that made her feel repeatedly guilty:

> It was more difficult for us, because I did not have the typical boyfriend who lived with his parents. . . . It was a major challenge, but it's good that I can say "Yes, it happened, but it was not so [frequent]." He wanted me to

live with him, but I didn't want to. [*Why not?*] Well, because I wanted a real commitment. I wanted to do the real transition from courtship to marriage.

Thomas, the 30-year-old married Catholic project manager from Austin, thought it was foolish not to live on your own: "You have to have, uh, experience just living on your own. . . . Away from home, basically." On the other hand, he drew a meandering line from independence to cohabitation and the complete loss of parental oversight in the lives of his peers—Christian or not:

> Especially here in Austin . . . because rent is so high, people are just kind of shacking up. And then they are already spending all their time together, and they're probably already sleeping together for the most part, so what is it to live together? . . . I have some friends from college doing this. Their parents used to have some pull, but in the new modern society, [young adults] kind of have all of the say now, especially if they have their own job. That's kind of the thing. If you are still in college, [the parents] have a little bit of pull, just because [they're] maybe paying for some [of it]. . . . But it's just gotten so out of hand, that everyone just does what they wish. And then the parents don't have any power anyways once you . . . start paying your own bills.

Nevertheless, Thomas maintains that living at home stalls the impulse to marry. He could be right. His cause-and-effect argument, however, is weak: "You have all these kids who didn't leave home because they couldn't afford it. . . . So the reason they haven't gotten married, ultimately, is because they don't know what it's like to be out on their own yet." Marriage, of course, is not about being on your own. Thomas's argument includes the question, "How can you care for another person if you haven't cared for yourself?" Easy, I say—if you've contributed to the activities of your family's household, learning to care for yourself, yes, and also others. (Note that this is a far cry from living as a dependent parasite in your parents' basement, playing video games while your mother does your wash and brings you dinner.) A scenario of mutual care, communication, and responsibility, I would argue, is a better preparation for the marital household than is independent living, in which a person's only concern is his or her own preferences and needs. If social isolation is on the rise, why create unnecessary solitude?

Consider also that consolidating expenses is a longstanding way in which households that include adult children can become economically stronger, especially in times of scarcity. If a young adult works full-time but lives at home—and contributes to the life and expenses of the household—this saves everyone money that would otherwise land in someone else's pocket (such as the landlord of the adult child's apartment complex). This is the kind of financial habit helpful for marriage. Szymon, a 32-year-old married computer programmer from Lublin, would agree, but he thinks some premarital independence is nevertheless beneficial to all parties:

> I lived too long with my parents. I know that [navigating marriage] is easier for parents and children if you separate from them for some time. I could have lived alone earlier. Generally speaking, I believe that living separately and then moving in together after the wedding has had a positive influence on us.

Father Bernardo, a priest from Guadalajara, told me that it's easier to transition to marriage in Mexico than in some other locales, since you're not used to doing what you want—because you live with your family. You're not independent. If you're 28 or 30 and you're unmarried, some independence and distance from your parents (via marriage) looks attractive. If you get used to living alone—and like it—it's a little harder to transition to married life. José Luis, a 26-year-old civil engineer from the same city, has been dating his girlfriend for eight years. He looks forward to both marriage and to moving out of his childhood home: "The first thing that attracts me is what I will be getting rid of—the way in which I live with my parents in my house. Because there are certain restrictions, rules, dealing with everyone, which is nice, but it is not always ideal."

Experiment with Prudent, Targeted State Investment in Marriage

All things considered, it might seem that this eighth suggestion—targeted state investment in marriage—is too risky and may do more harm than good, as we're talking about state intervention into something many consider sacred. I disagree with that perspective, insofar as marriage policy and family law are focused on actual marriage, rather than whatever sexually involved arrangement people dream up. Still, it is notoriously difficult to stimulate marriage via public policy. Some strategies are too expensive—especially when recovering from deep economic crises—or are too ambitious, yielding returns that seem modest in light of the costs. It's hard to know which will succeed, and how much success we ought to expect. So why not experiment?

The Oklahoma Marriage Initiative, one of the more well-known American state-level involvements in marriage, met limited success in its seventeen-year run and was suspended in 2016. Although hardly unhelpful, the initiative did not succeed in moving Oklahoma well down the list of states known for its high divorce rate. (Its ranking is currently third among the fifty.) Louisiana's experiment with "covenant marriage," which—among other things—makes it more difficult for the parties to divorce, has remained an opt-in possibility for marrying couples. Few elect it, however. We can blame our psychological preference for convenience; if significant thought is required to consider an option, the default choice nearly always wins.[31]

The seven countries in this study varied widely in marriage law but had in common that they seldom directly targeted marriage for subsidized investment.[32] Nigeria is in the toughest fiscal shape to do such a thing, so its population can only wish. And they do. Abraham, a 25-year-old self-employed and unmarried Methodist, believes his government could do a variety of things to encourage marriage in Nigeria: "Provision of job opportunities, job security. The government should be able to give, provide employment for the youth and for the general public." It's a pipe dream shared with other interviewees from Lagos, including Genevieve, the 25-year-old unmarried caterer: "Looking at developed countries, they give [their people] basic welfare; they have a strong social institution that caters to the welfare of their citizens," she pointed out. "So in a country like Nigeria, you can't just compare. We don't have job security, livelihood zero—so we just cannot compare."

Can Rewarding Fertility Stimulate Marriage?

State-sponsored marriage incentives are uncommon. More popular are fertility incentives. But insofar as marriage remains linked to childbearing—as is the case in several sites—supporting fertility may yet aid the marital impulse. Christians in Lagos, for example, still strongly associate childbearing with marriage; it's a package deal. (It's less true in the United States.) The idea of bringing children into the world in an unmarried setting there was almost unthinkable.[33] This sentiment was echoed by Solomon, a 26-year-old Catholic working in advertising on the more prosperous Victoria Island section of Lagos: "When people are not getting married, there will be no re-production. You understand?" I got the impression that Nigerians need not be active in their faith to agree on this matter.

And yet fertility rates typically increase only modestly when policymakers try to incentivize births.[34] Poland, however, is hoping that modestly is good enough as it works to turn around its dismal rate. Low Polish fertility is something of a conundrum, given the country's high marriage rate and conservative Catholic reputation. Other factors that might explain low birth rates elsewhere (like high unemployment or expensive housing) aren't applicable here. In theory, Poland ought to be exhibiting rates among the highest in Europe. But the opposite is the case.[35]

In response, its Family 500+ program, a 2016 initiative still in operation, rewards families with 500 złoty (around $130 USD) every month for each child. So, the more children in a family, the larger the family's monthly windfall. (Payments are higher for special-needs children.) As might be expected, then, far more Polish interviewees (than those from other sites) were bullish on incentive programs when asked if their government was doing anything to help with families and marriages. For Szymon, the married computer programmer from Lublin, the program is a real motivator, and he intends to capitalize on it: "I haven't experienced it yet, because I've got only one child. But it's a huge incentive."[36] Pawlina was likewise positive about the program, as well as another one, Housing for the Young, that aims to assist young Polish adults in securing affordable housing:

> [The policies] motivate people that maybe [family life] won't be so bad, that we will get married and have some money to maintain the children who will appear. . . . So we don't have to live with our parents for the rest of our life, but we can get married and try to do something on our own.

Szymon and Pawlina exhibited appreciation for their government's interest in the family lives of its people. It was a rare interviewee in other countries who felt the same way. Most perceived their government as either disinterested or positively seeking to undermine marriage (typically by endorsing same-sex marriage). But Pawlina's outlook is optimistic, even, as she described growing family size among her friends and peers:

I've recently been under the impression that people, when it comes to children, didn't decide to have bigger families for some time, within recent
years . . . because they lacked financial resources. . . . But now an increase in
such families can be observed. I can see in my district, among my friends,
that women give birth to children and then they are pregnant again, and
these families are much bigger.

Some in Poland, however, feel that the 500+ income is largely nullified by
rising costs. One of these is Agata, a 23-year-old (civilly) married veterinary
physiotherapist. "Fine, they've just given the 500+ benefit. So what?" she
scoffed. "All prices have risen. Even the insurance for the car has doubled."
She is also skeptical of her government's intentions with the program, perceiving unfair preferential treatment:

What if a couple has only one child, lives modestly, earns [the minimal
average salary], has to pay bills, and has to pay for day care because they
both work? They won't receive 500+ and are even in a worse situation than
before [the new program]. So, it seems to me that the government doesn't
really care.

But back to our original question: Can rewarding fertility stimulate marriage? Let's look at the data in Poland's case. Second and third births have certainly risen, while the total fertility rate has increased from 1.29 to 1.42.[37] The
program has also done a good deal to reduce child poverty in Poland.[38] But
will this improve the marriage rate? Maybe. It's too early to assess it, but I am
eager for the day the numbers come in. If Polish marriage rates since 2016
prove to have remained stable, climbed, or slid at a slower rate than those
of their neighbors, I'd consider any of those scenarios a signal of success.
(For what it's worth, Poland's northeastern neighbor Belarus is experiencing
a baby boom—and larger families—signaling what analysts are calling a
"retraditionalization" there.)[39]
    There are reasons why paying for fertility may not ultimately stimulate
marriage, but I see few reasons to think it would *harm* marriage.[40] Such
programs are a vote of confidence in the goodness of children. And since
having—and affording—a family remains a central motivation to marry,
among Christians and non-Christians alike, marriage rates may, indeed,
benefit.

There are, at the same time, legitimate worries about increasing the tax burden on unmarried and/or childless citizens in order to encourage family formation. The demographer authors of *Understanding Family Change and Variation* see this as a stumbling block to higher fertility in Poland's neighbor Germany: "The burden of [additional] taxes adds to the economic difficulty of younger adults and works against timely family formation." Hence, "even well-intentioned family policies," they observe, can have "antenatal consequences."[41] By contrast, the American system is not more profamily in its policies, but it makes up for it with greater opportunity for shift work, lower taxes, and more available day-care options.

In 2007, the Russian government, concerned about low fertility and its long-term effects on economic growth, began offering a one-time payment of around 450,000 rubles (equivalent to $9,600 USD in 2007) to families with more than one child. Money from the program—coined Maternity Capital—is not provided in cash but can be applied (via bank transfer) toward housing, a mother's pension, and/or children's education.[42] And yet family sizes remain small. Today, only 8 percent of Russian families have three or more children.

Fewer Russians than Poles brought up their government's fertility incentive program. Why is the Russian effort less popular and less effective? Because of the amount and the method: Poland not only offers more money but also pays it directly to the family as supplemental income with no use limitations. Moreover, the Russian program is forgettable because it is offered once, not monthly, and it is not repeated upon a successive birth. Viktor, the 29-year-old clinical psychologist from Moscow, was only vaguely aware of the Russian government's efforts: "I've heard that there are some programs . . . of material support when children are born, in particular the second child, the 'Maternity Capital,' if I am not mistaken, something like that."

The aid would be welcome, especially given the rising cost of living. Many of Moscow's middle class residents are economically squeezed, to say nothing of the working class and poor, and want no more than one or two children. My visit to a typical two-earner flat in suburban Moscow revealed a sparse and aging Soviet-era infrastructure, with little privacy or space for adding a child, let alone more than one. (Larger families there are more likely to be Muslim than Orthodox.) At the conclusion of the Soviet era, this small apartment would have been deeded by the state to its occupant, who was then free to sell, stay, or rent it out. In 2017, it rented for $450 USD per month and would sell for around $100,000. Average earnings in Moscow, however, fluctuate significantly and stood at just over $1,200 per month in 2018.[43] Not many can imagine fitting a multiple-child family into that scenario. "It's just, well, I don't know. It's just some kind of cynical mockery," said one Russian interviewee describing the government's profertility efforts. "I don't think that anything will change. We have a general problem with the social sector in our country. Both the pension system and social security. And healthcare. And education. It's no secret to anyone."

Indeed, in many of the most prosperous global cities, incomes—and apartments—are inadequate for even small families to enjoy a good quality of life. American urban dwellers in such expensive locales as San Francisco, Seattle, and Portland seem to fare no better. Cities—where the jobs are—are increasingly the haunts of the childless and single. Joel Kotkin, a modern-day authority on global political and social trends, maintains that housing costs are the key driver of delayed marriages in most of the world's cities.[44] However, he also considers housing a soluble problem, something that governments can help with—whether that's in zoning to add flexibility to housing design and density or requirements for additional green space (for family use).

Other "indirect effects" policy ideas on marriage include "wage subsidies," wherein workers would receive, for example, half the difference between the market wage (what they're paid) and the target (or living) wage, with the government depositing the subsidy amount directly into paychecks. Like Poland's 500+ program, the wage subsidy defies conventional labeling as conservative or progressive, free market or statist. Oren Cass, senior fellow at the Manhattan Institute, argues this idea as a substitute for the bounteous tax windfalls governments often provide to large companies willing to relocate to their state or country (in return for the promise of good jobs).[45] Such a subsidy diminishes inequality—without government interference or bloat—by diverting tax revenue from higher earners and directing it straight to the paychecks of lower earners. As is evident conceptually and in reality, marriageable men are employed men who earn a living wage—a moral and Christian notion.[46] So far, a wage subsidy only exists in theory, not reality.

Whether it's by way of cash for families or lower-wage workers, or subsidized mortgage rates for young couples, there are creative ways to enable more young people to envision themselves married and flourishing.

Countries and localities know better what might work where, and what's prone to fail. I just think experimenting to aid marriages—the building block of good societies—is a risk worth taking if economic circumstances permit it.

Conclusion

There are ways to stimulate marriage among Christians, and this chapter highlights eight of them. Some of them come from listening to this project's interviewees, while others have emerged from my own observations over the past decade.

First, we have compelling narratives about marriage. Human persons are, at bottom, story followers who are capable of being talked into, or out of, a marriage. There are a great many beautiful stories about marriage out there. Tell them. Second, let's cultivate marriage-friendly subcultures. This is tough to do today, however, since an emergent global "monoculture" diminishes the value of marriage and family. Some Christians and their congregations or parishes locate their efforts here in a recollection of local or national history—often connected to song and dance. Others manage to find it in a small-group experience with some component of commitment. Third, parents must bring the message of positive subculture home with them. Construct the home as a haven from the market mentalities of the world around you.

Fourth, seek improvement in marriage preparation. Our premarital programs need to be renewed and refashioned for the digital age. We can no longer bank on the stability of marriages around us to foster new couples. These young lovers need tools and the skills to use them to create and sustain a strong union from the beginning.

A fifth piece of advice is to aid suffering marriages in our midst. For many, marriage is more a source of suffering than they had anticipated. Can we help them understand that this doesn't mean the union ought to be canceled? Standards and expectations for marriage are high. Probably too high. But there is such a thing as the good-enough marriage, and it merits wide support. Sixth, parents need to be mindful of the advice they give (or fail to offer) their young adult children. Seventh, young adult children ought to weigh the costs and benefits of living at home until they are married. This sounds like heresy to the American ear, and there are good reasons to commend independence. Living away from home, however, is hardly an obvious good and shouldn't be assumed as such.

Finally, governments ought to consider creative ways to support marriage. Given the longstanding connection between fertility and marriage in much of the West and Global South, fostering fertility may also help our unions. The financial costs, of course, can run high, and nations may find such programming unsustainable. But I'm a fan of experimentation in search of the common good. It is far riskier to ignore the decline of marriage than to try out new ways to stimulate it.

7

The Future of Christian Marriage

Marriage rates in much of the West have been in decline for nearly forty years. The median age at first marriage for women has surged recently until it is now—in many places—over age 30, after fertility has begun to diminish. Given that many men and women still marry in order to start a family, this development is ironic. Why all this has happened in a few short decades is a question that has generated lots of answers, only some of which partially satisfy.

One answer that hasn't received attention is that fewer and fewer people are interested in participating in what marriage actually *is*. While few people marry without affection—and we rightly question those who do—marriage is still, at bottom, about the mutual provision and transfer of resources within a formalized sexual union. "All in all, if the basis of marriage is specialization and exchange," wrote the late UCLA demographer Valerie Oppenheimer, "then marriage seems an increasingly anachronistic social form."[1] She's right about the exchange part—and declining marriage rates appear to reinforce her point. But marriage is what it is. It's not *changing*; it's *receding*. Fewer people want it in an era of increasing technology, gender equality, expectations, and secularization.[2] But that doesn't mean a new kind of *marriage* will ultimately succeed it.

In a misguided attempt at discerning the legal meaning of marriage, University of Arizona law professor Barbara Atwood writes that "the declining marriage rate in the United States reflects the changing nature of the institution."[3] Atwood almost gets it right, but she has misplaced a few words. A more accurate statement would be that the declining marriage rate in the United States—and elsewhere—reflects changing *interest* in the nature of the institution. Its nature hasn't changed.

I didn't write this book as an act of protest or to resist changes in marriage laws. I am merely observing that when we expect the institution of marriage to change too much or bend to our wishes, we shouldn't be surprised to find it stubborn. Instead, fewer people are marrying, and I expect that pattern to accelerate rather than slow, at least for a time. A 2014 Urban Institute report estimates that up to 31 percent of American women and 35 percent of men born in 1990 will not marry by age 40.[4]

This is happening despite—or perhaps because of—how positive modernity has been for families. Higher average incomes, better health, and longer lives are good things, even though these are unevenly distributed (as always) and still greet us with seeds of unintended consequences. We can search widely and quickly for a mate now, and relationship possibilities are far more numerous. And yet these do not appear to reliably contribute to more settled relationships and higher marriage rates. On the contrary, they make for pickier people, and—for the manipulative—more sexual opportunity well short of commitment. Marriage, in turn, recedes. We seem to be creeping in the direction of relational autonomy. We're alone even when we're together.[5] Christians certainly differ from these patterns, but only by degree.

When Marriage Is Embattled, Can It Thrive?

Sociologists of religion have long studied the social influence of religion, but they have been of two minds about how such influence operates in the lives of adherents. One model of influence has been dubbed the "moral communities" theory, which argues that any impact of religion (positive or negative) on individuals' own personal behavior is felt or experienced more powerfully when that religion is widely practiced and socially affirmed. When this theory is applied to the study of Christian marriage, the logic goes something like this:

1. The expectations of Christianity about marital behavior are demanding.
2. It's easier to fulfill such expectations when they are shared among the general population.
3. Hence, the influence of my own personal religiousness on my marital behavior depends in part on my peers' beliefs and behavior.
4. As others around me cease exhibiting religiosity—as well as commitment to marriage—it becomes more difficult for me to stay committed to either one.

This is the moral communities effect: community norms that are in step with your personal beliefs enable you to accomplish your goals more effectively than you could on your own. It means, then, that churchgoing Christians are more apt to meet someone marriage minded, marry, have children, and remain married when more of their immediate peers and neighbors exhibit similar behaviors and beliefs.

The moral communities theory has the advantage of making logical sense. It builds on what we know about people—that they are powerfully influenced by peer pressure, at every age, and they are keenly oriented toward what is normative in their community. (In general, people want to be normal more than they want to be good.) If underage drinking is normal in a community, then we're more apt to allow our own adolescent children to do it. If it's normal to marry before age 25, then we're likely to do just that. If divorce is endemic around us, we've got plenty of exit examples to follow when our own marriage hits the rocks.[6] If splitting is rare, however, we're more apt to suck it up and hang in there, even if we're unhappy.

A second, quite different theory could be labeled the "embattled and thriving" model. It quite simply predicts the opposite. This theory, when applied to Christianity and marriage, would go something like this:

1. The expectations of Christianity about marital behavior are demanding.
2. The majority of people around me, including many Christians, don't live up to it.
3. But this ought not surprise me; we are in a struggle between what's right and what's popular.
4. An identity forms, and personal resolve strengthens, in part, due to perceptions that I am part of an "embattled" minority.

Moral communities theory holds that Christians are more apt to marry (and model Christian marriage traits) when lots of their peers are marrying, too. The embattled-and-thriving theory, however, thinks the opposite has a good chance—that it's when you perceive yourself surrounded by resistance that the influence of Christian faith becomes most evident. Tough times make for resilient Christians. The embattled-and-thriving theory would expect that serious young adult Christians within a largely secular population yawning at matrimony would perceive marriage as even more worthy of their careful attention than if they were mere drones in a large hive of conformity.

What do the data say? It's impossible to settle the question by way of talking to a couple hundred people (as we have done here), but the weight of evidence collected so far would seem to fall on the side of the moral communities theory. There is little qualitative evidence from the interviews that churchgoing Christians are systematically and consistently thumbing their noses at the marital norms around them by (1) marrying at younger ages, (2) marrying in spite of uncertainty about economic circumstances, (3) expressing more modest expectations for marriage, and/or (4) firmly resisting the impulse to cohabit or at least to commence a premarital sexual relationship. Some interviewees have done (or intend to do) all of these, but it would be false to suggest it is a majority that does so.

The embattled-and-thriving theory, if accurate, should reveal that it does not matter what the wider population does regarding marriage—because it would either not affect Christians or might even make their resolve stronger. But I see no wide evidence to support this optimistic conclusion. First, while there is a marriage market for, say, ultraorthodox Jews and for Mormons, there is no such thing as the "Christian" marriage market. They mix in with the wider marriage market. What affects that market affects them. This alone makes for far greater uncertainty among single Christians hoping to pair up. Second, most interviewees seemed quite sensitive to what is going on around them. One thing they mentioned consistently was their hope for good exemplars, as discussed in Chapter 6. They found it easier to do what they believed was right when they were not alone in making the relevant choices. Yana, a 27-year-old Muscovite who coordinates interactive workshops in science, knows something of the challenges of living a Christian life while married to an atheist. She captured the essence of the moral communities theory: "If everyone around [me] prays, then I pray. If everyone around is watching a movie, playing with toys, reading, or staring into the computer screen, I find it very hard to distance myself from it and do my own things."

The moral communities theory carries with it a variety of implications. It suggests that what affects marriage—state and national policies, as well as local norms—affects everyone, including Christians who might think they don't care what the government says. But what about the believers who find strength in their embattled position and work together to "circle the wagons"? It's an impulse many certainly feel. The problem is that true resistance is not a momentary act. It lives or dies by the level of steadfast commitment to doing things differently than your peer group day in and day out. This is far easier imagined than accomplished in reality. What's more, pulling away from what has become normative in society often yields alienation that makes normal life among one's fellow citizens more and more burdensome. No—being embattled is not a recipe for sustainable thriving. The future of

Christian marriage is tightly linked to the future of marriage in general. That means marriage is far from a private matter.

Marriage Is a Public Matter

My wife and I recently celebrated our twenty-fifth wedding anniversary. Planning how we would mark the occasion was left to my discretion. Maybe I should have taken her on a vacation—a second honeymoon of sorts. Instead, I planned a gathering of a few dozen friends at our house. Perhaps I'm cheap, but one of the key reasons I did so is that I think of our marriage as a public thing, even if few people actually know the inner workings of our marital life. My marriage, I hold, is an entity with ramifications and consequences that echo outside our home. The same is true in reverse: what happens in other marriages can affect ours. A marriage needs friends, and it can likewise supply friendship to others' unions.

It matters profoundly whether a society understands marriage as a public concern or merely a private matter. If marriage were simply and only a private matter, would there still need to be laws about it? Absolutely. Even an antimarriage activist like Clare Chambers is right about one thing: there's no getting away from public oversight of relationship and family matters. A marriage-free state would have no choice but to regulate romantic relationships and family ties in order "to protect vulnerable parties, to settle matters and disputes . . . and to ensure justice."[7] So breaking up marriage's privilege is a recipe for an unruly mess that would only extend state regulation ever further into our private lives. Chambers calls her idea "piecemeal regulation." In reality, it would be a zoo. (Even the early Soviets saw that coming.)[8] Priests, pastors, elders, or church councils would be in no position to regulate all the matters that would erupt within their flocks. Even Jesus refused to serve as a mediator between siblings on a point of inheritance law.[9] In other words, if marriage becomes a "private" matter, no relationship will actually be so. There won't be less regulation, but far more.

Few Christians spend much time thinking about whether marriage is fundamentally public or private—including many leaders and certainly most of my interviewees. Young adult Christians are not lacking intelligence about marriage, as revealed by their answers to the question about what marriage *is* (see Chapter 2), but the default mode is to consider marriage a private matter (with some public manifestations). The wedding is a public event, but the marriage itself is considered nobody's business. Decisions to divorce are private, though they entail public legal filings, and declarations, social shifts in relationship status, the creation of distinctive households, and so on. Westerners tend to minimize these public aspects of divorce, expecting little to no objection from others. Most do not share the perspective of Jessica—the 31-year-old engaged woman from Austin—who imagines marriage as creating circles that ripple out "to the extended family, to the community, to the nation, and to the entire society."

But that is exactly what marriage does—it creates concentric circles by building families, connecting generations, and forming friendships. Yana, quoted earlier in this chapter, similarly characterizes marriage as a public phenomenon by likening it to "a small reactor, a small power plant that produces more than enough energy to illuminate and warm itself." She continued: "I love it very much when a family is set so well, that this resource, this heat, that is inside, is also enough to bring it out, share with loved ones, distant relatives, at work, in the subway, in the street, in a shop." Yana's reactor metaphor is clever. But consider also what can happen inside a reactor if it is *not* maintained: a ruptured core and explosion that can contaminate everything around it.

Divorce severs far more than a solitary marriage, even if the union has yielded no children. In-laws are commonly cut off from an ex-spouse, and friends often wind up forced to pick sides. I'm not saying all marriages must endure. I'm simply observing that marriage is a public matter at least as much as it is a private one. I'm not only referring to its legal ramifications in the public sphere, like tax laws and inheritances. I'm saying it has extensive social ramifications in others' lives.

Confusion about the public aspects of marriage has led some Christians to support civil (but not religious) same-sex marriage.[10] For Thomas, the 30-year-old married Catholic telecommunications manager from Austin, civil marriage is "a contract to live together and reap benefits from the state." What he's saying is that marriage is fundamentally a private matter, with some public ramifications. And he's content with extending the benefits to alternative arrangements: "Basically, any two people can get married, which is fine, because you turn it into a contract."

This understanding enables Thomas to ignore much of the conflict between modern civil marriage and his faith's sacramental understanding of the union. "So kind of my argument is to get the government out of the marriage business," he explained, "and have it just be the church" (which doesn't account for the "contract" he just endorsed, which some entity must regulate). Thomas's idea allows him to operate at ease in a world where marriage is thought of as socially constructed—malleable. He can passively assent to civil marriage laws (which he holds should not exist):

> It's fine. It is what it is. Like I said, if they truly love each other and they want to live together, so be it. You can call it marriage, because that's what the government calls that, but ultimately, you know, the true believer of Christ knows that real marriage is based on natural law.

Thomas acknowledges that his coworkers would squabble with his distinction between what they consider marriage and the sacrament he considers "real marriage." But the tension is seldom, if ever, recognized (or addressed). This quiet enables him to acquiesce to whatever civil marriage definition holds, while retaining a religious definition in his heart. To fight over it is pointless, he figures, since "the Supreme Court has determined we're going to call it marriage, and that's what it's going to be."[11] Thomas knows that some other Christians are more perturbed about the matter than he is, but he finds a disinterested stance more reasonable: "I mean, the Church is actively fighting it, I guess, but I think it's futile, because it doesn't matter what the law says. Ultimately the Church hasn't changed." The law, however, is a teacher. It matters that American marriage law now teaches none of the core and supporting expectations that appear in Figure 3.1. Thomas is right about one thing: marriage has been reduced (in the United States) to a symbol and set of benefits. He's mistaken about another—that it doesn't matter.

Geoff, the 24-year-old Baptist from Austin, differs from Thomas in his opinion about state involvement in marriage. The state, he holds, has too much invested in the kinds of positive byproducts of marriage to just step out of the way now:

> I think the government should care about marriage because of economic reasons, because of societal reasons, because when you have a society where marriages are flourishing, you're inevitably going to have a society that is flourishing in other areas. . . . People who are married earn more, and they perform better in their work. They live longer. They build families and reproduce, which carries on the society and makes society more stable. So government should care about marriage.

Christians like Geoff will continue to dispute social change in civil marriage forms, while others (like Thomas) will take the libertarian route, that is, press for the state to get "out of the marriage business." An identical pattern has already emerged, or else will soon, in many other countries where there is comparable divergence between civil and religious marriage and a similar perspective on marriage as a (largely) private matter.

But libertarianism is not viable on this count. Again, we learn from the natural experiment detailed in Chapter 4: the early Soviet sexual revolution was undergirded by an explicitly libertarian approach to marriage. It minimized marriage law, recognized the "fluidity of personal relationships," and tried not to favor one union over another, stressing, as Goldman observed of 1920s Russia, "the right of the individual to be free of state interference."[12] It was a fiasco then, and it won't work now, so long as human beings act in predictable ways.

Christians who hold that marriage can recede around them without threatening their own—or their children's—commitment to a historically consistent understanding of marriage are unfortunately mistaken. It is a little like saying advertising doesn't work on me—it only affects other people. Such an escape from persistent influence is only conceptually possible. In lived social reality, that won't happen.[13]

How Central Is Marriage to the Future of Christianity?

Columnist Rod Dreher makes a compelling case in *The Benedict Option* that to cast off Christian teaching on sex and sexuality is to remove the factor that gives, or gave, Christianity its power as a social force.[14] Leaning on the work of the late sociologist and cultural critic Philip Rieff, Dreher maintains that "renouncing the sexual autonomy and sensuality of pagan culture was at the core of Christian culture—a culture that, crucially, did not merely renounce but redirected the erotic instinct. That the West was rapidly re-paganizing around sensuality and sexual liberation was a powerful sign of Christianity's demise."[15]

Although nothing seems so primal as sex, I would submit that marriage is even more central than sex to the future of Christianity.[16] The two are related, no doubt, but they're not the same. Consider the public nature of marriage and cohabitation versus the private nature of sex.

Sex is old news. Premarital intimacy (with and without pregnancy) has a very long history in the annals of Christian marriage.[17] Cohabitation, on the other hand, has a much shorter history within Christianity. And it's far more publicly apparent than is sexual intercourse. Dreher argues that "when people decide that historically normative Christianity is wrong about sex, they typically don't find a church that endorses their liberal views. They quit going to church altogether."[18] But they're more apt to quit going to church altogether *together*—that is, when they're cohabiting.

You can live your entire life thinking the your church is too restrictive on sexual matters, and it can remain a private rebellion in your mind. You can also live your life intermittently unchaste—and there's a decent chance that no one you wish to hide it from will find out. Many people do both of these. But living with someone you aren't married to but are in a sexual relationship with is by definition public. Not trying to hide. It is therefore "scandalous," to use the Catholic term, meaning it is not just personally wrong but publicly corrosive to the conduct of fellow believers (Luke 17:1).

Many Christians have long bristled (privately) under Christianity's sexual ethics, and marriage has been the institution that makes them "fit," even if awkwardly. This is exactly why I think Dreher's observation is not simply about sex. In Justyna's, Monika's, and Mateusz's cases, marrying is what they wanted to do and did, which also made their own sexual activities licit to their families and church communities.

My point here is that, ultimately, it is (public) cohabitation, and not simply (private) sexual activity, that is more corrosive to the social practice of Christianity. This is because cohabitation mimics, and arguably mocks, marriage, tacitly encouraging others to endorse the imitation by publicly recognizing the union, to say nothing of the tendency for the cohabiters themselves to leave the faith, at least for a time. Sexual intercourse, on the other hand, doesn't mimic something—you're either doing it or you're not. But you can feign marriage by exhibiting its exchange characteristics—including sex—while failing to endorse one or more of its central supports: fidelity, totality, children, and permanence.

Carlos, a 30-year-old engineer who now works for a Christian nonprofit organization in Mexico City, thinks marriage has not changed at all. What has shifted, he maintains, is the new ability of persons to mimic most of what marriage once encompassed and circumscribed. Aspects of cohabitation, such as mutual responsibilities, are "similar [to marriage] . . . but the bond is not the same." Marriage, on the other hand, involves "really committing, and looking to have and create a family with the other person." Carlos thinks premarital sex "lightens the commitment. That is, it's easier for people not to get married, because they get that more easily, more simply." This situation, as I noted earlier, is hardly new. What's new is the couple's bid for social support from fellow Christians for their marriage-like relationships.

Similarly novel (and more so) is the rapid surge in support for same-sex relationships. This shift composes the core of Dreher's argument about the death of Christianity as "a culturally determinative force."[19] But again, gay and lesbian sexual relations are private. As such, institutional Christianity has long tolerated (but not endorsed) the existence of such relations. Some Christians, and a few Christian denominations, have pressed for the normalization of same-sex sexual activity, and the matter now constitutes a central cleavage between mainline and evangelical Protestantism as well as orthodox and progressive Catholicism. But the sexual activity is still private. It is the public nature of same-sex marriage that prompts far greater angst. That's because it would seem to counterfeit marriage, even if a large majority of citizens or a plurality of judges or lawmakers consider it a socially constructible civil reality. How so?

Unlike cohabitation—which thwarts only marriage's four supporting bonds—same-sex unions undermine the core of marriage: the sexual union that marks the exchange relationship characterized by sexual difference. Justyna's, Monika's, and Mateusz's cohabiting unions could be made into marriages. But even if a gay couple covenanted to not pursue sexual activity with other people, sought to have children by alternative means, treated their union as comprehensive, and remained together until death—that is, if they successfully upheld the four key supports—they would still not have exhibited what marriage is at its core. This is why a major frame shift—not to mention a significant media and public-relations effort—has to occur in countries for same-sex marriage to be thinkable, then exhibited in a variety of locales, marketed to fellow citizens, and finally endorsed by a majority. But this is also why its civil achievement—as a social construction—will remain tentative and require consistent reinforcement and endorsement in a way that heterosexual cohabitation will not, because the core of marriage will remain missing.

Since they're far more numerous than same-sex relationships, how premarital heterosexual relationships are channeled toward marriage will remain a more persistent ongoing risk to Christian churches. Treating them as licit relationships will not serve the long-term health of Christian churches, even though this is what many cohabiters seem to prefer. That includes Justyna, who wishes the Catholic Church would exhibit a formal tolerance of such unions. If they did, she holds, more people would attend Mass. However, when religious organizations privilege social support (how can we reinforce what you wish to do) over social control (maybe you're better off not doing that), this yields fewer Christians equipped and prepared to do difficult things (like chastity . . . or sacrificial giving . . . or loving one's enemies). Christianity is, as journalist and apologist G. K. Chesterton popularly asserted, nothing if not difficult.[20] But there is a comfort found in clear norms that are consistently and fairly enforced. Indeed, like many Catholics (especially outside the United States), Justyna enforces the existing rules herself: she elects not to receive the Eucharist when she attends Mass. Many others in her state simply leave, perhaps returning of their own accord after marriage and childbearing.[21]

Some nevertheless hold out hope that we will witness a new *aggiornamento* on marriage and divorce. That is, that Christian leaders—in response to the behavior patterns of the people—will alter Christian teachings on marriage and the domains nearest to it: sexuality, sexual behavior, divorce, and childbearing and rearing. I doubt this will occur on a wide scale. But two things are already happening, and they're nearly as effective here as a shift in Christian doctrine.

First, there is a significant recession in religious authority and practice in much of the West. Clergy have witnessed their authority diminished, fed by sexual-abuse scandals that continue to reverberate through congregations and the public consciousness. Second, leaders are actively choosing to run silent, or at least quieter, on issues of marriage and sexuality to avoid sounding "controversial" or alienating the noncompliant. But to *say* nothing is not to *convey* nothing; their silence communicates complicity—though its source is actually timidity. Christian leaders seem increasingly afraid to acknowledge objective reality—which is irrational, given that their life's work is devoted to its proclamation. These twin developments—diminished authority coupled with fear of acknowledging reality—will undermine Christian understanding on marriage and sexuality almost as effectively as any formal *aggiornamento* could.

After Familism

Something significant has happened around the institution of marriage, to which the statistics displayed in Chapter 1's tables are a response. Many sociologists, including scholars of marriage, would nevertheless dispute my claim that something big has occurred at all. They would respond that people are simply getting married a bit later and that in some locales, long-term cohabitation is replacing formal marriage. But it's certainly nothing to be concerned about. In fact, they assure, wherever you see these phenomena happening, good economies, better human rights, and greater overall flourishing seem to follow in their footsteps.

I'm not so sure the causal order works like that. What if the West's vibrant economies, political stabilities, and legacy of recognizing genuine human rights have persisted—in part—because of the world that monogamous marriage (rooted in and reinforced by Christianity) helped make possible?[22] What if the West is living off the fumes of the countless sacrifices that husbands and wives, mothers and fathers, have been making for many decades—not because they always adored their spouse but because they understood that sacrifice is what marriage entails and is what is expected of them? What if we are now slowly dismantling a key social structure upon which the West's successes have been built, leaving us now far more vulnerable than we yet realize? Some argue the dismantling started long before demographers ever noticed it in the statistics about marriage and divorce. Where marriage is headed might be glimpsed by seeing where we've come from.

Familism, in its simplest sense, is a social structure wherein the family is prioritized over the individual in practice, norm, and law. Familism is not a term used by most people, though the idea carries a long history. Assumed within familism (or familialism, as some call it) are convictions about the reality of sexual difference between men and women, as well as the importance of mothers and fathers in the lives of their children. I'm neither interested in defending nor impugning familism here. I wish, instead, to talk about its significance—what it is, or was, and what it means that it is no more.

Familism is more than a mentality or pattern of behavior, such as the impulse to "put your family first." It is also not confined to that era in which "the family's importance in socialization" had not yet notably declined or in which the family was apt to be a more "closely knit unit," to cite David Riesman's observations in *The Lonely Crowd*.[23] Familism is bigger and more primal than that. In familism, the family is more important than its constituent components—those persons who compose it. Familism was a social *system*—the order of things. It was the air you breathed, even if some (or many) disliked it and resisted. Employers understood and affirmed marriage. The law privileged it. Peers expected it. Women and children were more vulnerable to strangers apart from it (and more vulnerable to husbands and fathers within it). Certainly sex differences characterized it and perhaps magnified it.

Many women flourished under familism, despite assumptions to the contrary. Economists Betsey Stevenson and Justin Wolfers are well known for documenting the paradoxical decline in women's happiness over the past four decades. It's a paradox, they say, because their happiness receded despite social, technological, and educational shifts that advantaged women and that were widely believed to have made them happier.[24] Perhaps these shifts only made some women happier, at the expense of others. And perhaps the collapse of familism as part of the cause is worth a look.

There is ample evidence of how far familism has receded in the past century. In American family law, the individual matters—not their unions—and since the early 1970s, one spouse can detonate a marriage, entirely apart from the will or interests of the other spouse or even the children. Laws criminalizing adultery have either been scrapped or ignored.

For a different kind of example, the university that employs me continues to add major courses of study—with ever more specific concentrations, including video game production—but offers little to no instruction on how to build a productive family life. (It either must not be very important, or it's considered strictly a private matter.) We no longer provide education in "home economics," that is, those mundane and seemingly intuitive activities that both create and sustain a household—things like money management, solving material problems, and communicating effectively.[25] But these valuable skills are anything but intuitive. To put it memorably, young adults are offered no guidance about maturation, mortgages, or marriage—save for words of caution, counsel to delay, and cost-benefit evaluation.

Meanwhile, our legislatures, courts, and communities are being compelled to ameliorate our neglect of the home. They do so by unwittingly withdrawing responsibilities and duties from parents and, in so doing, penalizing functioning marriages. Antonio, a 34-year-old recently married manager at a small Spanish transportation company in Pamplona, described such a situation to me:

> I know people who have pretended to be separated in order to get their children into a particular school [in Madrid]. Public schools follow a point system. If you live near a school, you get points. If your siblings attend the same school, you get points. Sometimes those criteria include if you're a

single mother or father, with the assumption that if you are together you have more resources to find a good school. I understand the logic behind that, but sometimes you end up promoting separation.

This is just one example of how governments underappreciate the document-able talents and efficiencies of functioning marriages, unwittingly penalizing them so that others are enabled to avoid them altogether.

Familism has been consonant with subsidiarity, an organizing proposition holding that problems should be addressed by the smallest competent social unit. And that smallest competent social unit for many of life's dilemmas and tasks—if even for sheer lack of alternatives—was long the family. For many, those days are over.

Critics of familism are quick to associate it with Christianity, or religion in general, together with political conservatism. This is not a new strategy. In fact, Harvard sociologist Carle Zimmerman heard the same accusations over seventy years ago, noting them in his 1947 omnibus evaluation of the family in social history, entitled *Family and Civilization*.[26] Zimmerman actually anticipated and addressed arguments about—and often against—marriage that wouldn't be floated until decades later. *Family and Civilization* is a rare 1940s book that remains sociologically fascinating and, it would seem, valuable so many years after it first appeared. This is all the more captivating in a discipline that is faddish and obsessed with novelty and criticism. I have not seen its equal in terms of historical and social depth and grasp.[27]

The family, in Zimmerman's perspective, is "a *natural, cumulative*, institutional group, generally so integrated that it has a realism above and different from the separate personalities of its members."[28] How sociological. Furthermore, the family is, for Zimmerman, far from only a private matter:

> It performs the basic functions of procreation, rearing, socialization, protection, and education of the new generation. It tries to make the individual into a person . . . a citizen of the world at large. Through the family, the individual gets the fundamental parts of his social position, his status. . . . The family is held together internally by all the forms of affection which attract one human being to another. On its external side, the family is kept

together by strong systems of mores or beliefs held by members of the community and by systems of law, either common or written (statute).

The late social critic Christopher Lasch noted that Zimmerman wanted to treat the family as interconnected with other social institutions, as distinct from his peers in the sociology of family, who largely perceived the family as an independent domain charged principally with companionate affection. Zimmerman clearly didn't buy it. He paid for his professional misstep thereafter, observing that scholars skeptical about claims that the family was a mere private-sphere matter "are just not considered 'in the groove.' "[29] (Don't I know it.) The public relations strategy leveraged by many of his fellow specialists, he maintained, was intended to undermine family itself, shifting more and more power away from it and toward the state (and the corporation, school, and even the church). The very foundations of social order were being put at risk, he believed. Zimmerman held that a great many social scientists were duplicit—assisting in the transition to individualism while claiming that families were stronger than ever. It spilled over into their sociological training:

> All any college student learned of social science and sociology from the nineteenth century to World War I was a theory of social relativism, the linear "evolution" of society through the nineteenth century, the need for challenging all social institutions including the family, and the possibility of continued improvement through the destruction of accepted values.[30]

The times have not changed.

While individuals can opt to prioritize their own family today, they no longer do so within a familist system, whether they live in Poland or Paraguay. Family no longer enjoys "most favored" status. Its privilege has been checked. How can you tell? Zimmerman offered a series of rhetorical questions that provide the answer:

> Of the total power in the society, how much belongs to the family? Of the total amount of control of action in the society, how much is left for the family? . . . If we want to marry or break up a family, whom do we consult, the family, the church, or the state? If we are in need, to whom do we go, the family or the community? If we violate a rule, who punishes us, the family or the state?[31]

We can add other observations here. Employers increasingly treat employees' partnered relationships equally, and governments, especially but not only in the West, are moving to do the same. Parents counsel their children to finish their education and get a good start on their career first, before giving thought to marriage and family—advice I have heard the world over—while many divorced parents practically beg their children to avoid ever being dependent on a spouse. Together with "widespread uncertainty and ambiguity," Pope Francis notes the threats these developments register as he observes the "extreme individualism which weakens family bonds and ends up considering each member of the family as an isolated unit, leading in some cases to the idea that one's personality is shaped by his or her desires, which are considered absolute."[32]

This is what Zimmerman identified as atomism—the system of extreme individualism that has replaced familism—decades before its effects began to be visible in the data (e.g., in rising divorce rates or declining marriage rates). Despite recurrent and increasingly unfounded concerns about overpopulation, we are actually far more solitary—and many are lonelier—than when the planet exhibited a fraction of its current population. Like familism, atomism is not a system that persons or families can opt out of—or into. This is why Christians aren't able to replicate it in miniature. The most they can do is prioritize their own families. They can no longer expect others, or the organizations which they inhabit, to do the same.

Writing in 2012, Joel Kotkin discerns this shift toward atomism in the West as well as in a variety of developing countries, like Brazil and Iran. Unlike Zimmerman, however, Kotkin believes the development of atomism is more recent—certainly so outside Europe and North America. "The new emerging social ethos," he asserts in his report *The Rise of Post-Familialism*, prioritizes "individual personal socioeconomic success as well as the personal quest for greater fulfilment."[33] It is as if Kotkin had listened in on my team's interviews in every location. He continues, with concern:

> The reasons for this shift are complex, and vary significantly in different countries and cultures. In some countries, particularly in East Asia, the nature of modern competitive capitalism often forces individuals to choose between career advancement and family formation. As a result, these economies are unwittingly setting into motion forces destructive to their future workforce, consumer base and long-term prosperity. The widespread

movement away from traditional values—Hindu, Muslim, Judeo-Christian, Buddhist or Confucian—has also undermined familialism. Traditional values have almost without exception been rooted in kinship relations.[34]

Zimmerman had long before concurred—bluntly—with Kotkin's claim about secularization and the shift away from tradition: "Anyone with the slightest perspective on all these sacred books and religions will know immediately that familism and domestic practices form their main central core."[35] Zimmerman singles out Christianity, however, asserting that by the sixth century, "*familism* was *the theme* of Christianity."[36] By contrast, "periods of atomism of the family are always periods of disbelief [in monotheism]."[37] "Virtually all religions," Kotkin similarly asserts, "are familialistic, and many rituals of religious life involve family."[38] Secularism, he argues, lacks the will to motivate sacrifice on behalf of future generations by appealing to the faith of previous ones. This doesn't characterize every self-identified secularist, of course. Whether Kotkin is right about secularism, time will tell. Recent predictions suggest that secularism's low rate of natural reproduction will limit its spread in the United States.[39] But American Christians' fertility rates are slowing, too.[40]

Some would suppose that Zimmerman would turn to Christianity for the rescue of familism. However, while he maintained that the Christian Church was not a force for atomism, he held that the Church was no longer one of "the directive forces of western society" at all.[41] While John Paul II's successful ecclesial efforts to undermine the Communist Bloc is one piece of evidence to the contrary, there may not be a great deal more. Zimmerman's skepticism of religion's influence here may be merited.

Zimmerman was frequently criticized for his "the sky is falling" attitude, including a critical remark from then-actor Ronald Reagan.[42] But his Harvard colleague Pitirim Sorokin had lamented the rise in atomism even earlier, in 1941:

> The family as a sacred union of husband and wife, of parents and children, will continue to disintegrate. Divorces and separations will increase until any profound difference between socially sanctioned marriages and illicit sex-relationship disappears. Children will be separated earlier and earlier from parents. The main sociocultural functions of the family will further decrease.[43]

The only indicators at the time of the family disintegration Sorokin predicted would have been indirect, in the form of Western art, literature, and film—of which he was a particular critic—as well as the nascent (and comparatively mild) sexual revolution for women (e.g., the "Roaring Twenties").[44] Sorokin in particular impugned American fiction writers of the twenties and thirties for glamorizing "the erotic excesses and disloyalties of their characters as perfectly normal," in contrast to "the great writers of the nineteenth century, like Tolstoy and Flaubert."[45] The former's *Anna Karenina*, considered by many one of the top works of literature ever produced, details the personal and social consequences of desire unshackled.

While it is reasonable to assume that the conservative Zimmerman and Sorokin were philosophically opposed to the changes they were witnessing, it doesn't follow that they were making it up. Zimmerman traced the earliest seeds of atomism's emergence to revolutionary theology and philosophy, then scholarly and popular literature, and finally law. First, the Reformation's squabble over marital oversight was consonant with a general turning away from church authority and toward the individual conscience. But even a Reformational vision of marriage as a semisacred institution was to be further stripped by revolutionary impulses to limit marriage, as Zimmerman observed, to a "private agreement of a secular nature."[46] Second, the French and Russian Revolutions made it clear that the family was to serve state (and individual) interests by way of freeing individuals to more readily enter and exit unions. Nevertheless, marriage among the masses typically rebounded from revolutionary impulses after a period of unsettledness, and the Protestant Reformation did not profoundly reorient the average marriage.

The urbanization prompted by the Industrial Revolution,[47] on the other hand, revealed to men and women how children—a key marital bond—had become net consumers. Fertility rates sank (well in advance of the contraceptive revolution that followed in the late sixties). Social historian Steven Seidman describes a "constellation of social developments" during this time, among them the growth of a national market amid the commercialization of banking and farming.[48] In my own family's case, both of my grandfathers had moved from farm to city (Chicago) by the early 1930s. The America of the small town was in the process of becoming the America of the city, and cities had long been culturally equated with antifamily norms. The family "unit" was becoming a cluster of individuals, and the free market both fostered and responded to this new definition.[49]

Seidman documents the emergence of more liberal intellectual voices about sex education—including Havelock Ellis and sociologists Ernest Burgess and William Ogburn—and also a popular shift in the culture of romance, a turn toward valuing "the sensual and expressive qualities of sex."[50]

A parallel revolution was occurring in family law. Divorces could be had in particular states—Nevada and Indiana were two of them—far more easily than in others, prompting a late-nineteenth-century divorce tourism industry. In an illuminating and innovative study of 1,225 divorce proceedings filed in Los Angeles and New Jersey in the 1880s and the 1920s, social historian Elaine Tyler May detected clear change in what men and women expected of matrimony:

> The marital conflicts that surfaced in the courts of Los Angeles in the 1880s reveal the fundamental principles upon which nineteenth-century marriages rested. Men and women had specific duties and lived with concrete restraints on their behavior and demeanor. Husbands were expected above all to provide adequate support for their families.[51]

By 1920, May detects, the consensus about what spouses expected from marriage and from each other was eroding, in capitalist and communist countries alike, as the Industrial Revolution altered the terms of labor, diminished the productive value of a large family, and shifted families from countryside to city. Divorce was growing (though still uncommon) and justified not because people believed less in marriage, but because they invested it with higher expectations for fulfillment. An unintended consequence was that spouses would no longer be content with a mediocre mate. Hence, the great American quest for marital satisfaction was well underway, long before demographers would note the surge in divorce and decline in marriage, consistently evident starting around 1970.[52]

Today, sociologist Andrew Cherlin argues that marriage is in the throes of deinstitutionalization.[53] But what are the differences between deinstitutionalization, the decline of familism/emergence of atomism, and indicators of the second demographic transition (such as low fertility)? Is everyone talking about the same thing? I don't think so. Cherlin and Zimmerman seem to be addressing a more seismic social shift than the demographers are. But their timetables are different. Zimmerman, and Sorokin with him, argued that familism eroded long before there were signs of the deinstitutionalization of marriage.

The deinstitutionalization of marriage that Cherlin asserts is, hence, not a last stage of receding familism but an advanced stage of atomism. The West's situation is not merely about delaying something that nearly everyone will still do—marriage—and from which most will benefit. Instead, our atomism is issuing forth a rise in solitary living—before, after, and instead of marriage. The number of American adults (of any age) living alone has leaped from 9 percent of households in 1950 to nearly 28 percent by 2018.[54] In Scandinavia, single households are even more common, at 40 to 45 percent of total. In fact, 31 percent of Norwegian adults under age 30 live alone, as do 29 percent of Danes and 27 percent of Swedes.[55]

Marriage is simply much less necessary today, and it is becoming less common by the decade, if not the year. Kotkin perceives beneficiaries of the new solitude—and offers them, and everyone, words of caution:

> Many forces—greens, urban land speculators and some feminists—may see the shift towards childless and single households as either a source of profit or a sign of social progress. Yet post-familialism remains at the most fundamental level demographically and socially unsustainable. In the coming decades, success will accrue to those cultures that preserve the family's place, not as the exclusive unit in society, but as the one truly indispensable for the ages.[56]

"The future of the world and of the Church," Pope John Paul II famously asserted, "passes by way of the family."[57] We underestimate its significance at our peril. If there is to be any newfound esteem for the family over the individual, it will not likely originate in the United States, a nation with deeply atomistic tendencies that have spawned a marriage-go-round.

Predictions

I've made the case that there has been significant upheaval in how the globe's Christian population meander toward marriage. But is there more to say about what may come next? Certainly, though here is where things tend to become more speculative than I prefer. As I said when I made predictions in *Cheap Sex*, the odds are against being right all the time. With that in mind, here are five predictions about Christians and marriage.

First, marriage among Christians will continue to recede some, in step with wider marital patterns and behaviors. The resistance among a minority, however, will become more visible.

Marriage rates have been sliding and the median age at first marriage rising. In the near term, I see nothing to halt that trend among Christians, since most of them consider marriage as much of a capstone as anyone else. But marriage will never disappear, both among Christians and non-Christians. Why? Because companionship, homebuilding, and economic interdependence remain compelling incentives to many. While the core of observed marriage (illustrated in Figure 3.1) is not uniquely Christian, Christians appear to find it and its four key supports more desirable than most—but only by degree. If a Christian marriage were a thing wholly apart from everyone else's marriage, then we would be witnessing far greater disparity in marriage rates and timing than we actually see between the two groups. But there is a gap.

When I think about the nearly two hundred interviewees with whom my team spoke, I come to a much weaker confidence that the average young adult Christian will resist those forces—described in the earlier chapters of this book—that appear to weaken marriage and emaciate family life. It's not that Christian teaching will change much. It won't. It's just that many Christians themselves have become moral libertarians—content to live and let live. What is *possible* (by way of consumer norms, marital expectations, and reproductive technology) becomes more and more *probable* for Christians as time passes.

A minority among them, however, continue to thwart cultural pressures. Almost always these resisters are deeply embedded in Christian communities—small groups, tight-knit congregations, or religious communities. These are the sources of vibrant marital subcultures and will stand out from the surrounding culture. But do not overestimate their size.

Progressive forces have and will continue to prompt the alteration of marriage policies, to thwart religious dissent, make civil marriage's legal boundaries more inclusive, and try to bend its norms and expectations. But this is no long-term strategy. Attempting to alter marriage—while retaining the title—is a losing proposition.

Church leaders—pastors, priests, and bishops—seem to act as if they, too, believe that marriage is fundamentally malleable and, hence, they must fight for a particular vision of it, one that will vary by denomination or tradition. They simply need to stably assert what marriage *is*, and what it will continue to be. If, however, Christian leaders back a fundamentally symbolic and capstone vision of marriage and neglect as central the functional, foundational good of it—what marriage accomplishes—I cannot see how their congregations will ultimately flourish over the long run.

Second, the connection between employment and marriageability will weaken further (without disappearing), because there is far more today to marriageability than there used to be.

The economic evidence for a strong connection between men's employment—both wages and stability—and their movement toward marriage is waning. Employability remains a marker of marriageability in men,[58] but where it was once primary, it's now one indicator among many. Why *so* many? Because in the West, marriage is far more voluntary than ever before; you don't need to marry in order to live a fulfilling, meaningful, prosperous life. That means men and women will be choosier and more apt to insist on a better fit—because they can. For example, a woman wants to marry a conservative Christian who loves God more than he loves her. Fine. But she also expects him to sacrifice for her across a host of domains: he must work, want (or not want) children, support her career, coparent with equality, listen to her with understanding, be her best friend, and defer to her interests when possible. (This is what social psychologist Eli Finkel has dubbed the "suffocation model" of marriage.)[59] Some of these expectations don't become obvious until after the couple marries, which makes for no shortage of compromising, squabbling, and not a little second-guessing. Some depart to try again.

High expectations accompany the capstone vision. Too high, perhaps. Much is expected from normal people with their own strengths and weaknesses. (An exchange model, on the other hand, capitalizes on both strength and weakness by matching deficits in one spouse with skill sets in another, and vice versa.)

Third, the gender revolution will overreach. Marriage will never be successfully, sustainably "queered."

Christians are pretty conventional about marriage, I learned. They don't like to rock the boat. They have high expectations for matrimony, and they don't really like to sacrifice too much. Christians remain pretty conventional about other matrimonial matters, too. Egalitarian marriages are growing among them, typically stimulated by economic need or aspirations. But since strictly egalitarian marriages are unions of two people who really don't trade strengths and weaknesses to build something together that they couldn't achieve by themselves, my bet is on a declining rate of such marriages. Future egalitarians will cohabit longer, marry less often, and spend plenty of time by themselves, because they're able to and because strict egalitarians' relationship standards are among the highest sociologists have encountered. Scandinavian data affirms all three of these.

There is much more to the gender revolution, however, than men adapting to a working wife who wants him to share chores and childrearing. An altogether different operation that has begun to emerge—the slow and steady degendering of relationships and the attempted erasure of sex distinctions altogether—enjoys far fewer endorsements among the faithful. If Christian young adults believed the gender revolution did not involve this surreptitious goal, most of them would perceive the movement as a good fit with their faith. But insofar as they discern this unwritten phase (many don't), most are opposed to it.

Queering means to bend something away from heterosexuality, away from historical-conventional understandings of sex and gender, and to refashion its norms. To successfully queer marriage would cause it to diminish and disappear, and that's not going to happen. Marriage will never successfully be queered by the gender revolution not because of the overwhelming resistance of Christians, but because to queer marriage is to move the union well afield of what it actually *is*. We have civil same-sex marriage because family law is malleable by legislators and judges. But marriage is not encompassed within the bounds of family law. It's not that theological, political, and legal squabbles over marriage are not important. But over the course of decades, the social practice of marriage proves robust, revealing what marriage actually is. Even same-sex marriage, a first stage in queering, will never become popular in the LGBTQ world, because marriage is, at its core, heteronormative. If I am mistaken about all this, the simple passage of time—followed by plenty of critics—will reveal my error. Only three years into nationwide same-sex marriage in the United States, rates of uptake remain a fraction of those among opposite-sex couples.[60]

The degendering of relationships amid the effort to either undermine marriage's significance or to queer it is frustrating not only to many Christians. The recent rightward turn in global politics—not just the United States, but Brazil, Italy, and multiple Central and Eastern European countries—is a signal of dissent here as well. The rise in what are called "nationalist" sentiments is about far more than immigration patterns in Europe and the United States. Rolled up into it is also concern over the attempted hijacking of what a majority understand as common sex differences, together with the legacy of mothers, fathers, their marriages, and family life in having helped bring about long-standing public good and social order. Many Christians and secular conservatives hold that these foundations of Western civilization are openly disparaged today, together with a flattening of culture and blurring of boundaries, all in the ironic name of "diversity." Dissent from this monoculture is increasingly suppressed or subsequently punished. And they resent it. In turn, this resentment—now making its presence felt at ballot boxes around the globe—angers supporters of the gender revolution, who perceive in their opponents' values darker motives, including racism, sexism, homophobia, and fascist intent. This cold war over the meaning and significance of the body, intimate relationships, families, and the survival of local culture is a global one, with much at stake.

Fourth, marriage will slowly but certainly become a religious thing.

The future of marriage is the future of religious marriage, not because faith is required for marriage, but because the faithful seem more interested in living out what marriage *is*.

This fourth prediction follows directly from the first. Insofar as marriage continues to recede universally, but to a lesser degree among active Christians, it will increasingly become a religious thing. Even a modest gap in marriage patterns between the more and less devout will amount to a far more significant difference over several decades. Table 1.2 all but confirms that this will occur.

So is marriage good for Christians, or are Christians good for marriage? This conundrum isn't likely to be solved, because of something called "social selectivity." That's the name for the processes, factors, and influences that affect why some people marry and others do not, as well as why some stay married—despite conflict—while others split. Harvard sociologist Carle Zimmerman wrestled over selectivity seventy years ago, wondering in print whether "the greater resistance to disease, suicide, mental and other troubles of the familistic [is] due to family environment or to the selection by the family of a 'healthier' type of person? No one has yet answered this question satisfactorily."[61] That's still the case today. Most students of marriage and the family, Zimmerman noted, "are satisfied to show the differences without explaining them."[62]

Marriage is nevertheless a "normal good" to Christians, more so than among the general population. A normal good, as you may recall from Chapter 4, is priced higher than "inferior goods," which tend to circulate more widely and be more easily accessible but are thought to lack the quality that the normal good enjoys. So what does this have to do with

Christianity? Plenty. Marriage is considered far superior in quality to co-habitation in the minds of most of our interviewees—whether they had ever cohabited or not.

Who is more likely to marry? Those for whom marriage remains a good worth pursuing even while peers are settling for, and mass culture promotes, inferior goods. That means that marriage will slowly but surely come to be associated with the most religious of the world's citizens—conservative Christians, Orthodox Jews, and Muslims.

The fifth—and most recent—prediction is perhaps the most vulnerable of them all. As I finished last-minute corrections to this manuscript, the COVID-19 (novel coronavirus) pandemic descended on the West, bringing normal life to a halt. The call for "social distancing" to slow the spread of the virus has pressed citizens homeward—wherever that is—a development that will privilege households occupied by stable marriages. Matrimony will re-veal its benefits (e.g., security, provision, care) yet again.

What else should we expect? The marriage rate will plummet more rap-idly for a time, given that weddings tend to be public events. Only those who are prepared to skip the public part will be marrying. Will Christians do that more than others? Perhaps, but again—only by degree. So, very many weddings will be delayed, if only briefly. More importantly, the mar-riage rate will not bounce back quickly, for several reasons. First, relationship development—the formation of future marriages—is going to slow down for a time. People will not meet new people, and many blossoming relationships will stall or be postponed. Online matching will take a hit, given that subse-quent meetups will plummet. These are some of the casualties of social dis-tancing. Add to that the turmoil of economic recession (or depression), and wages will seem too paltry to "merit" marriage, as described earlier in the book. (Sadly, "deaths of despair" will likely surge as uncertainty and isola-tion deepens.) Marriage as a foundation for survival and thriving may make a modest comeback of sorts—if the social conditions prove both severe and enduring (which no one wishes for). In a crisis, two are certainly better than one, on average. Cataclysms, moreover, have a way of altering or clarifying our priorities. But the marriage-as-capstone mentality will not falter easily. (Cognitive structures, once built, tend to be robust.) The post-pandemic world may feel and be quite different, or we may pick up where we left off in the early months of 2020. Either way, Christian commitment to marriage—culturally, socially, and theologically—is both solid and very old. It has been here before.

Conclusion

In the end, it is remarkable what has remained stable about marriage over millennia. Kingdoms have come and gone. Democracies and dictatorships have waxed and waned. Wars (and viruses) have wearied and horrified. Life has been brutal for many and pleasant for increasing numbers. Amid it all, marital love is still a valued ideal. The association of marriage with having children? Still there. The yearning to know and be known intimately by another person? Still strong. The concept of a man and a woman swearing to sacrifice for each other for a lifetime? Still compelling.

The penchant for splitting, however, seems poised to filter upward from the domain of marriage to our communities and nations. These are divisive times in global politics. Three social institutions are believed to be necessary for human happiness—the family, church, and civil society.[63] But even among these three, the family is primary. Writing in *First Things* in 2017, Russell Hittinger observes, "Marriage and family are not only the most vulnerable society [of the three], but also the most important one to get right. Whoever shrinks from that society is not well-prepared to live in the other two." Marriage not only unites two persons but two families. It is learning to get along, to navigate difference. Marriage is where love creates, is demonstrated, and learned. Why should we be surprised that communities and countries are fragmenting when their common experience of matrimony is becoming rarer?

Christians of the world have been particularly good to marriage. They have, at various turns, promoted prudent alterations—mutual consent, the turn away from polygamy, and equal property rights—that have benefitted women and men alike and enabled wider personal and social flourishing. But while Christians continue to value marriage, they inhabit an atomistic atmosphere now bending matrimony to fit expansive material and psychological expectations. The foundational vision of marriage as a load-bearing structure has receded. Almost without attracting notice, marriage has become a capstone—private, less central, and less necessary. Can Christianity still thrive if marriage retreats? Can civil society? We will find out.

Additional Survey Data Analyses

Table A1.1. Percent of Women Ages 30–34 Currently Married

Country	1980–1981	1990–1991	2000–2002	Most Recent
Australia	80.6	77.0	58.7	55.2
Czech Repub.	87.0	83.9	74.6	46.9
Denmark	—	79.7	55.0	43.0
Finland	75.9	64.4	51.4	45.7
France	83.6	69.2	56.0	48.2
Germany	—	74.8	56.0	48.2
Greece	86.2	84.1	71.9	63.0
Italy	85.2	78.2	70.5	49.9
Japan	88.1	82.9	69.0	61.0
Netherlands	—	73.2	53.9	43.4
Norway	81.8	67.2	53.1	41.4
Poland	86.6	85.9	80.8	74.9
Romania	—	89.2	76.1	72.9
Spain	85.1	78.6	63.6	70.6
Sweden	66.8	55.0	40.4	40.1
Switzerland	76.7	72.7	65.5	51.9

Note: "Most recent" estimates of percent currently married are as early as 2010 or as late as 2016. Wherever possible, consistency of figures from country census or estimates was maintained across rows. In a few instances, however, particular rows display both census numbers and estimates.

Source: World Marriage Data 2017 (New York: United Nations, Department of Economic and Social Affairs, Population Division, 2017).

Table A2.1. Estimated Postponement Effects on Ever-Married Rates

Area	Total Effect	Individuals 35–39	Individuals 40–44
Europe (1,385)	−3.44**	−2.50**	−1.29**
	(0.30)	(0.38)	(0.43)
	0.90	0.77	0.60
North America (443)	−3.59x**	−3.13**	−2.28**
	(0.28)	(0.30)	(0.33)
	0.44	0.53	0.35
South America (213)	−5.24**	−5.47**	−5.17**
	(0.83)	(0.93)	(1.07)
	0.62	0.57	0.50
Middle East (330)	−2.89*	−2.80*	−2.48
	(1.30)	(1.29)	(1.37)
	0.19	0.17	0.11
Africa (763)	−4.05**	−3.56**	−3.05**
	(0.41)	(0.53)	(0.57)
	0.56	0.37	0.26
Asia (332)	−4.11**	−4.48**	−4.21**
	(1.26)	(1.07)	(1.14)
	0.44	0.58	0.51
Australia (87)	−3.68**	−2.88**	−1.87*
	(0.35)	(0.50)	(0.50)
	0.90	0.76	0.64
Oceania (259)	−3.64**	−2.79**	−1.76**
	(0.44)	(0.57)	(0.63)
	0.71	0.45	0.23

Notes: Results in column 1 reflect a regression of total ever married rates for individuals 25–44 on age at first marriage with controls for sex and year with country fixed effects. Columns 2 and 3 reflect the same regressions with ever married rates for individuals 35–39 and 40–44, respectively. Each coefficient reflects percentages multiplied by 100. Below each coefficient appears a robust standard error (in parentheses) and, under it, the R-squared for the model. The number of observations appear in parentheses beside the region.

* $p < 0.05$

** $p < 0.01$

Source: Minnesota Population Center. Integrated Public Use Microdata Series, International. Minneapolis, MN: IPUMS, 2017.

In-Person Interview Questionnaire

The purpose of this study is to better understand how Christian young adults in their 20s and 30s think about marriage and romantic relationships. We will be conducting this research with about 250 other men and women around your age in several different countries.

This interview should last around 60 minutes. I will ask you to discuss sensitive issues about your relationship life and thoughts. You may find a few of these questions embarrassing and/or difficult to talk about. You may skip any question you'd rather not answer, or ask me to turn off the recorder; either is fine. Your privacy and confidentiality are very important and will be protected. The in-person interviews will be digitally recorded, but we will delete any personally identifying information, and they'll be destroyed after a transcript of the interview has been created.

- Is all that OK with you?
- We use these interviews to really hear from your perspective, and in your own words, how you're experiencing your 20s, how you think about relationships, marriage, and your opinions about each of these. This is a chance for you to talk openly about whatever you want to say, to express whatever ideas or feelings you have, to talk about things that might be too uncomfortable to tell other people.
- There are no right or wrong answers to this study. I just want to know whatever you honestly think or feel. If you don't understand a question, just tell me that you don't know the answer.

To begin, then:

- How old are you?
- Are you employed for pay? [IF YES] What do you do?
- How much education have you received?
- [IF COLLEGE] What was your major program of study?
- How's the economic outlook for you these days?

Switching gears a bit toward our primary topic . . .

- In (your country), the median age at marriage for men is around age X, and for women it's around age X, and fewer people are getting married at all. What do you think of that? Is that a good thing, a bad thing, or makes no difference?
  - Why do you think it is that people are marrying later today? Is it because they want to, or . . .?
  - [IF UNCLEAR, PRESS] Do you like it that many young people are waiting to marry, or not getting married at all?
- Has anything about marriage changed today, or do you think marriage is comparable to what it has long been before?
  - Is there something unique about marriage, or is it comparable to cohabitation (or living together)?

- Does conflict over gender roles and ideals have anything to do with how people think about marriage today, or not really?
- What's the purpose or point of marriage?
  ○ If you were going to convince a skeptic about its value, what would you say?
- In just a couple sentences, how would you describe what marriage *is*?
- Should couples "date" for a long time before getting married, or is that not helpful?
- What discourages people from getting married?
- What can be done to encourage marriages?
- Do parents play a role in who young people meet and how they approach marriage, or not really? Should they?
- Have you observed any efforts or initiatives in your community or country that seem to be, or could, improve the current situation?
- Have you seen student movements in universities working to change these trends, or not?
- Does the government in your country care if people get married or not? Do they reward marriage in any way? Do they care about fertility rates?

Now for a few questions about you personally:

- Do you intend to get married someday? [IF YES] When? [IF NO] Why not?
- Do you look forward to marriage, or is it something that makes you nervous?
- Is there an ideal age to get married?
- What attracts you about marriage? Does anything frighten you about it?
  ○ [IF FEMALE] Do you think men have a problem committing? [IF YES] How can you tell? Why do you think that is?
- [IF MALE] Have you ever asked someone to marry them? [IF NO] Ever thought of it?
- [IF FEMALE] Has someone every asked you to marry them?
- Is there a difference in what you wish for and what you think you can find in a marriage partner, or not?
- Do you feel pressure from peers either to get married or to wait? [IF YES] How so? Has that been steady over time or has that pressure changed?
- What does your priest or pastor say about marriage and relationships today?
  ○ Do you disagree with them about any marriage-related matter?
- Does your church do anything to promote meeting and marrying, or not?
  ○ [IF NO] Do you think they should, or not really?
  ○ [IF YES] What should your congregation be doing?
  ○ Are you aware of any organizations who promote marriage? [IF YES] How so?
- Do you see or hear any messages about marriage in the media?
  ○ [IF YES] Anything in particular come to mind?
- Are your biological parents (still) married?
  ○ [IF YES] Would you characterize their marriage as a happy one, or not?
  ○ [IF NO] Can you tell me what happened?
- Do you live with your parents? [IF NO] How far away are they?
- [IF NO] Do you live alone? Why? For how long?
- [IF NO] Who do you live with?
- How many siblings do you have? Are you close with any of them?
- Do you want to have children someday? [IF YES] How many? Why that number? Do you think you'll have that many? [IF NO] Why not?

I'd like to ask a few more-sensitive questions before we conclude this interview. Remember, all of this is confidential and your identity will not be revealed. We're just trying to get a full picture of what's going on with relationships today. However, remember that you do not have to answer any question that you would prefer not to.

- Have you ever tried online dating? Thought about it?
  - [IF YES] What's your experience of online dating been like?
  - Where do people tend to meet?
- Are you currently in a romantic relationship?
  - [IF NO] Have you ever been in a romantic relationship?
  - [IF YES] When did your last relationship end? Do you have other reasons for not being in a relationship?
- Are you *actively* trying to move the relationship forward, in terms of commitment? Or are you wishing it would be slow, or . . .?
- Are you currently in a sexual relationship?

  - [IF NO] Is sex "too easy" these days, or not? Does this matter for marriage, or not really?
  - [IF YES] So would you call that person a boy/girlfriend, or . . .? How long have you been in this relationship? Do you think you'll be with this person a year from now? Two years? 5? 10? Do you think you'll marry them, or not? Does he/she want to get married soon, or not? Do you feel any pressure to marry?
  - About how long was it before you started having sex? (Before the relationship officially started?)
  - Do your parents know?
    - [IF YES] What do they think?

[IF RESIDENTIAL STATUS IS UNCLEAR] Do you currently live with this person?

- [IF YES] When did you move in together? How did you decide to do that? Do you like the arrangement? What are the best aspects of it? Any down sides to it? Think you'll marry them, or not? Does *he/she* want to get married soon, or not?

Notes

Chapter 1

1. See Kutter Callaway, *Breaking the Marriage Idol: Reconstructing Our Cultural and Spiritual Norms* (Downers Grove, IL: InterVarsity Press, 2018). My interests in marriage are largely sociological in nature.
2. Actually, their effect on marriage and divorce rates is hardly uniform. See Kristen Harknett and Daniel Schneider, "Is a Bad Economy Good for Marriage? The Relationship between Macroeconomic Conditions and Marital Stability from 1998–2009," National Poverty Center Working Paper No. 12-06, January 2012, http://npc.umich.edu/publications/working_papers/?publication_id=234&. On page 4, the authors assert that "(t)he historical record from the twentieth century contains precedents for both economic downturns stabilizing *and* destabilizing marriages." A variety of economic indicators—including unemployment rates and median wages—affect marriage incentives differently. See Hamid Baghestani and Michael Malcolm, "Marriage, Divorce, and Economic Activity in the US: 1960–2008," *Applied Economic Letters* 21 (2014): 528–532. The authors note on page 528 that "(w)hile the economic climate can affect incentives to marry and divorce, the direction of these effects is theoretically ambiguous."
3. See Ron Lesthaeghe, "The Second Demographic Transition: A Concise Overview of Its Development," *Proceedings of the National Academy of Sciences*, 111 (2014): 18112–18115.
4. Harvard cultural sociologist Orlando Patterson sees it: "People are just not getting married and that tells you something. It's the natural tendency of human beings to want to get married and establish relationships. That's not happening." This remark appears on page 64 in his untitled chapter: Orlando Patterson, untitled chapter, in *Marriage—Just a Piece of Paper?*, eds. Katherine Anderson, Don Browning, and Brian Boyer (Grand Rapids, MI: Wm. B. Eerdmans Publishing Co., 2002), 62–67.
5. Robert E. Alvis, *White Eagle, Black Madonna: One Thousand Years of the Polish Catholic Tradition* (New York: Fordham University Press, 2016).
6. Pew Research Center, May 10, 2017, "Religious Belief and National Belonging in Central and Eastern Europe." http://assets.pewresearch.org/wp-content/uploads/sites/11/2017/05/15120244/CEUP-FULL-REPORT.pdf
7. "Marriage and Divorce Statistics," Eurostat Statistics Explained, http://ec.europa.eu/eurostat/statistics-explained/index.php/Marriage_and_divorce_statistics. For U.S. measures, see "Marriage and Divorce," National Center for Health Statistics, https://www.cdc.gov/nchs/fastats/marriage-divorce.htm

8. The general source for these estimates is the World Bank, although the partic-ular source can include the UN Population Division, the UN Statistics Division, or Eurostat.

9. Some Christians are happy about such developments—but most are not. And this varies by nation. Spain was an early adopter of legalized same-sex civil marriage, in 2005, whereas Poland has yet to signal serious debate about the matter.

10. Don S. Browning, *Marriage and Modernization: How Globalization Threatens Marriage and What to Do about It* (Grand Rapids, MI: Wm. B. Eerdmans Publishing Co., 2003). The quote is from page viii.

11. Michael J. Rosenfeld, "Who Wants the Breakup? Gender and Breakup in Heterosexual Couples," in *Social Networks and the Life Course: Integrating the Development of Human Lives and Social Relational Networks*, eds. Duane F. Alwin, Diane H. Felmlee, and Derek A. Kreager (Cham, Switzerland: Springer, 2018), 221–243.

12. Bella DePaulo, "Marriage Is Over—It Will Never Again Matter the Way It Once Did," *Medium*, June 17, 2019, https://medium.com/@BellaDePaulo/marriage-is-over-it-will-never-again-matter-the-way-it-once-did-e7c1c5084bdb. The quotes here are from paragraphs 12 and 16.

13. Joseph Lupton and James P. Smith, "Marriage, Assets and Savings," in *Marriage and the Economy: Theories from Advanced Industrial Societies*, ed. Shoshana A. Grossbard-Schectman (New York: Cambridge University Press, 2003), 129–152; Janet Wilmoth and Gregor Koso, "Does Marital History Matter? Marital Status and Wealth Outcomes among Preretirement Adults," *Journal of Marriage and Family*, 64 (2002): 254–268; Lingxin Hao, "Family Structure, Private Transfers, and the Economic Well-Being of Families with Children," *Social Forces* 75 (1996): 269–292; Lucie Schmidt and Purvi Sevak, "Gender, Marriage, and Asset Accumulation in the United States," *Feminist Economics* 12 (2006): 139–166; W. Bradford Wilcox, Jared R. Anderson, William J. Doherty, David Eggebeen, Christopher G. Ellison, William A. Galston, Neil Gilbert, John Gottman, Ron Haskins, Robert I. Lerman, et al., *Why Marriage Matters: 30 Conclusions from the Social Sciences* (New York: Institute for American Values/National Marriage Project, 2011); W. Bradford Wilcox and Joseph Price, "Families and the Wealth of Nations," in *Unequal Family Lives: Causes and Consequences in Europe and the Americas*, eds. Naomi R. Cahn, June Carbone, Laurie F. DeRose, and W. Bradford Wilcox (New York: Cambridge University Press, 2018), 179–195.

14. Nicholas Eberstadt, "Family Structure and the Decline of Work for Men in Postwar America," in *Unequal Family Lives: Causes and Consequences in Europe and the Americas*, ed. Naomi R. Cahn, June Carbone, Laurie F. DeRose, and W. Bradford Wilcox (New York: Cambridge University Press, 2018), 105–140; Nicholas Eberstadt, *Men without Work: America's Invisible Crisis* (West Conshohocken, PA: Templeton Press, 2016).

15. Allan V. Horwitz, Helene Raskin White, and Sandra Howell-White, "Becoming Married and Mental Health: A Longitudinal Study of a Cohort of Young Adults," *Journal of Marriage and Family*, 58 (1996): 895–907; Matthijs Kalmijn, "The Ambiguous Link between Marriage and Health: A Dynamic Reanalysis of Loss and

Gain Effects," *Social Forces* 95 (2017): 1607–1636; Kathleen A. Lamb, Gary R. Lee, and Alfred DeMaris, "Union Formation and Depression: Selection and Relationship Effects," *Journal of Marriage and Family*, 65 (2003): 953–962; Gary R. Lee, *The Limits of Marriage: Why Getting Everyone Married Won't Solve All Our Problems* (Lanham, MD: Lexington Books, 2015); Shanshan Li, Meir Stampfer, David R. Williams, and Tyler J. VanderWeele, "Association of Religious Service Attendance with Mortality among Women," *JAMA Internal Medicine*, 176 (2016): 777–785; Nadine F. Marks and James David Lambert, "Marital Status Continuity and Change among Young and Midlife Adults: Longitudinal Effects on Psychological Well-Being," *Journal of Family Issues*, 19 (1998): 652–686; Alois Stutzer and Bruno S. Frey, "Does Marriage Make People Happy, or Do Happy People Get Married?," *The Journal of Socio-Economics*, 35 (2006): 326–347; Jeremy E. Uecker, "Marriage and Mental Health among Young Adults," *Journal of Health and Social Behavior*, 53 (2012): 67–83; Linda J. Waite and Maggie Gallagher, *The Case for Marriage* (New York: Doubleday, 2000); Robert G. Wood, Brian Goesling, and Sarah Avellar, *The Effects of Marriage on Health: A Synthesis of Recent Research Evidence* (Princeton, NJ: Mathematica Policy Research Inc., 2007), https://aspe.hhs.gov/system/files/pdf/75106/report.pdf

16. Tyler J. VanderWeele, "On the Promotion of Human Flourishing," *Proceedings of the National Academy of Sciences*, 114 (2017): 8148–8156.

17. Third Extraordinary General Assembly of the Synod of Bishops, *Relatio Synodi* (Vatican City: Vatican Publishing House, 2014). The quote appears in paragraph 2.

18. See U.S. Census Bureau, American Community Survey, 2014, https://www.census.gov/acs/www/data/data-tables-and-tools/data-profiles/2014/

19. Some scholars see the world only in terms of narratives or personal accounts, ignoring how selective their samples may be. Others, including demographers, tend to see the world in terms of large-scale data and draw their conclusions entirely from that, risking the common mistake of interpreting the persons around them as fitting what the official, population-based data sources tell them. Both risk missing out on valuable material the others can supply. This book, like my previous ones, contains both forms of data. (However, in line with its goals, this book is more heavily weighted toward the interview narratives.)

20. Mark Regnerus, *Cheap Sex: The Transformation of Men, Marriage, and Monogamy* (New York: Oxford University Press, 2017).

21. Nigeria, Lebanon, and Russia were all single-city sites (Lagos, Beirut, and Moscow). The other four countries featured multiple sites: In Poland, interviews were conducted in Lublin, Krakow, and Warsaw; American interviews were conducted in Austin, Texas, and Howell, Michigan; Mexican interviews were conducted in Guadalajara and Mexico City; and while most Spanish interviews were conducted in Pamplona, several also took place in Madrid and Barcelona.

22. If such leaders veered too far or too quickly into idealism—that is, answering my questions with sermonettes about the subject matter—I pressed them back to the practicalities of what was actually going on with the people they served. Sometimes I got help, too. For example, when I asked Nina and Lawrence Khong, copastors at the Faith Community Baptist megachurch in Singapore, about how they deal with the

skewed sex ratio (that is, more women than men) in their congregation, Lawrence started quoting Scripture and relaying maxims about the importance of "waiting on the Lord" (for a spouse). His wife, however, wouldn't hear it, shook her head, and interrupted him to level with me about the practical problems this scenario creates. This resulted in a rich conversation about a challenge I discuss at length in Chapter 4.

23. Hence, while the basic Christian self-identification rules out just under 70 percent of the world's citizens, leaving two billion eligible (see Pew Research Center, Religion and Public Life, April 2, 2015, "The Future of World Religions: Population Growth Projections, 2010–2050," https://www.pewforum.org/2015/04/02/religious-projections-2010-2050/), the attendance criterion shaves far more off the sampling frame. And since this is not a random sample, I make no claims that churchgoing Christians in Spain or Nigeria or Poland all tend to think and act just like the ones we interviewed. They may or they may not. On the other hand, the questions I posed are quite general. Hence, I think the samples in each country yield information that is in line with what other churchgoing Christians there would have said.

24. This group nevertheless constituted a minority of the sample. Most attended services weekly.

25. This term was used by numerous Russian interviewees. It refers both to a mentality about marriage that denigrates or minimizes it as of no great consequence, of modest importance, and scripted, as well as to a literal stamp or demarcation of marital status in one's (domestic) Russian passport.

26. Most of global Christianity does not recognize the civil or religious legitimacy of such unions. (Some do, of course.) Also, this arrangement constitutes a tiny fraction of all marriages. Hence, it would be myopic and distracting to focus considerable attention on the very small share of the globe's Christian citizens who wish to pursue a same-sex marriage. When the subject of same-sex relationships arose in the interviews, I certainly did not stifle discussion about it.

27. David B. Dunson, Bernardo Colombo, and Donna D. Baird, "Changes with Age in the Level and Duration of Fertility in the Menstrual Cycle," *Human Reproduction*, 17 (2002): 1399–1403.

28. Table A1.1 (in Appendix A) displays the percentage of women ages 30 through 34 who are *currently* married in these countries, for comparison purposes.

29. See "World Marriage Data 2017," United Nations—Department of Economic and Social Affairs Population Division, https://www.un.org/en/development/desa/population/theme/marriage-unions/WMD2017.asp

30. Jonathan Evans, "Unlike Their Central and Eastern European Neighbors, Most Czechs Don't Believe in God," *Pew Research Center*, June 19, 2017, http://www.pewresearch.org/fact-tank/2017/06/19/unlike-their-central-and-eastern-european-neighbors-most-czechs-dont-believe-in-god/

31. It can get lower, however: only 18 percent of 25- to 29-year-old women had ever been married in Lithuania and Greenland as of 2015–2016.

32. Paul Hamilos, "Spain's Divorce Rate Soars after Rules Relaxed," *The Guardian*, November 17, 2007, https://www.theguardian.com/world/2007/nov/17/spain.international

33. "Bulletin on Population and Vital Statistics in the Arab Region No. 16" (New York: United Nations Economic and Social Commission for Western Asia, 2013), https://www.unescwa.org/publications/bulletin-population-and-vital-statistics-escwa-region-issue-no-16

34. "Frequently Requested Church Statistics," Center for Applied Research in the Apostolate, http://cara.georgetown.edu/frequently-requested-church-statistics/

35. Ibid.

36. As a worldwide measurement of sociocultural and political change, the World Values Survey (WVS, http://www.worldvaluessurvey.org/wvs.jsp) consists of nationally representative surveys of adults (18 and older) in almost one hundred countries. These surveys are based on a common questionnaire administered by national research teams in each country at each survey wave. The minimum sample size per country is 1,200 completed interviews, which are conducted face-to-face or by phone and must be representative of all adults within the private households participating. Survey quality varies crossnationally. In general, advanced industrial societies with decades of survey research experience have higher quality samples, compared with countries with little or no such experience. Furthermore, as part of a confederation of researchers (rather than a centralized research organization), each national team is responsible for its own expenses and often relies on local funding for fieldwork and analysis, which further increases crossnational variation in sample quality. To mitigate this variation, WVS data archive staff oversee internal consistency checks between the sampling design and the outcome and engage in rigorous data-cleaning procedures. Furthermore, no country is included in a wave before full documentation has been delivered.

37. The estimates appearing in the table are predicted probabilities generated from a basic logistic regression model, using the WVS's most recent iteration in each country (between 2010 and 2014), sorted by sex, setting Muslim = 0 and Hindu = 0 (where applicable), literate = 1, and the modal values for respondents' education and income category (by country).

38. Fewer than 5 percent of Russians report attending religious services at least once a week, compared with 50 percent in Poland, 46 percent in Mexico, and 14 percent in Spain.

39. OECD Family Database, http://www.oecd.org/els/family/database.htm

40. Christian Smith, *American Evangelicalism: Embattled and Thriving* (Chicago: University of Chicago Press, 1998).

Chapter 2

1. The two rites (there are others as well) differ in some ways but are considered in full communion with one another.

2. "Bulletin on Population and Vital Statistics in the Arab Region No. 16."

3. Don Browning, "Critical Familism, Civil Society, and the Law," *Hofstra Law Review*, 32 (2003–04): 313–329.

4. William Countryman, *Dirt, Greed, and Sex: Sexual Ethics in the New Testament and Their Implications for Today* (Minneapolis: Fortress Press, 1988).
5. Carle C. Zimmerman, *Family and Civilization* (New York: Harper & Brothers, 1947).
6. Genesis 25:6.
7. David de la Croix and Fabio Mariani, "From Polygyny to Serial Monogamy: A Unified Theory of Marriage Institutions," IZA Discussion Paper No. 6599 (2012), Institute for the Study of Labor, Bonn, Germany.
8. Deuteronomy 24.
9. Deuteronomy 22:28–29.
10. Matthew 19; Mark 10.
11. Mark 10:11.
12. Matthew 22:30.
13. Countryman, *Dirt, Greed, and Sex*.
14. John 8:1–11.
15. Acts of the Apostles 15.
16. Sarah Ruden, *Paul among the People: The Apostle Reinterpreted and Reimagined in His Own Time* (New York: Image Books, 2010); Rodney Stark, *The Rise of Christianity: A Sociologist Reconsiders History* (Princeton, NJ: Princeton University Press, 1996).
17. N. T. Wright, *Paul for Everyone: The Prison Letters* (Louisville, KY: Westminster John Knox Press, 2004). The quote is from page 67.
18. Ruden, *Paul among the People*. See also Rodney Stark, *The Rise of Christianity: How the Obscure, Marginal Jesus Movement Became the Dominant Religious Force in the Western World in a Few Centuries* (San Francisco: HarperCollins, 1997).
19. 1 Corinthians 7.
20. David J. Ayers, *Christian Marriage: A Comprehensive Introduction* (Bellingham, WA: Lexham Press, 2018). Calvinists like Ayers consider marriage as part of God's "common-grace care for the human race," something intended to bless and assist everyone, not just Christians. The quote appears on page 23.
21. The *American Political and Social Behavior* survey interviewed 5,285 Americans in November 2018. The data collection was conducted by Ipsos, formerly Knowledge Networks (or KN), a research firm with a very strong record of generating high-quality data for academic projects. They maintain the KnowledgePanel', a well-regarded survey pool that does not accept self-selected volunteers. As a result, it is a random, nationally representative sample of the American population and compares favorably with other large population-based data collection efforts. This data will be made publicly available by early 2021.
22. Browning, "Critical Familism, Civil Society, and the Law." The quote here appears on page 324.
23. Joel F. Harrington, *Reordering Marriage and Society in Reformation Germany* (Cambridge: Cambridge University Press, 1995). Russell Hittinger concurs that "[t]he institution of marriage was not radically affected by the Reformation." See F. Russell Hittinger, "Marriage as *Imago Dei*: Developments in Catholic Social Thought," *The Family in America*, 28 (2014): 313–327. The quote is from page 315.
24. Ayers, *Christian Marriage*, 261.

25. When I refer to "legal" marriage, I am referring to a marriage that can be legally entered into according to prevailing civil laws. Validity and legality tend to mean the same thing concerning civil marriage but different things when religion is involved. Religious organizations often regulate the marriages of their members and subject them to rules that may alter their validity but not their (civil) legality. For example, the Catholic Church would not recognize a parishioner's second marriage (after a civil divorce) as valid prima facie. Nor does it recognize same-sex marriages as valid, legal though both examples may be in the United States and in a variety of other countries.

26. In *Christian Marriage*, Ayers notes that for the first sixty-five years in New England, Puritan ministers in the colonies were forbidden to perform marriages. That role was reserved for civil magistrates. Moreover, according to Harvard sociologist Carle Zimmerman, "courtship, bundling, precontracts, marriage, adultery, and behavior of children were all subjects of lawmaking" in seventeenth-century New England. And it was not until 1733 that all ministers were enabled to perform wedding ceremonies. See Zimmerman, *Family and Civilization*, 537.

27. Moore, the Southern Baptist head of the Ethics and Religious Liberty Commission, observes: "It is quite common to hear ministers (and I am one of them) who will say that they would rather do a funeral than a wedding." See page 102 of Russell Moore, *The Storm-Tossed Family: How the Cross Reshapes the Home* (Nashville, TN: B&H Publishing Group, 2018).

28. Martin Luther, *The Estate of Marriage* [1522], as excerpted in *Luther on Women: A Sourcebook*, ed. and trans. Susan C. Karant-Nunn and Merry E. Wiesner-Hanks (Cambridge: Cambridge University Press, 2003). The quote appears on page 100.

29. Steven Ozment and John Witte Jr., "Martin Luther," in *Christianity and Family Law: An Introduction*, eds. John Witte Jr., and Gary S. Hauk (Cambridge: Cambridge University Press, 2017), 195–210. The quote is from page 209.

30. It may, however, take less time than in the past. See Jim Yardley and Elisabetta Povoledo, "Pope Francis Announces Changes for Easier Marriage Annulments," *New York Times*, September 8, 2015, https://www.nytimes.com/2015/09/09/world/europe/pope-francis-marriage-annulment-reforms.html

31. This statement refers to the union of Adam and Eve in Genesis 2 and the "wedding supper of the Lamb" (that is, of Christ to his purified Church) in Revelation 19.

32. The status of polygamy was settled—and multiple wives or concubines prohibited—in the West with two major Church councils (the Fourth Lateran in 1215 and Trent in 1563). See de la Croix and Mariani, "From Polygyny to Serial Monogamy."

33. Catholic Church, *Catechism of the Catholic Church, Second Edition* (Washington, DC: United States Conference of Catholic Bishops—Libreria Editrice Vaticana, 2000), 1601.

34. Timothy Keller, *The Meaning of Marriage: Facing the Complexities of Commitment with the Wisdom of God* (New York: Penguin Books, 2013). The quote appears on page 111.

35. "The 2000 Baptist Faith and Message," Southern Baptist Convention, http://www.sbc.net/bfm2000/bfm2000.asp. The quote here is from section XVIII.

36. Moore, *The Storm-Tossed Family*, 103.

37. *Catechism of the Catholic Church*, 1601: "The matrimonial covenant, by which a man and a woman establish between themselves a partnership of the whole of life, is by its nature ordered toward the good of the spouses and the procreation and education of offspring; this covenant between baptized persons has been raised by Christ the Lord to the dignity of a sacrament."

38. The Nigerian interviewees were more apt to mention the legal aspects of marriage than were those from other sites.

39. Chrysostom's writings appear more popular among the Orthodox than Catholics, although Vatican II's *Lumen Gentium* popularized the phrase *domestic church*. See Paul VI, *Lumen Gentium* (Vatican City: Vatican Publishing House, 1964). Pope John Paul II further popularized the term, citing it in *Familiaris Consortio*. See John Paul II, *Familiaris Consortio* (Vatican City: Vatican Publishing House, 1981).

40. I realize that the population of active Christians is itself a rather selective group. On the other hand, the sample of young adults was not handpicked for their thoughts on marriage, but only included for their tendency to attend church regularly.

41. Wendy Z. Goldman, *Women, the State, and Revolution: Soviet Family Policy and Social Life, 1917–1936* (Cambridge: Cambridge University Press, 1993), 216–217.

42. Andrew J. Cherlin, "The Deinstitutionalization of American Marriage," *Journal of Marriage and Family*, 66 (2004): 848–861.

43. See Andrew Cherlin, *The Marriage-Go-Round: The State of Marriage and the Family in America Today* (New York: Vintage, 2010); Andrew Cherlin, "Marriage Has Become a Trophy," *The Atlantic*, March 20, 2018, https://www.theatlantic.com/family/archive/2018/03/incredible-everlasting-institution-marriage/555320/. See also the work of sociologist Kathryn Edin, including Kathryn Edin and Joanna M. Reed, "Why Don't They Just Get Married? Barriers to Marriage among the Disadvantaged," *The Future of Children* 15 (2005): 117–137.

44. Maria J. Kefalas, Frank F. Furstenberg, Patrick J. Carr, and Laura Napolitano, "Marriage Is More Than Being Together: The Meaning of Marriage for Young Adults," *Journal of Family Issues* 32 (2011): 845–875.

45. Daniel Schneider, "Wealth and the Marital Divide," *American Journal of Sociology* 117 (2011): 627–667. The quote is from page 633.

46. Daniel Schneider and Orestes P. Hastings, "Socioeconomic Variation in the Effect of Economic Conditions on Marriage and Nonmarital Fertility in the United States: Evidence from the Great Recession," *Demography* 52 (2015): 1893–1915.

47. Pamela J. Smock, Wendy D. Manning, and Meredith Porter, "'Everything's There Except Money': How Money Shapes Decisions to Marry among Cohabitors," *Journal of Marriage and Family* 67 (2005): 680–696. The quote is from page 688.

48. Ibid., 687.

49. Jennifer Johnson-Hanks, Christine Bachrach, S. Philip Morgan, and Hans-Peter Kohler, *Understanding Family Change and Variation: Structure, Conjuncture, and Action* (New York: Springer, 2011). The quote is from page 67.

50. Ibid., 68. See Arland Thornton, *Reading History Sideways: The Fallacy and Enduring Impact of the Developmental Paradigm on Family Life* (Chicago: University of Chicago Press, 2005). The quoted phrase appears on page 136.

51. Inés San Martín, "Pope Calls Gender Theory a 'Global War' against the Family," *Crux*, October 1, 2016, https://cruxnow.com/global-church/2016/10/01/pope-calls-gender-theory-global-war-family/

52. Inés San Martín, "Pope Francis: Ideological Colonization a 'Blasphemy against God,'" *Crux*, November 21, 2017, https://cruxnow.com/vatican/2017/11/21/pope-francis-ideological-colonization-blasphemy-god/

53. Lesthaeghe, "The Second Demographic Transition."

54. Miguel Requena, "The Secularization of Spanish Society: Change in Religious Practice," *South European Society and Politics* 10 (2005): 369–390; Miguel Requena and Mikolaj Stanek, "Secularization in Poland and Spain after the Democratic Transition: A Cohort Analysis," *International Sociology* 28 (2013): 84–101.

55. Maurizio Rossi and Ettore Scappini, "The Dynamics of Religious Practice in Spain from the Mid-19th Century to 2010," *Journal for the Scientific Study of Religion* 55 (2016): 579–596.

56. See, for example, Sharon Jayson, "Sooner vs. Later: Is There an Ideal Age for First Marriage?," *USA Today*, November 9, 2008, https://usatoday30.usatoday.com/news/health/2008-11-09-delayed-marriage_N.htm

57. Analyses of data from five different American survey projects suggest that "the greatest indicated likelihood of being in an intact marriage of the highest quality is among those who married at ages 22–25, net of the estimated effects of time since first marriage and several variables that might commonly affect age at marriage and marital outcomes." The quote is from page 787 of Norval D. Glenn, Jeremy E. Uecker, and Robert W. B. Love, Jr., "Later First Marriage and Marital Success," *Social Science Research* 39 (2010): 787–800.

58. These numbers should not be taken as representative of active Christians in these countries, given the nonrandom sampling strategy by which we located them.

59. Demographers have assessed whether "tempo" effects have lowered fertility rates in "lowest-low" fertility countries. That is, they have asked whether temporary postponements—often until better economic conditions materialize—ultimately reduce the number of children women have, or whether they have the same number but later. See, for example, Sam Hyun Yoo and Tomáš Sobotka, "Ultra-Low Fertility in South Korea: The Role of the Tempo Effect," *Demographic Research* 38 (2018): 549–576.

60. For those who don't deal with data like this every day, "regression" analysis involves estimating the effect of one variable on another variable, usually while holding other variables constant (i.e., controlling for them). In this case, sex (male/female) and the year the data was collected were the variables controlled for.

61. Missing data for age at first marriage is filled in using data from the Organisation for Economic Co-operation and Development (OECD). The United Nations data has ever-married rates as a percentage from each five-year age category (25–29, 30–34, etc.). For the regression models in Table A2.1, I used individual-level data from IPUMS International to calculate the total ever-married rates for each five-year category and for the total age range 25–44. Where possible, I used total population counts in our calculations of the ever-married rates for the total age range 25–44. I used the

calculated rates to fill in missing values in the UN data for ever-married rates in each age category and the total age range 25–44. If a country was missing the ever-married rate for the total age range 25–44 and was in the UN data but not in the IPUMS data, the missing rate was filled in by averaging the ever-married rates for each age category.

62. Johnson-Hanks, Bachrach, Morgan, and Kohler, *Understanding Family Change and Variation*.

63. The matter of numeric marital decline, however, appears to be of far less concern to demographers, economists, policy analysts, and politicians, who are focused on assessing future labor force composition.

Chapter 3

1. Didem Tüzeman, "Why Are Prime-Age Men Vanishing from the Labor Force?," *Economic Review—Federal Reserve Bank of Kansas City*, 103 (2018): 5–30.

2. Some interviewees answered our question about change in marriage over time with something that had nothing to do with gender roles, but we eventually asked all of them about the topic: "Does conflict over gender roles and ideals have anything to do with how people think about marriage today, or not really?" In that way, we were able to gather thoughts on the matter from all participants.

3. When I refer to gender, I am talking about the social and cultural attitudes, expectations, and patterns of thought and behavior that accompany sexual dimorphism but are not constrained by it. A helpful way of distinguishing gender from sex is by borrowing from probability theory: it can help to think of gender as overlapping normal curves of behavior, attitudes, and preferences that range from what is understood to be the very masculine to the very feminine. While they may vary across cultures, this doesn't mean that there's no such thing as normal preferences for men (i.e., what most men prefer) and normal preferences for women. Would these persist if not for the cultures in which they exist? And do masculinity and femininity shape culture, or is it the other way around? Judith Butler, author of the book *Gender Trouble* (New York: Routledge, 1990) and key contributor to what its critics call "the theory of gender," sits firmly in the "culture shaping gender" camp. To her, gender constitutes unconscious, culturally compelled "performance" and is entirely socially constructed. Her influence on contemporary gender matters, including the transgender movement, is extensive. I, on the other hand, tend to hold that gender, undergirded by sex differences, is more apt to shape culture than the other way around.

4. Enrique is a member of Opus Dei, a Catholic organization founded in Spain in the 1920s. Its primary concern is the spiritual health of Catholics in their vocations—to work and to family. Its view of women in the workforce began avant-garde, supporting and esteeming working women as a bit of a revolution from traditionalist religious practice. As a religiously conservative yet somewhat socially progressive group, Opus Dei has been most popular among Catholics in the professional class.

5. The "persistent familism" observed in Mexico as recently as 2000, which issued in a "marriage regime" as a means of "countering the vicissitudes of the economy," has

apparently come undone in the past two decades. See Elizabeth Fussell and Alberto Palloni, "Persistent Marriage Regimes in Changing Times," *Journal of Marriage and Family*, 66 (2004): 1201–1213. The quotes appear on page 1201.

6. Eli J. Finkel, Elaine O. Cheung, Lydia F. Emery, Kathleen L. Carswell, and Grace M. Larson, "The Suffocation Model: Why Marriage in America Is Becoming an All-or-Nothing Institution," *Current Directions in Psychological Science*, 24 (2015): 238–244.

7. Moore, *The Storm-Tossed Family*, 102.

8. Keller, *The Meaning of Marriage*, 30.

9. Richard A. Easterlin, "Relative Economic Status and the American Fertility Swing," in *Family Economic Behavior: Problems and Prospects*, ed. Eleanor Bernert Sheldon (Philadelphia: J.B. Lippincott, 1973), 170–223.

10. The matter of "Western ideologies" hits close to home for Magdalena. Her only sibling, an older sister studying for a Ph.D. in a city several hours from Lublin, "has completely different views than mine. . . [O]ur relation has never been a cordial one. My sister is an LGBT activist and she's an atheist, so it can have a huge influence on our relations." How different are their perspectives? Very. Magdalena elaborates: "I believe that Western ideologies which are imposed on our system of beliefs are trying to destroy our concept of family so that we will think that there is no difference between a sacramental relationship, cohabitation, homosexual or heterosexual relationship. . . . However, I cannot make those relationships equal. I think that a sacramental marriage is something completely different and incomparable. I think that due to such ideologies, the concept of marriage changes among people who are not well grounded in religion, uncertain of their beliefs. I know many people who state that they are religious, yet they change their views depending on what somebody tells them. I know many people who state that they are religious, yet they think that there's nothing wrong with homosexual relationships and adopting children by such couples. I think that these ideologies exert a huge influence on how people perceive marriage."

11. Hyunbae Chun and Injae Lee, "Why Do Married Men Earn More: Productivity or Marriage Selection?," *Economic Inquiry*, 39 (2001): 307–319; Alexandra Killewald and Margaret Gough, "Does Specialization Explain Marriage Penalties and Premiums?," *American Sociological Review*, 78 (2013): 477–502; Alexandra Killewald and Ian Lundberg, "New Evidence Against a Causal Marriage Wage Premium," *Demography*, 54 (2017): 1007–1028; Megan M. Sweeney, "Two Decades of Family Change: The Shifting Economic Foundations of Marriage," *American Sociological Review*, 67 (2002): 132–147; Janet Chen-Lan Kuo and R. Kelly Raley, "Is It All About Money? Work Characteristics and Women's and Men's Marriage Formation in Early Adulthood," *Journal of Family Issues*, 37 (2016): 1046–1073; Daniel Schneider, Kristen Harknett, and Matthew Stimpson, "What Explains the Decline in First Marriage in the United States? Evidence from the Panel Study of Income Dynamics, 1969–2013," *Journal of Marriage and Family*, 80 (2018): 791–811; Daniel Schneider, Kristen Harknett, and Matthew Stimpson, "Job Quality and the Educational Gradient in Entry into Marriage and Cohabitation," Washington Center for Equitable Growth Working Paper, November 2018, https://equitablegrowth.org/working-papers/job-quality-and-the-educational-gradient-in-entry-into-marriage-and-cohabitation/

12. Schneider, Harknett, and Stimpson, "What Explains the Decline in First Marriage in the United States?"

13. Ibid. Incarceration—being unavailable to the marriage market—didn't matter as much as anticipated for men, but affected black women's marriage rate, dropping it 29 percent. The authors nevertheless hold out hope that there is more to the story of economics: "We expect that some of the unexplained variance could be accounted for by more nuanced measures of economic security that are unobserved in our data, such as benefits, autonomy, work schedules, job security, and opportunity for advancement." Hope springs eternal for the convinced. The quote is from page 806.

14. Ibid., 807.

15. Too few scholars seem interested in the sex ratio disparities that arise when men's marriageability declines and incarceration rates are elevated. When there are fewer marriageable men, the marriage-minded among them—a smaller group by definition—are far more apt to perceive a dating environment that favors their interests, and to capitalize on it accordingly, by pursuing sex earlier in relationships and delaying marriage until they feel "ready to settle down."

16. The quote appears on page 65 in an untitled chapter by Patterson in Anderson, Browning, and Boyer, eds., *Marriage—Just a Piece of Paper?*.

17. William Julius Wilson, *The Truly Disadvantaged: The Inner City, the Underclass, and Public Policy* (Chicago: University of Chicago Press, 1990).

18. The quote appears on pages 400–401 in an untitled chapter by Wilson in Anderson, Browning, and Boyer, eds., *Marriage—Just a Piece of Paper?*.

19. Edin and Reed, "Why Don't They Just Get Married?" The quote is from page 126.

20. Daniel T. Lichter, Joseph P. Price, and Jeffrey M. Swigert, "Mismatches in the Marriage Market," *Journal of Marriage and Family* (in press, 2019), https://doi.org/10.1111/jomf.12603

21. Melissa S. Kearney and Riley Wilson, "Male Earnings, Marriageable Men, and Nonmarital Fertility: Evidence from the Fracking Boom," National Bureau of Economic Research Working Paper 23408, May 2017, https://www.nber.org/papers/w23408

22. The authors control for a pair of sensible pathways of influence—changes in house prices and changes in sex ratios—as well as experiment with lagged effects.

23. Kearney and Wilson, "Male Earnings, Marriageable Men, and Nonmarital Fertility," 5, 31–32.

24. Perhaps a simpler explanation is also worth considering—that oil-industry laborers took their money (and their marital intentions) with them to other locations besides North Dakota.

25. David Autor, David Dorn, and Gordon Hanson, "When Work Disappears: Manufacturing Decline and the Falling Marriage Market Value of Young Men," National Bureau of Economic Research Working Paper 23173, April 2018, https://www.nber.org/papers/w23173

26. See, as an example of this, Alexandra Killewald, "Money, Work, and Marital Stability: Assessing Change in the Gendered Determinants of Divorce," *American Sociological Review*, 81 (2016): 696–719.

27. Marianne Bertrand, Emir Kamenica, and Jessica Pan, "Gender Identity and Relative Income within Households," *The Quarterly Journal of Economics*, 130 (2015): 571–614. It is hardly a new conclusion; rather, it is one that has yet to expire. Economist Isabel Sawhill noted the empirical observation in 1977. See Isabel Sawhill, "Economic Perspectives on the Family," *Daedalus*, 106 (1977): 115–125.

28. These estimates come from analysis of the Census Bureau's American Community Survey.

29. A pair of sociologists suggest that more recent marriages—which are more selective in general—are less apt to split when wives outearn their husbands. They sort their sample (from the Panel Study of Income Dynamics) into more finely graded earnings differentials than did the *QJE* study. However, all of the authors agree that wives are apt to cut back on their labor-force participation so as to avoid outearning their husbands. See Christine R. Schwartz and Pilar Gonalons-Pons, "Trends in Relative Earnings and Marital Dissolution: Are Wives Who Outearn Their Husbands Still More Likely to Divorce?," *RSF: The Russell Sage Foundation Journal of the Social Sciences*, 2 (2016): 218–36.

30. Bertrand, Kamenica, and Pan, "Gender Identity and Relative Income within Households."

31. Ibid., 601. Additionally, if the wife earns more than the husband, spouses are 15 percent less likely to report that their marriage is very happy, 32 percent more likely to report marital troubles in the past year, and 46 percent more likely to have discussed separating in the past year.

32. Arlie Hochschild and Anne Machung, *The Second Shift: Working Parents and the Revolution at Home* (New York: Penguin Books, 1989).

33. Bertrand, Kamenica, and Pan, "Gender Identity and Relative Income within Households," 606.

34. Gary S. Becker, "A Theory of Marriage: Part I," *The Journal of Political Economy*, 81 (1973): 813–846.

35. Julie Matthaei, "Consequences of the Rise of Two Income Families: The Breakdown of the Sexual Division of Labor," *American Economic Review*, 70 (1980): 198–202.

36. If a couple publicly characterize themselves as married, refer to each other as husband and wife, use the same last name, and file joint tax returns, some civil authorities will treat them as married, even though no wedding took place and no marriage license was secured. Szymon, a 32-year-old computer programmer from Lublin, wouldn't be surprised at such a judgment. When asked if cohabitation was comparable to marriage, he responded, "If somebody isn't religious, thinks that cohabitation is good and doesn't base his decision on faith, it may seem to him that marriage is synonymous with cohabitation." Ndidi, the 28-year-old Pentecostal woman from Lagos, hewed closely to Becker's equivalence. When asked how a cohabiting couple differed from a married one, there wasn't much: "They live together, they bear children together, they do everything together. Most times [in cohabitation], the name doesn't change; the lady still bears her maiden name. That is the only thing." Fewer than a dozen of the U.S. states still recognize "common law marriages," but some are currently phasing out the privilege.

37. Laurie DeRose, Mark Lyons-Amos, W. Bradford Wilcox, and Gloria Huarcaya, *The Cohabitation-Go-Round: Cohabitation and Family Instability across the Globe* (New York: Social Trends Institute, 2017). See also Daniel T. Lichter, Katherine Michelmore, Richard N. Turner, and Sharon Sassler, "Pathways to a Stable Union? Pregnancy and Childbearing among Cohabiting and Married Couples," *Population Research and Policy Review*, 35 (2016): 377–399.

38. Bruce Wydick, "Why Married Sex Is Social Justice," *Christianity Today*, June 23, 2016, paragraph 14, http://www.christianitytoday.com/ct/2016/julaug/why-married-sex-is-social-justice.html

39. Matthijs Kalmijn, "Explaining Cross-National Differences in Marriage, Cohabitation, and Divorce in Europe, 1990–2000," *Population Studies*, 61 (2007): 243–263; Lynn Prince Cooke, Jani Erola, Marie Evertsson, Michael Gähler, Juho Härkönen, Belinda Hewitt, Marika Jalovaara, Man-Yee Kan, Torkild Hovde Lyngstad, Letizia Mencarini et al., "Labor and Love: Wives' Employment and Divorce Risk in Its Socio-Political Context," *Social Politics: International Studies in Gender, State and Society*, 20 (2013): 482–509.

40. See "Feminism, the Body, and the Machine" in Wendell Berry, *What Are People for?:Essays* (New York: North Point Press, 1990), 178–196. The quotes appear on page 180.

41. As in any empirical argument, some object. In a formative study now nearly 20 years old, sociologist Megan Sweeney contested Becker's "economic independence hypothesis," a theory that she claims "assumes that women with good prospects in the labor market will be less likely to marry than will women with relatively poorer prospects." (See Megan M. Sweeney, "Two Decades of Family Change: The Shifting Economic Foundations of Marriage," *American Sociological Review*, 67 (2002): 132–147. The quote is from page 132.) Sweeney wondered if the nature of the marital bargain has changed—that women's economic contribution now carries equal weight. It doesn't. Women's earnings are welcome, but they don't replace the pivotal importance of a man's income, which is a baseline indicator of marriageability in a way that a woman's income is not. What Sweeney finds is that men's economic prospects matter even more than they did in the past, whereas their education is less important. For women, it's the reverse; her education predicts marrying, but her earnings do not. Sweeney's findings don't undermine Becker. Rather, they affirm Cherlin's claim that marriage is now considered an achievement, not an aid to subsequently accomplishing things. Inexplicably, Sweeney ignores the role of religion in predicting marital decisions. Demographer Matthijs Kalmijn's does not, however, in a crossnational study of European marriage, cohabitation, and divorce rates. (See Kalmijn, "Explaining Cross-National Differences in Marriage, Cohabitation, and Divorce in Europe.") His conclusions reinforce hypotheses rooted in the second demographic transition—the share of adults pursuing higher education predicts higher marriage *and* higher divorce rates, while rising unemployment predicts subsequent lower marriage rates. It makes sense. But what matters most? Gender roles and religion, he concludes. In more religious countries, people are more likely to marry and less likely to split up.

42. Cherlin, *The Marriage-Go-Round*.

43. Waite and Gallagher, *The Case for Marriage*.

44. W. Bradford Wilcox and Robert I. Lerman, "For Richer, for Poorer: How Family Structures Economic Success in America," Research Brief, American Enterprise Institute and Institute for Family Studies, October 2014, https://ifstudies.org/ifs-admin/resources/for-richer-or-poorer-hep-2014.pdf

45. Robert I. Lerman, "Impacts of Marital Status and Parental Presence on the Material Hardship of Families with Children," Research Brief, Urban Institute, July 2002, https://www.urban.org/research/publication/impacts-marital-status-and-parental-presence-material-hardship-families-children/view/full_report; Robert I. Lerman, "Married and Unmarried Parenthood and Economic Well-Being: A Dynamic Analysis of a Recent Cohort," Research Brief, Urban Institute, http://webarchive. urban.org/publications/410540.html; Daniel T. Lichter, Deborah Roempke Graefe, and J. Brian Brown, "Is Marriage a Panacea? Union Formation among Economically Disadvantaged Unwed Mothers," *Social Problems*, 5 (2003): 60–86.

46. Kathryn Edin and Maria J. Kefalas, *Promises I Can Keep: Why Poor Women Put Motherhood before Marriage* (Berkeley: University of California Press, 2007).

47. Wilcox et al., *Why Marriage Matters*; Lorraine Blackman, Obie Clayton, Norval Glenn, Linda Malone-Colon, and Alex Roberts, *The Consequences of Marriage for African Americans: A Comprehensive Literature Review* (New York: Institute for American Values, 2005).

48. See William Fielding Ogburn, *Social Change with Respect to Culture and Original Nature* (New York: B. W. Huebsch, Inc., 1922).

49. Kim Parker and Wendy Wang, "Modern Parenthood: Roles of Moms and Dads Converge as They Balance Work and Family," *Pew Research Center*, March 14, 2013, http://www.pewsocialtrends.org/2013/03/14/modern-parenthood-roles-of-moms-and-dads-converge-as-they-balance-work-and-family/

50. Kristin Donnelly, Jean M. Twenge, Malissa A. Clark, Samia K. Shaikh, Angela Beiler-May, and Nathan T. Carter, "Attitudes toward Women's Work and Family Roles in the United States, 1976–2013," *Psychology of Women Quarterly*, 40 (2015): 41–54. To be sure, overall trends suggest change is still afoot, especially among adults. However, discourse about the "stalled gender revolution" suggests there are indicators of a limit. See Paula England, "The Gender Revolution: Uneven and Stalled," *Gender and Society*, 24 (2010): 149–166.

51. See, for example, Cherlin, *The Marriage-Go-Round*; Edin and Kefalas, *Promises I Can Keep*.

52. While he objects to same-sex marriage, something Spain legalized in 2005, Ander understands the logic of it within the current thought climate: "If gender differences are rejected, then I think that it makes perfect sense that a man marries another man."

53. Kathleen Gerson, *The Unfinished Revolution: How a New Generation Is Reshaping Family, Work, and Gender in America* (New York: Oxford University Press, 2009).

54. J. Richard Udry, "Biological Limits of Gender Construction," *American Sociological Review*, 65 (2000): 443–457. The quote is from page 454.

55. A forerunner of social network analysis, Georg Simmel asserted that marriage is anchored in sexual intercourse, an act that is "alone . . . common to all historically known forms of marriage, while perhaps no other characteristic can be found without exceptions." Like Simmel, recall that Hegel held that it is unacceptable to equate marriage with love, because love is "too contingent." Love is not meant to be transient in Bauman's "liquid" or Giddens's "confluent" sense. Marriage is not merely a sexual relationship. It is also not simply a civil contract, a notion Hegel labels "crude." See Kurt H. Wolff, *The Sociology of Georg Simmel* (New York: Simon and Schuster, 1950), 131 (note 10); Zygmunt Bauman, *Liquid Love* (Cambridge: Polity Press, 2003); Anthony Giddens, *The Transformation of Intimacy* (Stanford, CA: Stanford University Press, 1992). Even Erich Fromm, the famous German social psychologist, psychoanalyst, and socialist humanist, was far more skeptical about what the results of sexual attraction without sustained love would accomplish than are most moderns. The latter are delusional, Fromm would say. See Erich Fromm, *The Art of Loving* (New York: Harper, 1956).

56. Dietrich von Hildebrand, *Marriage: The Mystery of Faithful Love* (Manchester, NH: Sophia Institute Press, 1997). The quote comes from pages 10–11.

57. In the United States, for example, the most common reasons for sham marriage are to secure immigration benefits or—in the military—housing benefits and additional privileges reserved for married soldiers. See, as one example, Gabrielle Banks, "Fake Wedding Albums in Lucrative Scheme That Allegedly Paired Immigrants from Vietnam with U.S. Citizens," *Houston Chronicle*, June 29, 2019, https://www.houstonchronicle.com/news/houston-texas/houston/article/Fake-wedding-albums-in-lucrative-scheme-that-14072590.php. On the flip side, some people put on weddings that aren't actually legally valid, for the purpose of enjoying (or in the case of social media stars, profiting from) the attention. Just how common this is would be difficult to ascertain.

58. "'Til 2013 Do Us Part? Mexico Mulls 2-Year Marriage," *Reuters*, September 29, 2011, https://www.reuters.com/article/us-mexico-marriage/til-2013-do-us-part-mexico-mulls-2-year-marriage-idUSTRE78S6TX20110929

59. It is the case that two in three American divorces are more her idea than his (see Regnerus, *Cheap Sex*, page 161, Figure 5.2). Why? Because in today's marriage market, her net gain from marriage is less than it once was. When marriage is notably more difficult than they anticipated, women are more apt than men to perceive themselves fundamentally worse off inside marriage than outside of it (see Timothy Reichert, "Bitter Pill," *First Things*, May 2010, https://www.firstthings.com/article/2010/05/bitter-pill). This leads to women's higher support for, and actual interest in, divorce.

60. Dalton Conley, *Elsewhere, U.S.A: How We Got from the Company Man, Family Dinners, and the Affluent Society to the Home Office, BlackBerry Moms, and Economic Anxiety* (New York: Vintage Books, 2009). Other scholars label it similarly, as an "inter-temporal kind of polygamy" (de la Croix and Mariani, "From Polygyny to Serial Monogamy," 566).

61. In addition to this, von Hildebrand sensibly pits the comprehensive nature of the union against violations of fidelity: "The characteristics of complete, mutual

self-giving, and of being exclusively turned toward the beloved, as well as the fact that the two partners form a couple, exclude in themselves the possibility that this love can be directed simultaneously to more than one person." See page 20 of von Hildebrand, *Marriage*.

62. De la Croix and Mariani observe that "if we related polygyny to the possibility of fathering children from multiple women simultaneously, it seems safe to affirm that Europe . . . had become monogamous after the spread of Christianity." The quote appears on page 570 in "From Polygyny to Serial Monogamy."

63. Judith Stacey, *Unhitched: Love, Marriage, and Family Values from West Hollywood to Western China* (New York: New York University Press, 2012).

64. Indeed, a gay couple could marry civilly in a variety of Western countries, share beds with other men, never conceive a child, and split, only to subsequently marry new partners. And it's all still marriage in the eyes of the state. Some Christians could (and do) claim this scenario makes a mockery of their vision of marriage, but critics could (and do) counter with the claim that marriage is simply a social construction and, hence, reworkable. The notion that marriage—something ancient—is socially constructed, but sexual orientation—something discerned in the past century—is not, is a particularly bewildering assessment. Hence, it is no surprise that scholars of sexuality are beginning to embrace the notion that sexuality, too, is constructed and malleable.

65. Sociologist Judith Stacey accounts for gay unions' greater display of nonmonogamy by an appeal to sex differences: "They are men," and, hence, she holds that it is easier for them to separate emotional from physical intimacy. I believe her, but it is ironic to see sociologists of gender describe sexual differences in such robust terms. Stacey's remark appears in Mark Oppenheimer, "Married, with Infidelities," *New York Times*, June 30, 2011, paragraph 41, http://www.nytimes.com/2011/07/03/magazine/ infidelity-will-keep-us-together.html

66. Such a conclusion was reached by sociologist Debra Umberson in her qualitative study of gay, lesbian, and straight couples: "Men partnered with men were more likely . . . to indicate that such (extradyadic) sexual encounters posed minimal threat to their long-term relationship, as long as emotional intimacy was absent." In other words, sex with someone besides their primary partner is not the same as cheating, the latter of which remains a transgression. See Debra Umberson, Mieke Beth Thomeer, and Amy C. Lodge, "Intimacy and Emotion Work in Lesbian, Gay, and Heterosexual Relationships," *Journal of Marriage and Family*, 77 (2015): 542–556. The quote here is from page 551.

67. Stephen Macedo, *Just Married: Same-Sex Couples, Monogamy, and the Future of Marriage* (Princeton, NJ: Princeton University Press, 2015). See also Amy L. Wax, "Experiments in Matrimony," *First Things*, February 2017, https://www.firstthings. com/article/2017/02/experiments-in-matrimony

68. See supplemental materials for Joseph Henrich, Robert Boyd, and Peter J. Richerson, "The Puzzle of Monogamous Marriage," *Philosophical Transactions of the Royal Society B*, 367 (2012): 657–669.

69. de la Croix and Mariani, "From Polygyny to Serial Monogamy." Increasing secularization, however, means growing interest in serial monogamy and polyamory. In the

2018 American Political and Social Behavior survey, 56 percent of the least religious Americans between ages 20 and 65 agreed that "it's okay for three or more consenting adults to live together in a sexual/romantic relationship," far above the 5 percent found among the most religious Americans.

70. Chambers outlines, over the course of two chapters in her book, a contracts-based system to replace legal marriage. It is mind-boggling all the scenarios that would need regulatory oversight, to say nothing of how such contracts should be drawn up. "For example," Chambers writes, "partners could choose to contract such that any breach of sexual fidelity incurs an increase in housework." See Clare Chambers, *Against Marriage: An Egalitarian Defence of the Marriage-Free State* (Oxford, UK: Oxford University Press, 2017). The quote is from page 118. That's generous, by historical standards, and naïve about sex differences in how men and women punish infidelity. See David M. Buss, "Sexual and Emotional Infidelity: Evolved Gender Differences in Jealousy Prove Robust and Replicable," *Perspectives on Psychological Science*, 13 (2018): 155–160.

71. See Kurt H. Wolff, *The Sociology of Georg Simmel* (New York: Simon and Schuster, 1950). The quote is from page 130.

72. Bella DePaulo, "The Great Unraveling: Marriage Liberated Us by Coming Undone," *Psychology Today*, October 1, 2018, https://www.psychologytoday.com/us/blog/living-single/201810/the-great-unraveling-marriage-liberated-us-coming-undone. The quote is from paragraph 2.

73. Christian Smith, *What Is a Person? Rethinking Humanity, Social Life, and the Moral Good from the Person Up* (Chicago: University of Chicago Press, 2010).

74. Ibid.

75. For a few examples of social scientific writing toward such ends, see: Maggie Astor, "No Children Because of Climate Change? Some People Are Considering It," *New York Times*, Feb. 5, 2018, https://www.nytimes.com/2018/02/05/climate/climate-change-children.html; Bella DePaulo, *How We Live Now: Redefining Home and Family in the 21st Century* (New York: Atria Books, 2015); Eric Klinenberg, *Going Solo: The Extraordinary Rise and Surprising Appeal of Living Alone* (New York: Penguin Books, 2012); Christopher Ryan and Cacilda Jethá, *Sex at Dawn: The Prehistoric Origins of Modern Sexuality* (New York: HarperCollins, 2010).

76. It is helpful here to revisit the Catholic Church's recognition of the reality of marriage—once enacted it cannot be undone by any human power. It has a reality of its own. Others, including many Christians and not a few Catholics—hold that marriage can be undone by the couple and then certified by the state. The Catholic Church, on the other hand, holds that marriage precedes the advent of the state in time and in order of being, in keeping with the Aristotelian conviction that the family is the foundation of all other societies.

77. Edward Westermarck, *The Future of Marriage in Western Civilisation* (London: Macmillan and Co., Limited, 1936). The quote is from page 170.

78. Wolff, *The Sociology of Georg Simmel*. The quote is from page 130.

79. Meaning, it becomes unpopular and less often practiced. To be sure, aberrant "marital" behavior can be sparingly tolerated so long as it is recognized as such. An

intentionally childless union or sexually "open" marriage can be accommodated, like the occasional scofflaw who doesn't brake for the stop sign. But these are enabled to do so only by the institutionalized actions of the rest of us.

80. This is the reason why the scholarly and public relations effort to document the competence of gay parents was pivotal for the success of the same-sex marriage movement in the United States. That intellectual and legal squabble was staked, in no small part, on the longstanding link between marriage and childrearing.

Chapter 4

1. Russian wheat production—and with it, exports to half of the globe's countries—has surged in the past decade. See Anatoly Medetsky, "How an Oil Giant (Russia) Came to Dominate Wheat," *Bloomberg*, November 12, 2017, https://www.bloomberg. com/news/articles/2017-11-13/how-an-oil-giant-russia-came-to-dominate-wheat-quicktake-q-a. See also James Marson and Josh Chin, "Russia and China Show Off Ties with Putin Visit," *Wall Street Journal*, June 8, 2018, https://www.wsj.com/articles/russia-and-china-show-off-ties-with-putin-visit-1528467295

2. Boris Knorre, "Contemporary Russian Orthodoxy: From the Social Paradoxes to the Cultural Model," in *Culture Matters in Russia—and Everywhere*, eds. Lawrence Harrison and Evgeny Yasin (Lanham, MD: Lexington Books, 2015), 127–144.

3. Many Muscovites fear Putin's eventual departure from power not because they so adore him or his political decisions but because he is equated with restoration, stability, and strength. Many young adults don't know a Russia without him at the helm, and to imagine it fosters anxiety.

4. An exception to this is Paul Froese's *The Plot to Kill God: Findings from the Soviet Experiment in Secularization* (Berkeley: University of California Press, 2008).

5. Aleksandr I. Solzhenitsyn, *The Gulag Archipelago, 1918–1956, I–II* (New York: Harper & Row, 1973).

6. There are, so far as I can discern, some pragmatic reasons for this. First, the liturgy can run over ninety minutes, and healthy attendees are expected to stand the entire time (there are no pews). Second, the language isn't Russian but, rather, "Church Slavonic," which most of the people don't understand. Finally, unlike in Catholicism, there is no requirement in Russian Orthodoxy to attend weekly. This tends to weed out all but the most committed, limiting Orthodoxy's influence on the personal decision-making of the average Russian. See also John P. Burgess, "In-Churching Russia," *First Things*, May 2014, https://www.firstthings.com/article/2014/05/in-churching-russia

7. Russian Soviet Government, *The Marriage Laws of Soviet Russia* (New York: The Russian Soviet Government Bureau, 1921). The quote appears on pages 11–12.

8. Goldman, *Women, the State and Revolution*. The quote is from page 3.

9. Friedrich Engels, *The Origin of the Family, Property and the State* (New York: Pathfinder, 1972). The quote is from page 109.

10. Pitirim A. Sorokin, *The American Sex Revolution* (Boston, MA: Porter Sargent, 1956). The quote is from page 113.

11. Wendy Z. Goldman, "Freedom and Its Consequences: The Debate on the Soviet Family Code of 1926," *Russian History*, 11 (1984): 362–388. The quote is from page 363.

12. Ibid.

13. Wendy Z. Goldman, *Women, the State, and Revolution.* The quote appears on pages 216–217.

14. An argument can be made that the French Revolution provoked something similar in France, with the advent of a no-fault divorce decree.

15. Kristen R. Ghodsee, "Why Women Had Better Sex under Socialism," *New York Times*, August 12, 2017, https://www.nytimes.com/2017/08/12/opinion/why-women-had-better-sex-under-socialism.html. I do not disagree with Ghodsee's criticisms of the challenges posed to women and their marriages by contemporary capitalist economies in Eastern Europe. Her discussion of the Bolshevik family laws, however, is one-sided, especially when contrasted with Wendy Goldman's work on the same. I return to this subject in Chapters 5 and 7.

16. Wendy Goldman, "Freedom and Its Consequences."

17. Ibid.; de la Croix and Mariani, "From Polygyny to Serial Monogamy"; Goldman, *Women, the State and Revolution.* Demographer Sergei Zakharov observes that a mass abortion culture developed in part as a response to such "sharp changes in the social environment, which occurred all too often in the first half of the 20th century." See Sergei Zakharov, "Russian Federation: From the First to the Second Demographic Transition," *Demographic Research*, 19 (2008): 907–972. The quote is from page 911.

18. Ibid.

19. Regnerus, *Cheap Sex.*

20. David M. Buss, *The Evolution of Desire: Strategies of Human Mating* (New York: Basic Books, 2003).

21. Keep in mind that this is a nonrepresentative sample, not to be used for generating statistical estimates—or even expectations or presumptions about such statistics—concerning the population of churchgoing Christians.

22. See, for example, Tristan Bridges and Jesse M. Philbin, "Gender Convergence over 'Cheap Sex,'" *Contexts*, 18 (2019): 72–75.

23. Jean M. Twenge, Ryne A. Sherman, and Brooke E. Wells, "Declines in Sexual Frequency among American Adults, 1989–2014," *Archives of Sexual Behavior*, 46 (2017): 2389–2401. I have no dispute with the data on declining sexual frequency, only with what it means for the price of sex.

24. I use the term *chastity* because it is more versatile and comprehensive than a term like *abstinence*. Chastity is not, as many dictionaries define it, another term for avoiding sexual behavior. It is about integrating one's sexuality into one's state in life. While one could define chastity in terms of rules (such as, no sex outside of marriage), author George Weigel refers to Pope John Paul II's description of it as "the integrity of love" and "putting one's emotional center, and, in a sense, one's self, in the custody of another." Lust as the opposite of chastity desires pleasure through the *use* of another human being rather than through mutual self-giving. See George Weigel, *Witness*

to Hope: The Biography of Pope John Paul II (New York: HarperCollins, 1999). The quotes here are from page 142.

25. Meanwhile, the correlation between frequency of sex and religious service attendance is positive and statistically significant among married adults in nationally representative data from both 2014 and 2018. In regression models predicting frequency of sex in both the 2014 *Relationships in America* survey and the 2018 *American Political and Social Behavior* survey, greater church attendance remains significantly associated with more married sex even after controlling for age, race, physical health, depression, political affiliation, and a variety of other variables.

26. Roy Baumeister and Kathleen Vohs, "Sexual Economics: Sex as Female Resource for Social Exchange in Heterosexual Interactions," *Personality and Social Psychology Review*, 8 (2004): 339–363; Roy F. Baumeister, Kathleen R. Catanese, and Kathleen D. Vohs, "Is There a Gender Difference in Strength of Sex Drive? Theoretical Views, Conceptual Distinctions, and a Review of Relevant Evidence," *Personality and Social Psychology Review*, 5 (2001): 242–273; Letitia Anne Peplau, "Human Sexuality: How Do Men and Women Differ?," *Current Directions in Psychological Science*, 12 (2003): 37–40; Pamela C. Regan and Leah Atkins, "Sex Differences and Similarities in Frequency and Intensity of Sexual Desire," *Social Behavior and Personality: An International Journal*, 34 (2006): 95–102.

27. Paula England and Jonathan Bearak, "The Sexual Double Standard and Gender Differences in Attitudes toward Casual Sex among U.S. University Students," *Demographic Research*, 30 (2014): 1327–1338.

28. David M. Heer and Amyra Grossbard-Shechtman, "The Impact of the Female Marriage Squeeze and the Contraceptive Revolution on Sex Roles and the Women's Liberation Movement in the United States, 1960 to 1975," *Journal of Marriage and the Family*, 43 (1981): 49–65. The quote is from page 54.

29. Social scientists know, however, that when cohabitants *do* go on to marry, they are more likely to divorce than are those couples who had not lived together before marriage. See Michael J. Rosenfeld and Katharina Roesler, "Cohabitation Experience and Cohabitation's Association with Marital Dissolution," *Journal of Marriage and Family*, 81(2019): 42–58; Scott Stanley and Galena Rhoades, "Premarital Cohabitation Is Still Associated with Greater Odds of Divorce," *Institute for Family Studies*, October 17, 2018, https://ifstudies.org/blog/premarital-cohabitation-is-still-associated-with-greater-odds-of-divorce

30. Valentina wasn't speaking from experience but, rather, observation. She and her husband didn't sleep together before marrying, aided in this effort by the challenge of distance—he lived in Ukraine. Having parents who respected her freedom while setting expectations for her and her sister, together with ensuring they had a "confessor," a priest who knew them and to whom they could speak openly, also helped. (Comparatively few Russian Orthodox have a primary confessor.) The distance, however, proved challenging in other ways. They didn't know each other as well when they got married: "In reality, it was pretty difficult. We had to overcome a lot of things."

31. In his theory of personhood, sociologist Christian Smith identifies human dignity as "an inherent worth of immeasurable value that is deserving of certain morally

appropriate responses." (See Smith, *What Is a Person?* The quote is from page 435.) Still, why connect dignity with one's own relational and sexual behavior? This, too, has a history. In the mid-400s, Pope Leo the Great wrote the following admonition: "Christian, recognize your dignity and, now that you share in God's own nature, do not return to your former base condition by sinning. Remember who is your head and of whose body you are a member. Never forget that you have been rescued from the power of darkness and brought into the light of the Kingdom of God." (See Catholic Church, *Catechism.* The quote is from section 1691.)

32. Reinhard Hütter, "Pornography and Acedia," *First Things*, April 2012, http://www. firstthings.com/article/2012/04/pornography-and-acedia. The quote is from paragraph 14.

33. Rule 90, embedded within Chapter 32 (on "Fundamental Guarantees"), covers the prohibitions that particularly fail to recognize human dignity. See "Rule 90. Torture and Cruel, Inhuman or Degrading Treatment," International Committee of the Red Cross IHL Database, https://ihl-databases.icrc.org/customary-ihl/eng/docs/v1_cha_chapter32_rule90

34. Roy Baumeister and Kathleen Vohs, "Sexual Economics."

35. Gavin W. Jones, "Delayed Marriage and Very Low Fertility in Pacific Asia," *Population and Development Review*, 33 (2007): 453–478. The quote is from page 465. Jones's claim stands in contrast to other demographers who have argued that the sex ratio problem was overblown—that since women are apt to consider a wider (age) range of men, the actual marriage market contains more men than women, which ought to afford women "greater marital bargaining power" over the former. For two examples of this logic, see Thomas Anderson and Hans-Peter Kohler, "Low Fertility, Socioeconomic Development, and Gender Equity," *Population and Development Review*, 41 (2015): 381–407; Paula England and Elizabeth Aura McClintock, "The Gendered Double Standard of Aging in US Marriage Markets," *Population and Development Review*, 35 (2009): 797–816. Nevertheless, I think any bargaining power gained by age range is lost in other ways. For example, women have long preferred marrying men with at least as much education as they have. And in my study, they additionally prefer to marry men with Christian convictions and an active faith.

36. Geoff, the 24-year-old part-time electrician and full-time university student in Austin, thought his Southern Baptist congregation had the opposite problem—too many men: "Yeah, so in my church there's a lot of guys that are my age that are kind of like college age or whatever, and there's very few girls. There's very few." But even Geoff knew that this was an anomaly.

37. Bruce Wydick, "Why Married Sex Is Social Justice."

38. These estimates come from my own analyses of 2013–2015 data from the National Survey of Family Growth. The models include controls for religious affiliation, religious service attendance, age at marriage, marital status of the respondent's parents, as well as several standard demographic predictors (e.g., age, race/ethnicity, education).

39. Scott M. Stanley, Galena Kline Rhoades, and Howard J. Markman, "Sliding versus Deciding: Inertia and the Premarital Cohabitation Effect," *Family Relations*, 55 (2006): 499–509. Stanley, in turn, borrowed the notion from my late colleague Norval

Glenn. See Norval D. Glenn, "A Plea for Greater Concern about the Quality of Marital Matching," in *Revitalizing the Institution of Marriage for the Twenty-First Century: An Agenda for Strengthening Marriage*, eds. Alan J. Hawkins, Lynn D. Wardle, and David O. Coolidge (Westport, CT: Praeger, 2002), 45–58.

40. As an interesting aside, Noor's disdain for passivity and inaction, on top of having endured a dysfunctional family while growing up, contributed to a years-long secretive sexual relationship with a woman she described as someone who "takes action, a strong woman," who provided Noor with feelings of security. Noor does not, however, identify as bisexual. Some would suppose that's because she lives in a conservative culture. But she said she was not attracted to women, despite the sexual nature of this relationship. Instead, she held that she was attracted to men—and to that one woman. "She was my escape," she admitted, "for so many years. I know the relationship [with her was] toxic on so many levels, but part of me doesn't want to forget the positive emotions I felt with her."

41. George A. Akerlof, Janet L. Yellen, and Michael L. Katz, "An Analysis of Out-of-Wedlock Childbearing in the United States," *Quarterly Journal of Economics*, 41 (1996): 277–317; see also Regnerus, *Cheap Sex*. An unusual exception to this explanation came in an interview with Darren, a 30-year-old Catholic from suburban Detroit, who broke up with the mother of his only child "before I found out she was pregnant, for reasons like she had no ambition, she did not want to go to college, she just wanted to be a stay-at-home mom and live her life happy at home. Uh, so there's reasons it didn't work out. I believe she tried to—she stopped taking birth control to get me to stay. She told me that. But that's why I broke up with her." Not only does this type of "entrapment" barely exist as a practice, if Darren's case is any indication, such efforts not only fail to keep a man in a relationship, they backfire.

42. This section includes content that first appeared and is elaborated upon in *Cheap Sex*.

43. Reichert, "Bitter Pill."

44. Economist Tim Reichert, writing in the journal *First Things*, says that women in today's post-Pill mating market often find themselves in a "prisoner's dilemma." As Reichert describes it, a prisoner's dilemma (as discerned by mathematicians in the mid-20th century) is "any social setting wherein all parties have a choice between cooperation and noncooperation, and where all parties would be better off if they choose cooperation. But because people in a prisoner's-dilemma setting cannot effectively coordinate and enforce cooperation, all parties choose the best individual choice, which is noncooperation. The social result is disastrous, and everyone is made poorer." See Reichert, "Bitter Pill." The quote is from paragraph 44.

45. Peter S. Arcidiacono, Ahmed Khwaja, and Lijing Ouyang, "Habit Persistence and Teen Sex: Could Increased Access to Contraception Have Unintended Consequences for Teen Pregnancies?," *Journal of Business and Economic Statistics*, 30 (2012): 312–325.

46. Pope John Paul II, *Familiaris Consortio*. The quoted phrase is from section 6.

47. See Chapter 3 of Regnerus, *Cheap Sex*.

48. Akerlof, Yellen, and Katz, "An Analysis of Out-of-Wedlock Childbearing in the United States."

49. Giddens, *The Transformation of Intimacy*.

50. Pope Paul VI, *Humanae Vitae* (Vatican City: Vatican Publishing House, 1968). The quote is from section 17.

51. Ibid.

52. Barbara J. Risman, "Is Recreational Sex a Social Problem? Or, What's Wrong with Kids Today?," *Contemporary Sociology*, 48 (2019): 123–129. See also, in response, Mark Regnerus, "Comment on Barbara Risman's review of *Cheap Sex: The Transformation of Men, Marriage, and Monogamy*," *Contemporary Sociology*, 48 (2019): 130–131.

53. We did not ask interviewees if they were planning on using Catholic-approved family-planning methods (such as the Creighton Model).

54. Social theorist Anthony Giddens was an early predictor of significant ramifications from fertility control. See Giddens, *The Transformation of Intimacy*. The president of the National Institute for Reproductive Health said the Pill created the most profound change in human history. See Vanessa Grigoriadis, "Waking Up from the Pill," *New York Magazine*, November 28, 2010, http://nymag.com/news/features/69789. See also Claudia Goldin and Lawrence F. Katz, "Career and Marriage in the Age of the Pill," *American Economic Review*, 90 (2000): 461–465.

55. Janet Saltzman Chafetz, "Chicken or Egg? A Theory of the Relationship between Feminist Movements and Family Change," in *Gender and Family Change in Industrialized Countries*, eds. Karen Oppenheim Mason and An-Magritt Jensen (Oxford: Clarendon Press, 1995), 63–81. The quote is from page 69, italics original.

56. Tanya's husband would "translate," in American terms, to being mildly religious, like an occasional evangelical or Catholic. He is neither antagonistic to, nor encouraging of, her faith. Perhaps as a consequence, she is not as active in her parish as she once was.

57. Although I do not cover the concept at length, "infantilism" was mentioned as a problem by several interviewees, including multiple Russian Orthodox. In fact, Tanya's account of meeting her husband began with a discussion of infantile Orthodox men, which seems to be synonymous with indecisive and self-centered. She described a young adult trip to the Monastery of Optina, southwest of Moscow: "Everyone was like, 'Great! Let's go!' But then even those who had cars were not eager to drive, like, 'What if something happens? What direction should we take?' And when they didn't like something, they stood in the middle of the road like, 'We are not going anywhere. We want to have a swim in the lake.' In the end, one girl . . . asked to stop the car. I stopped and asked what had happened. And she was like, 'I won't be in his car anymore.' So she got into my car. . . . In general, girls are less infantile than boys. Girls are generally independent, ambitious, while boys . . . I see less of these qualities in them."

58. Arcidiacono, Khwaja, and Ouyang, "Habit Persistence and Teen Sex."

59. Brian Hollar, "Holy Matrimony, Batman! Why Do the Devout Pay So Much for Marriage?" Paper presented at the annual meeting of the Association for the Study of Religion, Economics, and Culture, Arlington, VA, April 2013.

60. I benefitted tremendously here from remarks by Carrie Miles, author of *The Redemption of Love: Rescuing Marriage and Sexuality from the Economics of a Fallen World* (Grand Rapids, MI: Brazos Press, 2006), offered in commentary on my book

Cheap Sex at the 2018 annual meeting of the Society for the Scientific Study of Religion.

61. W. Bradford Wilcox, "It's (Not Just) the Economy, Stupid," *Institute for Family Studies*, December 11, 2014, https://ifstudies.org/blog/its-not-just-the-economy-stupid-why-is-the-working-class-family-really-coming-apart

62. Brad, a 31-year-old engineer and Catholic newlywed in Austin, is convinced pornography is harming marriage. "Your brain," he explains, "will neurologically adapt to what you expose yourself to. So you train yourself about what a normal relationship is while watching all these fantasies that are totally ludicrous." The result, Brad surmises, is a drug that "satisfies better than any relationship ever could." While others may quibble about his last assertion, there's no arguing that pornography is a very popular inferior good today.

63. Hollar warns that if marriage is linked to men's better labor force performance, an extended recession in marriage may have wide ramifications for their productivity.

64. Beirut's Christians also, according to numerous conversations, exhibit higher average economic expectations than its Muslims—hence a higher barrier to marriageability. Interviewees noted that Christians expect to send their (few) children to private schooling and then to college, while Muslims leaned more heavily on free public schooling and exhibited more modest standard-of-living expectations to help raise their (commonly larger) families. Some wealthier Muslims prefer to live in or near Beirut's Christian neighborhoods and to send their children to Christian (Catholic or evangelical) schools.

65. Multiple interviewees noted that this ability to flaunt (even imaginary) wealth is also the reason for the popularity of certain Western social media, like Facebook, Instagram, and Snapchat (but not, interestingly, online dating sites).

66. Ben Hubbard, "Here Comes the Bride. And the Bride. And the Bride. Mass Weddings Boom in Lebanon," *New York Times*, September 15, 2019, https://www.nytimes.com/2019/09/15/world/middleeast/lebanon-weddings.html

Chapter 5

1. William Alex Pridemore, "Measuring Homicide in Russia: A Comparison of Estimates from the Crime and Vital Statistics Reporting Systems," *Social Science and Medicine*, 57 (2003): 1343–1354.

2. Moscow is "not just the capital and seat of government," former NPR correspondent Anne Garrels observes in her book *Putin Country*. "It is also the financial, commercial, cultural, and entertainment center—Washington, New York, Chicago, and L.A. all wrapped into one." See Anne Garrels, *Putin Country: A Journey into the Real Russia* (New York: Farrar, Straus and Giroux, 2016). The quote is from pages 4–5.

3. Becker, "A Theory of Marriage: Part I."

4. According to the World Bank, "In the 25 years from 1990 to 2015, the extreme poverty rate dropped an average of a percentage point per year—from nearly 36% to 10%. . . . The World Bank's preliminary forecast is that extreme poverty has declined

to 8.6 percent in 2018." See "Decline of Global Extreme Poverty Continues but Has Slowed: World Bank," *The World Bank*, September 19, 2018, https://www.worldbank. org/en/news/press-release/2018/09/19/decline-of-global-extreme-poverty-continues-but-has-slowed-world-bank. The quotes are from paragraphs 6 and 8.

5. Eric Morath, "Was the Gig Economy Overblown?," *Wall Street Journal*, June 7, 2018, paragraph 1, https://www.wsj.com/articles/was-the-gig-economy-overblown-1528403201

6. Lawrence F. Katz and Alan B. Krueger, "Understanding Trends in Alternative Work Arrangements in the United States," National Bureau of Economic Research Working Paper 25425, January 2019, https://www.nber.org/papers/w25425.pdf. The quote is from page 3. See also Josh Zumbrun, "How Estimates of the Gig Economy Went Wrong," *Wall Street Journal*, January 7, 2019, https://www.wsj.com/articles/how-estimates-of-the-gig-economy-went-wrong-11546857000

7. One aspect of a social structure is its reinforcement by culturally sensible cognitive categories. That is, what we think about a pattern enhances the durability of that pattern, even in the presence of sensible alternatives. Uncertainty could yield more marriages if we thought about marriage differently, as insurance against instability. But for the most part, we don't.

8. Additionally, Jerzy maintained that Polish communism lost its revolutionary sense long before its collapse in the face of the Solidarity movement. The government had, in the end, amounted to nothing more than an elite holding onto its political power and economic privileges.

9. Christopher Lasch, *Haven in a Heartless World: The Family Besieged* (New York: W.W. Norton & Company, 1977). The quote is from page xxiii.

10. Andrew J. Cherlin, *Labor's Love Lost: The Rise and Fall of the Working-Class Family in America* (New York: Russell Sage Foundation, 2014).

11. See Patrick J. Deneen, *Why Liberalism Failed* (New Haven, CT: Yale University Press, 2018). In a personal conversation, political theorist Kevin Stuart relayed the following apt analogy: "Free markets are like a river. The river is a powerful force for good. It made the land fertile, food plentiful, and communities wealthier. But the river wants to get out of its boundaries. It works relentlessly to escape its banks. And whenever it succeeds, it destroys things and kills people."

12. See "The Three Foes of the Family" in G. K. Chesterton, *The Well and the Shallows* (San Francisco: Ignatius Press, [1935] 2006), 111–113. The quote appears on page 111.

13. Leo XIII, *Rerum Novarum* (Vatican City: Vatican Publishing House, 1891). The quote appears in section 13.

14. The "invisible hand" refers to Adam Smith's description in his book, *The Theory of Moral Sentiments* (Boston: Wells and Lilly, 1817), of the unintended social benefits of the individual's self-interested behavior.

15. Nearly disappeared, but not entirely: see Christina Maxouris and Leah Asmelash, "A North Carolina Man Just Won a $750,000 Lawsuit after Suing His Wife's Lover," *CNN*, October 2, 2019, https://www.cnn.com/2019/10/02/us/alienation-of-affection-laws-north-carolina-lawsuit-trnd/index.html

16. Both in Marxist theory as well as in lived history, communism has tended to be antagonistic to organized religion. Dissident Aleksandr Solzhenitsyn describes in

The Gulag Archipelago how, even after the toxic reforms of 1926 were overturned, Christian families in Stalinist Russia were regularly broken up. Wives—who tended to be more religious than their husbands—were given the standard ten-year prison term and never allowed to reunite with their children. It is, therefore, difficult to suggest that Christian marriage would flourish under socialism or communism, at least of the sort the world has witnessed to date. While nascent socialist forces at work in America seem decidedly antagonistic to long-standing Christian notions about marriage and sexuality, such an observation should not be considered a blanket endorsement of present economic conditions.

17. Pope Francis, *Amoris Laetitia* (Vatican City: Vatican Publishing House, 2016), section 39.

18. Francis predicted this: a "weakening of faith and religious practice," leaving people "more isolated amid their difficulties." This "loneliness, arising from the absence of God in a person's life and the fragility of relationships," together with a sense of powerlessness, should surprise no one. The result, the pope concludes, is "widespread uncertainty and ambiguity." Ibid.

19. Vatican Secretary of State, "Statistical Yearbook of the Church 2015" (Vatican City: Vatican Publishing House, 2017).

20. Veronica was married briefly, for just over a year. In a sad, even bizarre account, she described a "normal" premarital sex life that ended promptly with the wedding. After that, she and her husband had sex "only once." He was uninterested. "That's why I think he's either gay, [was] with someone else, or has a lot of issues." Her ex took up with his secretary within a week of the divorce; that relationship, too, failed. Now he lives with a woman who has several children and is thirteen years his senior. He wanted a family, Veronica believes, but not a marriage.

21. Steven Ruggles and Sheela Kennedy, "Trends in Union Instability in the United States, 1980s–2010s," Minnesota Population Center Working Paper No. 2015-1, May 2015, https://pop.umn.edu/sites/pop.umn.edu/files/wp-2015-1.pdf. The quote is from page 8.

22. DeRose et al., *The Cohabitation-Go-Round*.

23. Arielle Kuperberg, "Age at Coresidence, Premarital Cohabitation, and Marriage Dissolution: 1985–2009," *Journal of Marriage and Family*, 76 (2014): 352–369; Wendy D. Manning and Jessica A. Cohen, "Premarital Cohabitation and Marital Dissolution: An Examination of Recent Marriages," *Journal of Marriage and Family*, 74 (2012): 377–387; Steffen Reinhold, "Reassessing the Link between Premarital Cohabitation and Marital Instability," *Demography*, 47 (2010): 719–733; Jay Teachman, "Premarital Sex, Premarital Cohabitation, and the Risk of Subsequent Marital Dissolution among Women," *Journal of Marriage and Family*, 65 (2003): 444–455.

24. Daniel T. Lichter and Zhenchao Qian, "Serial Cohabitation and the Marital Life Course," *Journal of Marriage and Family*, 70 (2008): 861–878. See also Daniel T. Lichter, Richard N. Turner, and Sharon Sassler, "National Estimates of the Rise in Serial Cohabitation," *Social Science Research*, 39 (2010): 754–765.

25. Colleen N. Nugent and Jill Daugherty, "A Demographic, Attitudinal, and Behavioral Profile of Cohabiting Adults in the United States, 2011–2015," National Health

Statistics Report No. 111 (Washington, DC: National Center for Health Statistics, 2018), https://www.cdc.gov/nchs/data/nhsr/nhsr111.pdf

26. Stanley, Rhoades, and Markham, "Sliding vs. Deciding."

27. In Lagos, such parental influence is not just imaginable, but common. One 24-year-old Anglican interviewee noted that if men can get a good job—which was challenging—they will "want to get married, even if they don't want to," because "most of them will be forced by their parents to [marry]."

28. Source: American Political and Social Behavior survey, 2018.

29. Stanley, Rhoades, and Markham, "Sliding vs. Deciding."

30. Enrique, quoted at several points in this book, describes something similar in his own orbit: "All my father's siblings are married; nobody is divorced. On my mother's side, it's the same thing. Everyone is very close to God. Both my grandmothers are very pious. I'm not an example of the difficulty." The interviewer responded by observing that Enrique is "not afraid to marry, and you expect to marry," to which Enrique responded, "Exactly."

31. Rose McDermott, James Fowler, and Nicholas Christakis, "Breaking Up Is Hard to Do, Unless Everyone Else Is Doing It Too: Social Network Effects on Divorce in a Longitudinal Sample," *Social Forces*, 92 (2013): 491–519.

32. Norval D. Glenn, "How Good for Children Is the 'Good Divorce'?," Institute for American Values Working Paper 78, April 2012, http://americanvalues.org/catalog/pdfs/good-divorce.pdf

33. Sebastián Valenzuela, Daniel Halpern, and James E. Katz, "Social Network Sites, Marriage Well-Being and Divorce: Survey and State-Level Evidence from the United States," *Computers in Human Behavior*, 36 (2014): 94–101.

34. Amanda M. Kimbrough, Rosanna E. Guadagno, Nicole L. Muscanell, and Janeann Dill, "Gender Differences in Mediated Communication: Women Connect More than Men Do," *Computers in Human Behavior*, 29 (2013): 896–900; H. Andrew Schwartz, Johannes C. Eichstaedt, Margaret L. Kern, Lukasz Dziurzynski, Stephanie M. Ramones, Megha Agrawal, Achal Shah, Michal Kosinski, David Stillwell, Martin E. P. Seligman et al., "Personality, Gender, and Age in the Language of Social Media: The Open-Vocabulary Approach," *PLoS ONE*, 8 (2013): e73791.

35. Nicole L. Muscanell and Rosanna E. Guadagno, "Make New Friends or Keep the Old: Gender and Personality Differences in Social Networking Use," *Computers in Human Behavior*, 28 (2012): 107–112.

36. Valenzuela, Halpern, and Katz, "Social Network Sites, Marriage Well-Being and Divorce."

37. Michael J. Rosenfeld, Reuben J. Thomas, and Sonia Hausen, "Disintermediating Your Friends: How Online Dating in the United States Displaces Other Ways of Meeting," *Proceedings of the National Academy of Sciences*, 116 (2019): 17753–17758.

38. Dan Slater, *Love in the Time of Algorithms: What Technology Does to Meeting and Mating* (New York: Current, Penguin Group, 2013).

39. Solange V. Manche, "Tinder, Destroyer of Cities—When Capital Abandons Sex," *Strelka Mag*, September 20, 2019, https://strelkamag.com/en/article/tinder-destroyer-of-cities-when-capital-abandons-sex

40. CatholicMatch Institute, *Online Dating: A Simple Guide for Catholics* (Zelienople, PA: CatholicMatch Institute, 2015). The quotes appear on pages 18 and 9, respectively.

41. Rosenfeld, Thomas, and Hausen, "Disintermediating Your Friends."

42. Yoosik Youm and Anthony Paik, "The Sex Market and Its Implications for Family Formation," in *The Sexual Organization of the City*, eds. Edward O. Laumann, Stephen Ellingson, Jenna Mahay, Anthony Paik, and Yoosik Youm (Chicago: University of Chicago Press, 2004), 165–193.

Chapter 6

1. Other accounts of this union and its participants paint a far more mixed portrait—and a darker impression of Sergei—than Katerina relays. The point is not so much whether a narrative's facts are agreed upon but, rather, how it has shaped its hearers.

2. Stephanie Coontz, *The Way We Never Were: American Families and the Nostalgia Trap* (New York: Basic Books, 1993).

3. William I. Thomas and Dorothy S. Thomas, *The Child in America: Behavior Problems and Programs* (New York: Alfred A. Knopf, 1928), 571–572.

4. David Popenoe, *War over the Family* (Piscataway, NJ: Transaction Publishers, 2008); Waite and Gallagher, *The Case for Marriage*.

5. Deneen, *Why Liberalism Failed*, 64–65.

6. Ibid., 66.

7. Rod Dreher, *The Benedict Option: A Strategy for Christians in a Post-Christian Nation* (New York: Sentinel, 2017). In a globalized and media-saturated world, however, even these are subject to colonization, to say nothing of a leaky pipeline by which the next generation can drift away.

8. Andy Crouch, *Culture Making: Recovering Our Creative Calling* (Downers Grove, IL: InterVarsity Press, 2009). The quote is from page 67.

9. Ibid., 248.

10. Robert Louis Wilken, "The Church as Culture," *First Things*, April 2004, paragraph 15, https://www.firstthings.com/article/2004/04/the-church-as-culture

11. Crouch, *Culture Making*. The quote is from page 75.

12. These two paragraphs are a summary of Środowisko as described in George Weigel's book *Witness to Hope*.

13. Ibid., 100.

14. Wojtyła's regard for the exchange that is marriage comes through clearly in a letter he wrote to an early member of Środowisko as she approached her own marriage: "After many experiences and a lot of thinking, I am convinced that the (objective) starting point of love is the realization that I am needed by another. The person who objectively needs me most is also, for me, objectively, the person I most need. This is a fragment of life's deep logic, and also a fragment of trusting in the Creator and in Providence." Ibid., 102.

15. Dietrich Bonhoeffer, *Life Together: The Classic Exploration of Christian Community* (San Francisco: HarperOne, [1939] 2009).

16. Crouch, *Culture Making*, 248.

17. Wilken, "The Church as Culture," paragraph 36.

18. C. S. Lewis, *Mere Christianity* (San Francisco: HarperOne, 2015), 134.

19. Arlie Hochschild, *The Time Bind: When Work Becomes Home and Home Becomes Work* (New York: Metropolitan Books, 1997).

20. 1 Timothy 1: 15.

21. Lasch, *Haven in a Heartless World*.

22. Ibid., especially pages xix–xxiv.

23. The quote appears on page 395 in an untitled chapter by William Doherty in *Marriage—Just a Piece of Paper?*, eds. Anderson, Browning, and Boyer.

24. While divorce is dipping in many locales as fewer couples marry, the Jacksonville figure nevertheless stands out. See Lee Habeeb, "The Incredible Success Story Behind One County's Plummeting Divorce Rate Should Inspire Us All," *Newsweek*, July 26, 2019, https://www.newsweek.com/incredible-success-story-behind-one-countys-plummeting-divorce-rate-should-inspire-us-all-1451188; W. Bradford Wilcox and Spencer James, "Divorce Is Down in Duval County: A Preliminary Evaluation of the Culture of Freedom Initiative in Florida" (Washington, DC: Philanthropy Roundtable, 2018), http://mediad.publicbroadcasting.net/p/wjct/files/201809/divorce_is_down_in_duval_county_by_brad_wilcox.pdf

25. See *Witness to Love*, https://witnesstolove.org/

26. Additionally, 32 percent of heavy users thought about leaving their spouse, double the estimated rate (16 percent) among nonusers. See Valenzuela, Halpern, and Katz, "Social Network Sites, Marriage Well-Being and Divorce."

27. Mark Regnerus, "How Different Are the Adult Children of Parents Who Have Same-Sex Relationships? Findings from the New Family Structures Study," *Social Science Research*, 41 (2012): 752–770.

28. Mark 8:34–36.

29. Pilar Urbano, *The Man of Villa Tevere* (Strongsville, OH: Scepter Publishers, 2011).

30. This and the quote above it appear on page 278 of Claire Russell, ed., *Glimpses of the Church Fathers* (Strongsville, OH: Scepter Publishers, 2008).

31. Policies that require opt-out rather than opt-in decisions, like Austria's organ donation program, enjoy far higher compliance rates. See Stanford SPARQ, "'Opt Out' Policies Increase Organ Donation," https://sparq.stanford.edu/solutions/opt-out-policies-increase-organ-donation

32. Rashid, a Muslim convert living in Austin, reflected on his childhood years in the United Arab Emirates: "In the UAE they do care [about marriage]. They actually offer financial help for people who want to get married. [*Interesting. Like a loan or stipend?*] Very much free money. Sort of like a scholarship. [*Really? So they really want people to get married?*] (Laughs) Yeah. [*Is this in response to people not getting married?*] Yes, that's one reason, because of the expenses. And two, it's from their belief as well. It's from what the government believes—that marriage is important. I don't think they have the right view of marriage, because you can marry multiple wives, [but] they believe in marriage and it's important, so they promote it that way."

33. Fertility remains elevated in Nigeria, at an average of 5.5 births per woman, though efforts to reduce family size in Lagos are apparent—and effective. Kingsley, the 29-year-old evangelical, was adamant about the fertility-marriage link: "The reason why I can't have a baby mama is because there is nothing like that in my family. You don't get pregnant before marriage."

34. University of Pennsylvania demographer Hans-Peter Kohler responds to a question on this topic with a frank assessment: "The benefit-cost ratios for policies to increase fertility through generous parental leave, child benefit and related social programs in low fertility settings are likely to be fairly low. For many policy options that have been considered, the empirical support for sustained effects on fertility levels is relatively weak, despite substantial private and/or social costs of such policies." See page 10 of Hans-Peter Kohler and Thomas Anderson, "Divergent Demographic Destinies." Paper presented at the annual meeting of the Population Association of America, Washington, DC, April 2016.

35. They're not alone: Central and Eastern European states formerly under the thumb of the Soviet Union all exhibit comparable fertility rates today. Each declined precipitously after the end of the communist era, signaling heightened uncertainty that has not yet abated.

36. When interviews were conducted, the program only rewarded families with at least two children. That has since shifted to families with any children.

37. Lyman Stone, "Poland's Baby Bump," *First Things*, March 2, 2018, https://www.firstthings.com/web-exclusives/2018/03/polands-baby-bump

38. See Karolina Goraus-Tańska and Gabriela Inchauste, "The Family 500+: Battling Child Poverty in Poland," *World Bank Blogs*, December 22, 2017, https://blogs.worldbank.org/europeandcentralasia/family-500-battling-child-poverty-poland

39. Sebastian Klüsener, Aiva Jasilioniene, and Victoria Yuodeshko, "Retraditionalization as a Pathway to Escape Lowest-Low Fertility? Characteristics and Prospects of the Eastern European 'Baby Boom.'" Paper presented at the annual meeting of the Population Association of America, Austin, TX, April 2019.

40. We're not talking about replacing the income of a spouse, for those concerned that such a plan would be a boon for single mothers. (To be sure, the culture of "the Polish family" helps reduce opportunism that some might otherwise perceive in the 500+ program.)

41. Johnson-Hanks, Bachrach, Morgan, and Kohler, *Understanding Family Change and Variation*, 79–80.

42. Zakharov, "Russian Federation."

43. "Moscow Salaries See Double-Digit Growth in 2018, Official Figures Say," *The Moscow Times*, February 5, 2019, https://www.themoscowtimes.com/2019/02/05/moscow-salaries-see-double-digit-growth-2018-official-figures-say-a64402

44. Joel Kotkin, Anuradha Shroff, Ali Modarres, and Wendell Cox, ed. Zina Klapper, *The Rise of Post-Familialism: Humanity's Future?* (Singapore: Civil Service College, 2012).

45. Oren Kass, *The Once and Future Worker: A Vision for Renewal of Work in America* (New York: Encounter Books, 2018). Kass points out that a consistent wage subsidy is more helpful than a tax credit, which is paid out only once a year.

46. See references to living wages, as well as state investment in the same, in at least three different papal encyclicals: Leo XIII, *Rerum Novarum*; Pope John XXIII, *Mater et Magistra* (Vatican City: Vatican Publishing House, 1961); Pius XI, *Quadragesimo Anno* (Vatican City: Vatican Publishing House, 1931).

Chapter 7

1. Valerie K. Oppenheimer, "Women's Rising Employment and the Future of the Family in Industrial Societies," *Population and Development Review*, 20 (1994): 293–342. The quote is from page 333.
2. In a popular essay, writer Mandy Len Cantron observed, "When my partner, Mark, and I talk about whether or not we want to get married, friends tend to assume that we are trying to decide whether or not we are 'serious' about our relationship. But I'm not expressing doubts about my relationship; I'm doubting the institution itself." This is accurate. Cantron is observing the thing itself and wondering aloud whether she wants it or not. The quote comes from paragraph 4 of Mandy Len Cantron, "What You Lose When You Gain a Spouse," *The Atlantic Monthly*, July 2, 2019, https://www.theatlantic.com/family/archive/2019/07/case-against-marriage/591973/
3. Barbara Atwood, "Marital Contracts and the Meaning of Marriage," *Arizona Law Review* 54 (2012): 11–42. The quote appears on page 19. Atwood is hardly alone. Many scholars, politicians, and observers presume that marriage's raison d'être is entirely socially constructed and, hence, quite malleable.
4. Steven P. Martin, Nan Marie Astone, and H. Elizabeth Peters, "Fewer Marriages, More Divergence: Marriage Projections for Millennials to Age 40," Research Brief, Urban Institute, April 2014, https://www.urban.org/research/publication/fewer-marriages-more-divergence-marriage-projections-millennials-age-40/view/full_report
5. Sherry Turkle, *Alone Together: Why We Expect More from Technology and Less from Each Other* (New York: Basic Books, 2011).
6. Sociologist Nicholas Christakis and his colleagues noted that divorce is, indeed, infectious, out to the third degree—that is, friends of one's friends. See McDermott, Fowler, and Christakis, "Breaking Up Is Hard to Do, Unless Everyone Else Is Doing It Too." To be fair, this study has its critics. Nevertheless, studies in the sociology of religion provide support for the thesis as well, including Mark Regnerus, "Moral Communities and Adolescent Delinquency: Religious Contexts and Community Social Control," *Sociological Quarterly*, 44 (2003): 523–554.
7. Chambers, *Against Marriage*, 3.
8. Historian Wendy Goldman documents concern from multiple Soviet leadership figures about the premature unraveling of marriage. Recognizing cohabiting unions "would prompt endless disputes between partners that the courts would have to resolve," asserted one. See Goldman, *Women, the State, and Revolution*, 227.
9. Luke 12:13 and following.
10. Discussion of same-sex marriage among interviewees was not extensive, in part because we did not specifically inquire about the matter. Where it came up—most

typically when inquiring about government interest in marriage—the average respondent indicated disapproval. A small minority considered the topic irrelevant. No interviewee signaled open endorsement of same-sex Christian matrimony, while a minority—like Thomas—were content with a distinction between religious and civil marriage. Thomas was unusual (though not alone) in his more extensive conversation about the tensions between the two.

11. This echoes a similar conclusion offered by Cardinal Donald Wuerl, former Archbishop of Washington, who said in a news conference after the *Obergefell* decision, "The law of the land is the law of the land" and "We certainly follow what the law says," even while he noted that the Church's definition of marriage would remain distinctive. See Lou Chibarro Jr., "Cardinal Wuerl Conciliatory on Marriage Ruling?," *Washington Blade*, July 7, 2015, https://www.washingtonblade.com/2015/07/07/cardinal-wuerl-conciliatory-on-marriage-ruling/. The quotes are from paragraphs 2 and 3.

12. Goldman, *Women, the State, and Revolution*, 186.

13. Islam appears far more adept at maintaining its distinctive marriage and family norms in societies in which it finds itself, including historically Christian or secular nations. And Muslims maintain a notably higher birth rate to boot. Demographically, theirs is the future, when glimpsed over the course of hundreds of years. Of course, history has a way of not turning out the way that demographic projections suggest, and it is subject to unforeseen events and circumstances (like pandemics).

14. Dreher, *The Benedict Option*; see also Rod Dreher, "Sex after Christianity," *The American Conservative*, April 11, 2013, http://www.theamericanconservative.com/articles/sex-after-christianity

15. Ibid., paragraph 19. What takes the place of Christianity in this framework? That's the subject of Rieff's final book, *My Life among the Deathworks*, where he argues that a new world culture is emerging whose social order rests on no preexisting sacred order—such as found in the monotheistic religions—and whose cultural artifacts serve primarily as sites to "transgress" or deconstruct. See Philip Rieff, *My Life among the Deathworks: Illustrations of the Aesthetics of Authority, Sacred Order/ Social Order, Volume I*, ed. Kenneth S. Piver (Charlottesville: University of Virginia Press, 2006).

16. Readers should not interpret any of this discussion as reflecting my own personal endorsement of behavioral forms, their seriousness (or lack thereof), or any commentary on the moral status of particular actions.

17. Pregnancy has preceded matrimony in many a marriage among believers, though this is seldom the case anymore in an era in which fertility is now primarily an optional result of sex rather than a predictable one. See George Akerlof, Janet L. Yellen, and Michael L. Katz, "An Analysis of Out-of-Wedlock Births in the United States," *Quarterly Journal of Economics*, 111 (1996): 277–317.

18. Dreher, "Sex after Christianity," paragraph 14.

19. Ibid., paragraph 19.

20. G. K. Chesterton, *What's Wrong with the World* (1910) (Whitefish, MT: Kessinger Publishing, 2010).

21. But fewer return today than in the past. See Vern L. Bengtson, *Families and Faith: How Religion Is Passed Down across Generations* (New York: Oxford University Press, 2017); Cyrus Schleifer and Mark Chaves, "Family Formation and Religious Service Attendance: Untangling Marital and Parental Effects," *Sociological Methods and Research*, 46 (2017): 125–152; Ross M. Stolzenberg, Mary Blair-Loy, and Linda J. Waite, "Religious Participation in Early Adulthood: Age and Family Life Cycle Effects on Church Membership," *American Sociological Review*, 60 (1995): 84–103; Jeremy E. Uecker, Damon Mayrl, and Samuel Stroope, "Family Formation and Returning to Institutional Religion in Young Adulthood," *Journal for the Scientific Study of Religion*, 55 (2016): 384–406.

22. Henrich, Boyd, and Richerson, "The Puzzle of Monogamous Marriage."

23. David Reisman, *The Lonely Crowd: A Study of the Changing American Character* (New Haven, CT: Yale University Press, 1950), 56.

24. It's not just a statistical fluke, either. Women's declining relative well-being "is found across various datasets, measures of subjective well-being, demographic groups, and industrialized countries." See Betsey Stevenson and Justin Wolfers, "The Paradox of Declining Female Happiness," *American Economic Journal: Economic Policy*, 1 (2009): 190–225. The quote is from the study's abstract.

25. This despite Don Browning's prescient observation and advice: "Marriage is a complex intersubjective communicative process that needs advanced levels of 'communicative competence'. . . . Hence, just as we train people to drive well and safely, society through its various educational and religious institutions should teach people to handle the communicative, cultural, and bio-economic realities of marriage. This is primarily a task for the institutions of civil society rather than law or government, although both can, in limited ways, support this cultural task." See Browning, "Critical Familism, Civil Society, and the Law." The quote here appears on page 324.

26. Zimmerman, *Family and Civilization.*

27. *Family and Civilization* was published in the days when scholars were expected to work on fewer (but more significant) projects, rather than lend their name to a glut of small, self-interested projects with little comprehensive investigation. The difference is palpable. The book is certainly not above criticism, of course. *Family and Civilization* is neither an easy nor a short read. (The original is 810 pages.) It ranges widely, is organized awkwardly, and displays no shortage of disjointed redundancy. And yet a more comprehensive evaluation of the intellectual, philosophical, historical, and (early) sociological treatment of marriage in the West you will not find. John Witte Jr.'s treatment of the religious history of marriage (in *From Sacrament to Contract*) outpaces Zimmerman's talent here, but that is high praise for Witte, because Zimmerman does better justice to the theological debates around marriage than I (could ever) accomplish here. To be sure, Zimmerman and Sorokin—as all scholars of an era—were creatures of their time. They used terms we no longer recognize. They had biases that are easier to detect in hindsight. They were not passive recorders of historical and sociological events and processes but displayed preferences for particular arrangements, using terms like "the great cultures" (41). In that, they are no different from my contemporary peers—or from me.

28. Zimmerman, *Family and Civilization*, 41.

29. Ibid., 57. Among many such gems, this one from page 807 stands out: Zimmerman observed "the tendency of the elite to call any suggestion antithetical to extended and decadent atomism to be fascism."

30. Ibid., 558.

31. Ibid., 125.

32. Pope Francis, *Amoris Laetitia*, section 33.

33. Kotkin et al., *The Rise of Post-Familialism*, 1.

34. Ibid.

35. Zimmerman, *Family and Civilization*, 780.

36. Ibid. The emphasis is Zimmerman's.

37. Ibid., 781.

38. Kotkin et al., *The Rise of Post-Familialism*, 9.

39. According to a "cohort-component projection of the religious composition of the United States," the "low fertility of secular Americans and the religiosity of immigrants provide a countervailing force to secularization, causing the nonreligious population share to peak before 2043." See Vegard Skirbekk, Eric Kaufmann, and Anne Goujon, "Secularism, Fundamentalism, or Catholicism? The Religious Composition of the United States to 2043," *Journal for the Scientific Study of Religion*, 49 (2010): 293–310. The quote above is from the article's abstract.

40. Samuel L. Perry and Cyrus Schleifer, "Are the Faithful Becoming Less Fruitful? The Decline of Conservative Protestant Fertility and the Growing Importance of Religious Practice and Belief in Childbearing in the US," *Social Science Research*, 78 (2019): 137–155.

41. Zimmerman, *Family and Civilization*, 806.

42. Zimmerman retained a disdain for Hollywood, and they got the message. In response to a remark by Zimmerman that the film industry comprised a "synthetic childless population," then-actor Ronald Reagan retorted: "Never having been on the Harvard campus, I feel no more qualified to discuss the professor than he is to discuss Hollywood and the motion picture people. If the professor could be persuaded to leave the cloistered halls where intellectual inbreeding substitutes for the 'synthetic' life of Hollywood, I believe we could show him that the people in the studios, gathered from the cities, towns and farms, are a pretty good cross section of American life, no better, no worse. As to fertility, I believe that movie families could match that of the Harvard professor both as to numbers and quality." This appeared as an Associated Press story entitled "Film Stars' Harvard Critic 'Just Trying to Get in Act,'" *Boston Herald*, December 19, 1946.

43. Pitirim Sorokin, *Social and Cultural Dynamics, Volume 4* (Cincinnati, OH: American Book Company, 1941). The quote is from page 776.

44. Neither Zimmerman's nor Sorokin's predictions were a reaction to the work of Alfred Kinsey, since *Sexual Behavior in the Human Male* (Philadephia: W.B. Saunders, 1948) did not emerge until after *Family and Civilization* had been published. While divorce rates had noticeably crept upward, there was yet little published sociological data on sexual behavior.

45. Pitirim A. Sorokin, *The American Sex Revolution* (Boston: Porter Sargent, 1956), 23.

46. Zimmerman, *Family and Civilization*, 525. The independence of the family from the state is formally evident in Catholic social thought as early as *Rerum Novarum*, though subsidiarity is more explicitly discussed in *Quadragesimo Anno* (1931). Among Protestants, the idea of "sphere sovereignty" was central to the political thought of late-nineteenth-century political philosopher and statesman Abraham Kuyper.

47. Christopher Lasch held that such revolutions—especially the French and Industrial ones—were particularly corrosive to the family: "Contractual labor succeeded permanent labor and families became unstable, no longer able to support themselves without governmental assistance or to transmit traditional learning from one generation to the next. The spread of modernist ideas undermined religion and respect for paternal authority, leaving behind a vast moral devastation." See Lasch, *Haven in a Heartless World*, page 46.

48. Steven Seidman, *Romantic Longings: Love in America, 1830–1980* (New York: Routledge, 1991), 66.

49. Joanna L. Grossman and Lawrence M. Friedman, *Inside the Castle: Law and the Family in 20th Century America* (Princeton, NJ: Princeton University Press, 2011).

50. Seidman, *Romantic Longings*, 66.

51. Elaine Tyler May, *Great Expectations: Marriage and Divorce in Post-Victorian America* (Chicago: University of Chicago Press, 1980). The quote is from page 27.

52. I say "consistently evident" here because the leap in divorce and marriage rates immediately following the end of the Second World War was a temporary aberration. The stable shifts in divorce and marriage rates begin around 1970.

53. Cherlin, *The Marriage-Go-Round*.

54. Ellen Byron, "More Americans Are Living Solo, and Companies Want Their Business," *Wall Street Journal*, June 2, 2019, https://www.wsj.com/articles/more-americans-are-living-solo-and-companies-want-their-business-11559497606

55. OECD, "Society at a Glance 2016: OECD Social Indicators" (Paris: OECD Publishing, 2016), https://doi.org/10.1787/9789264261488-en. Estimates are for persons ages 15–29.

56. Kotkin et al., *The Rise of Post-Familialism*. The quote is from page 35.

57. John Paul II, *Address to the Confederation of Family Advisory Bureaus of Christian Inspiration* (November 29, 1980), 3–4, in *Insegnamenti, Volume III, Part 2* (Vatican City: Vatican Publishing House, 1980), 1453–1454. John Paul II reiterates this quote in *Familiaris Consortio*, section 75.

58. I realize that college-educated women are now the most likely to marry. That simply reveals that marriageability is a two-way street; in a world in which men still make the marriage propositions, marriageability is not simply about him. It's about her, too.

59. Finkel et al., "The Suffocation Model."

60. Data from the (large) 2018 National Health Interview Survey reveals that LGBT adult men are married at one-third the rate of heterosexual men (16 percent vs. 48 percent, respectively), while LGBT women display a rate one-half that of heterosexual women (23 percent vs. 47 percent). The picture may be clouded, however, since NHIS does

not distinguish the sexual orientation of the spouse. A 2017 Gallup poll—which did distinguish spousal orientation—revealed that 10 percent of LGBT Americans were in a same-sex marriage, while noting that *more* of them (13 percent) reported being married to someone of the opposite sex. Hence the real NHIS gap in marriage may be at least twice as large as it appears. See Jeffrey M. Jones, "In U.S., 10% of LGBT Adults Now Married to Same-Sex Spouse," *Gallup Social and Policy Issues*, June 22, 2017, https://news.gallup.com/poll/212702/lgbt-adults-married-sex-spouse.aspx. Additionally, recent analyses of tax returns show that while 92 percent of opposite-sex married couples file "jointly" (something only married couples can do), only 59 percent of same-sex couples do so, signaling the likelihood that census estimates of one million Americans in a same-sex marriage are dramatically overstated and that a significant share of same-sex "marriages" may not actually be legally formalized. There may be as few as five or six same-sex marriages for every 1,000 opposite-sex marriages. See Robin Fisher, Geof Gee, and Adam Looney, "Same-Sex Married Tax Filers after *Windsor* and *Obergefell*," *Demography*, 55 (2018): 1423–1446.

61. Zimmerman, *Family and Civilization*, 681.

62. Ibid.

63. Russell Hittinger, "The Social Vision of Pope Leo XIII in the Twenty-First Century," *First Things*, March 2017, https://www.firstthings.com/media/the-social-vision-of-pope-leo-xiii-in-the-twenty-first-century; Pius XI, *Divini Illius Magistri* (Vatican City: Vatican Publishing House, 1929), 11. The term Hittinger uses is *polity*, meaning the political organization of our communities—including local government and civic organizations (like the local chapter of the Girl Scouts or the Knights of Columbus). See Russell Hittinger, "The Three Necessary Societies," *First Things*, June 2017, paragraph 35, https://www.firstthings.com/article/2017/06/the-three-necessary-societies

Index

Tables and figures are indicated by *t* and *f* following the page number.

For the benefit of digital users, indexed terms that span two pages (e.g., 52–53) may, on occasion, appear on only one of those pages.